An Innocent Yank at Home Abroad

Footnotes to History
1922–1945

An Innocent Yank at Home Abroad

Footnotes to History
1922–1945

by
Max Oppenheimer, Jr.

Sunflower University Press®

1531 Yuma • P. O. Box 1009 • Manhattan, Kansas 66505-1009 USA

Cover art, by Rodney L. Hoover.

Layout by Lori L. Daniel

ISBN 0-89745-230-5

Sunflower University Press is a wholly-owned subsidiary
of the non-profit 501(c)3 Journal of the West, Inc.

Oh! Fortunate eyes,
Whatever you've seen,
No matter the guise,
Pure beauty it's been!

— Johann Wolfgang von Goethe,
1749–1832

To My Father, in Remembrance

For Ed and Lyn

Acknowledgments

M Y HEARTFELT GRATITUDE goes to Carol A. Williams and Robin Higham for graciously smiling on my literary effort, presenting it in such an attractive guise, and giving me lunch to boot. My special thanks to Lew Singer for giving me the final shove to get me to my word processor.

Max Oppenheimer, March 9, 1929, in Hamburg, dressed as "Uncle Sam" for a costume ball.

Contents

Prologue

Synchronicity in the Search for My Roots

*T*HERE ARE MOMENTS when I have wondered whether the Three Parcae — Nona,
Decuma, and Morta, as the Romans called them
— also known as the Three Fates, always have
their act flawlessly together. Might not all those
fine and fragile threads, that supposedly reflect and control our individual destinies, inextricably intertwine and
slip from their nimble fingers? Especially suspicious
would be Nona, the one with the spindle. Might she not,
on occasion, allow the threads of life to become hopelessly entangled or even knotted beyond repair, when
they should unravel in a neat, orderly fashion? And what
if then, solely inspired by some mischievous playfulness,

arbitrary whim, or willful cunning, she compounds her actions by cutting and tying the threads together in an arbitrarily bizarre pattern? This could explain these extraordinary cases of synchronicity we often encounter in our lives.

My father spoke little of his childhood, volunteering but sketchy details of his early life. One of 13 children, he was born in Rimbach, Germany, a small community in the Odenwald near Heidelberg. His father, whom I never knew, understood nothing about farming and had lost the farm handed down to him as an inheritance. The family was very poor and my father suffered a deprived childhood, even hunger and meager care. Under circumstances never made clear to me, he was brought up in Frankfurt on the Main. Under quite austere conditions, he stayed in a kind of boarding school with other children. In jest — or in earnest — he told me how he and his comrades, when served frankfurters for lunch, would eat the skin but save the best meaty part for supper. Hearing these appalling stories, I could almost picture him as an abused Dickens waif.

He told me about being apprenticed to a merchant where he learned the rudiments of trade and commerce. As soon as he had completed his apprenticeship, he emigrated to Spain. There, over 16 or so years, he managed to make something of himself as a salesman, acquiring a certain amount of wealth as well as a lumberyard and a maritime salvage business on the side.

He never once spoke of his father or mother. When I asked about my grandparents and ancestors, he advised me not to search for my roots or rummage around in genealogy, since I might "run into a horse thief" somewhere in the family. I never knew whether or not he was serious. He claimed some members of our family had known the legendary Schinder Hannes (*schinden* is to flay, abuse, ill-treat in German; *Hannes* is John), a rogue and robber who plied his trade (if one might call it that) in the region adjacent to the Neckar Valley, robbing the rich, much like Robin Hood, and remaining on good terms with the poor.

The few uncles and aunts I met on my father's side of the family, eight in all out of thirteen, never mentioned their parents or their childhood. And I did not pry any further, because, at that time in my life, it did not much matter to me. My thoughts were focused on the future rather than the past.

My father was not a churchgoing man. In fact, I don't ever remember seeing him at a church service. Still he was interested in and knowledgeable about religion, talking to me often about the Bible and the New Testament, sharing with me his views on the various possible interpretations of the parables of Jesus. He once confided that he had thought of converting to Catholicism while living in Spain.

I never knew my last name might be viewed as Jewish until I was 20 years old and applied for membership in a YMCA. I had been christened Lutheran-Evangelical and raised in the Protestant faith. My mother, of Huguenot and Protestant ancestry, was the determining factor in my religious background, upbringing, and inclination. Nothing in our lifestyle or in the way others behaved toward me gave me any reason whatsoever to think of myself as anything but Protestant.

I was never aware that any member of my father's side of the family professed to be orthodox Jews. Religion never came up when we met. To my knowledge, they never observed Jewish holidays. I could then and can now only surmise that my father, for reasons of his own, had drawn a curtain behind this part of his past, which also explains why he named me Max, Jr. — a practice, I understand, not condoned by the Jewish faith.

In the 1950s, while I was working in Frankfurt, Germany, I drove to nearby Rimbach to see if I could find out something about my father's origins and family. The persons I spoke with discouraged me from any further search, claiming there were no archives available after World War II. Everything had been pretty much destroyed.

I did not insist, either remembering my father's warning about horse thieves or merely considering it quite unessential to investigate my roots. I dismissed the matter once and for all, even discarding the few papers I had concerning my father, including a birth certificate. The date of the certificate did not seem to jibe with the one we had observed every year in the family. The subject was closed, and I never planned to reopen it.

While this particular thread spun from Nona's spindle was woven into the design of my destiny's warp, another one originated, quite independently, at the very end of 1981 in Mexico. While visiting Yucatán, my wife and I drove from Mérida to the nearby Mayan archeological site of Dzibilchaltún. We found ourselves alone on the grounds except for one lonely tourist perched on top of the imposing stone structure known as the Temple of the Seven Dolls. We joined him, and from his accent, as he returned our "hello," I gathered he was from Germany.

Günther Augspurger was a young German addicted to perennial foreign travel. He availed himself of every opportunity to visit strange lands, often in connection with rugby games played abroad by the amateur league of which he was an active member. We talked a while, and because he was without transportation, I offered him a ride back to Mérida. I never expected to see him again, but, lo and behold, we ran into him that evening when walking in the town's crowded streets. Destiny obviously willed it thus, and surprisingly, before parting that afternoon, Günther had prophesied, "We shall meet again!"

We spent quite some time together that evening. Learning that I was interested in foreign languages and language *per se*, he told me that near where he lived, in Mosbach, in the Neckar region not far from Heidelberg, a paleolinguist named Richard Fester had written interesting books about the origins of language and the first primeval sounds possibly uttered by prehistoric man. We exchanged addresses and promised to keep in touch. And so we did.

Günther sent me Fester's address and one of his books, *Primeval Words of Man*. I corresponded with Fester and ordered from him a second work on primeval language of the Ice Age. Ironically, both the book and a letter bordered in black from Frau Fester, the author's wife, informing me of her husband's death, reached me on the very same day at my home in Santa Fe, New Mexico — another case of strange synchronicity, since the letter and package had been mailed on different dates.

Günther and I wrote each other occasionally, mostly exchanging Christmas cards and small presents. In 1986, when teaching English in Kunming, Yunnan Province, in south-central China, I was Günther's host. I arranged for his sojourn in a university guesthouse, showed him around the area — including the famous Shi Lin or Stone Forest, and invited him to attend some of my classes and lectures, all of which strengthened the friendship formed in 1981. Again we kept in sporadic contact.

Suddenly, in the summer of 1997 I felt the urge to phone Günther and tell him I might be paying him a visit in October when on a planned trip to France. Thus, on a Thursday, October 2, 1997, I showed up at the gate of the remodeled farmhouse in Schwarzach im Odenwald, a small community approximately 25 miles from Heidelberg, where my friend was

living with his identical twin brother, Dieter. Finding myself heartily
welcomed by the two men and without previous plans as to my length of
stay, I ended up remaining in Schwarzach through October 7th, taking a
room at a local inn. As it turned out, the Friday after my arrival was a new
German holiday, Unity Day, instituted by German Chancellor Helmut
Kohl to celebrate the reunification of West and East Germany. On Friday
and Saturday, the three of us visited old familiar places like Worms (where
Martin Luther appeared before the Diet and was placed under the ban of
the Holy Roman Empire), Speyer, and the Neckar Valley region.

On Sunday, Günther had to play senior league rugby with his "Oldies"
team in a crucial final game he did not care to miss. Dieter and I planned
to come along and watch it, but in the last minute failed to make it, as
Günther had left earlier than expected while we had gone sightseeing.
Evidently, Nona was fiercely spinning her thread, weaving mysterious
new patterns into my life.

On a sudden impulse, I proposed to Dieter a drive to nearby Rimbach,
just for kicks, on the chance I might find out something more about my
father's origins. Upon our arrival we walked through town and noticed
a Protestant church on which a plaque announced that it had previously
been a Jewish synagogue. While we were standing in front of the closed
building, pondering this interesting conversion, a man connected with
the church asked whether he could be of help. I explained that my father
was originally from Rimbach and that I was interested in learning about
his ancestors. The man advised us to consult the Community Administrative offices on Monday and in the meantime to visit an old Jewish
cemetery.

Following his instructions, we finally found the cemetery. The gate was
locked. Without hesitation, I climbed the wall and Dieter followed. And
there, as if staring back at us, were rows of tombstones, many of them with
my own last name inscribed thereon. I was confronted with the graves of
my forebears.

Dieter and I had planned to take the TVA — the extremely fast train —
to Hamburg on Monday to visit the city where I had spent over seven
years of my childhood. Again, on impulse, I changed my mind. I was compelled to return to Rimbach!

We reached my father's birthplace purposely after the lunch hour. As
we entered the city hall, pondering whom to ask for information, a young
man entered the building. We told him what we were looking for and he

invited us to his office. I briefly told him about my residence in Germany as a child and my father's roots in Rimbach. He immediately reached in his desk and produced a book entitled *History of the Rimbach Jews,* by Wolfgang Gebhard, a local teacher now retired and still residing there.

In 1985, on the 50th anniversary of the infamous Hitler Reich Crystal Night, the municipality of Rimbach had decided to preserve, as a reminder and warning for future generations, an essential aspect of the community's history under National Socialism. The committee established for this purpose recommended that Wolfgang Gebhard's 1965 research on the subject be revised, expanded, and published as a book. The project was intended to recognize Hitler's cruelty toward the Jews, to commemorate the cause of freedom and human dignity, and to make certain personal liberties would never again be abused as they were under National Socialism. Schmidt handed us the book and I started scanning its pages. Somehow, I immediately found a list of families in alphabetical order, among which I recognized my father's name and those of his 12 brothers and sisters.

Herr Schmidt informed us that Mr. Gebhard might be available and, after a quick phone call, confirmed that we would be welcome to see him at three o'clock that very afternoon. I was really getting excited. I could not keep from looking again and again at the page with my father's name, misspelled as "Marx" instead of "Max." Neatly listed were also my grandparents' names and those of my aunts and uncles. I was furthermore told by Schmidt that the house my grandfather had lived in and had presumably lost for financial reasons, Bismarckstrasse 10, originally built in 1758, was still standing. It had been rebuilt and was now an Adidas sporting goods store. There was even a photograph of it in the book. Schmidt also remembered that when he was a child, his grandmother had told him that the family occupying the house was *bettelarm*, literally "poor like beggars."

We proceeded to the home of Wolfgang Gebhard, where we were graciously received. Mr. Gebhard produced some of his original research notes, which appeared to correct a misprint in the book and listed my father's given name as Max and not Marx. The notes, however, showed my father's date of birth as March 31, 1870. We had always celebrated his birthday on March 24th. Perhaps, Gebhard surmised, the birth had been reported late to the authorities. I promised to send Gebhard all the information I remembered about the members of my family as soon as I returned home: where they had moved, whom they had married, and the names of their offspring. None of these details had been found by Gebhard in the Rimbach hall of records. On the other hand, he was interested in any possible corrections or addenda I could supply.

After leaving the Gebhards, Dieter and I again climbed the walls of the cemetery. As we had been warned, the graves had been seriously vandalized during the Hitler period. Many of the tombstones had been overturned or broken. However, we had already noticed that someone was rehabilitating the cemetery. A mobile scaffold used to right and restore the stones stood by the graves. In fact, certain improvements and the repositioning of the scaffold testified to the fact that someone had been working there that day and since our first visit on Sunday. We found some of the graves listed in Gebhard's book, which included a map of the cemetery and the location of various tombstones. Not having had the time to study the lists in more detail, we merely identified those of more distant relatives, such as two belonging to another son of my great-great-grandfather and his wife. On a later visit, in October 1998, I located the graves of my great-grandfather Salomon (1795-1859) and my great-grandmother Jette (born Zacharias 1794-1877).

Gebhard's work allowed me to trace my family back to my great-great-grandfather, Gumbrich Oppenheimer (1751–1830). What it does not explain and what still remains a mystery is why my father wanted to put all his past behind him. According to the book's genealogical details, my grandfather and grandmother vanished without a trace from Rimbach. Neither their whereabouts, place of burial, nor their dates of death are known. Did my father merely want to forget an unhappy and deprived childhood, or were there other reasons for his advice not to rummage among the family ancestors?

As for now, I can only reflect on this fragile insecure society of ours, many members of which derive their self-esteem and their confidence in their own worth by deluding themselves with racial superiority over others and by invoking artificially discriminatory religious biases toward them. Is it not strange that such discrimination is often tenuously based on naught but a label, a name through custom or tradition identified with a clan or tribe, deemed different, inferior, or even tainted?

What's in a name, indeed? Had I been aware of such nonsense when a

child, I might have changed my own to my mother's maiden name Pour-
fürst, and no one would have been the wiser. Significant is also my
encounter with Günther on top of a pyramid in Yucatán. Had it not been
for this chance meeting, had he and I been minutes apart on the site, had
we not somehow instinctively bonded, none of this would have happened!
I might never have thought of returning to Rimbach to stumble across the
graves of my ancestors, discovering in the process a mysterious side to my
father's life.

Memory affords us a window into the past, a second glance at events
witnessed, experiences enjoyed, endured or shared, and persons encountered. Now and then, willy-nilly, familiar figures — some sharp and clear,
some vague and uncertain — loom before us, staggering, beckoned or
uninvited, into our conscious mind. Be it by childish insouciance, adult
preoccupation with daily challenges and concerns, old-age jaded or worn
by surfeit of emotions and feelings experienced over the slow march of
time, we may be inclined to keep shadowy ghosts from the past at bay. Let
down your guard, though, provide them with a breach, and they burst upon
us, crowding into our present, flooding our consciousness, irrepressible,
unrestrainable, with remembrances long forgotten or previously ignored.

Better still. Why not be daring and step boldly through the breach, meet
our ghosts from the past halfway, retrace our steps once more, revisit
familiar places, relive the good and the bad, and account for it all to ourselves, to those close to us, and perhaps to a curious sympathetic reader?
When we travel to strange cities and lands, are we not inclined first to take
a whirlwind tour, strike a preliminary acquaintance, then return and take a
closer look with eyes and minds, sensitized, sharpened, and alerted by the
previous experience, now encompassing immeasurably more from the
vantage point of anticipation? Why not apply this lesson to our own life,
unquestionably a journey worthy of a second glance?

A final motive for indulging in autobiography is to learn more about
one's self. We learn not only from maxims — wise saws and sentences,
philosophical writings — but also, often more graphically, from examples
and, as the French 16th-century author Montaigne pointed out in his
Essays (1595), from painting one's self: *"Everyone recognizes me in my
book and my book in me." "Every individual carries the entire form of the
human condition,"* and the individual exhibits all the characteristics of the
human species. For better or for worse, we may learn from our own lives,
from those of others, and others from ours. Hence my modest effort.

Introduction

What You Danced
Is Yours to Keep

S I LOOK BACK at my life spanning four-fifths of a century and recall how, with both cautious hesitation and hopeful excitement, I trod the paths before me, I see the road taken not as a meandering, sketchy line, but as a bold one firmly traced, as though a benevolent destiny had drawn especially for me a clear map to follow. I no longer see myself blindly groping my way or as a knight of yore, erring about in confusion through daunting labyrinthine forests and thick underbrush, in quest of honor, fortune, or some mythical coveted grail. Nor do I see in my past tantalizing "roads diverging in a yellow wood," as Robert Frost writes with exquisite lyrical concision in "The Road Not Taken," wondering which one to choose "and sorry I could not travel both." I now know I took the fairest one, pointed out by a guiding spirit with my best interests and welfare at heart. Today, ages later, I know the road I took was the right one for me, and the difference in my favor.

When I was a young boy, my father often quoted a Spanish proverb I have treasured all these years. In my mind it embodies, as many proverbs do, the fossilized wisdom of generations and a profound human truth: *No se le quita a uno lo bailado* — one cannot take away from someone what he has danced. Its message is crystal clear: when looking at life, be grateful for whatever you have tasted of it! Don't quibble, weighing the good versus the bad, which ultimately are mere semantic artifices beyond definitive human judgment or evaluation. What is important is having lived your life, savored each experience, grown with the knowledge acquired, enjoyed to the fullest the relationships and bonding established with others, coped with the events that befell you — pleasurable or not, endured the grief, savored the happiness; all of it, without exception, is inalienably yours to keep. And finally, when all is said and done, don't take your life lightly and for granted. Be forever conscious of and grateful for having lived it. The true meaning of *carpe diem* — pluck, put to use, enjoy the present day — consists in both the living and the enduring consciousness of having done so.

This — not to alarm the skeptics among us — requires trust and faith, at least in some spirituality above and beyond the human sphere. The argument from the great French 17th-century mathematician, philosopher, and mystic Blaise Pascal states that we incur absolutely no risk whatsoever and have everything to gain, nothing to lose, if when offered a bet regarding faith — in the broadest sense of the word, be it in the existence of God, a Supreme Being, or some Universal Power — we wager in the affirmative, opting for belief and faith rather than skepticism, agnosticism, and atheism. Be astute! Play the odds, they are in your favor! Indeed, should you win the bet, you hit the jackpot, having cast your lot with a Higher Being. Should there be no God, you will not, by losing your wager, suffer any negative consequences, since there is no one whose wrath you need fear. Such reasoning has served me well and has, after initial misgivings, uncertainty, and fretting, rewarded me with peace of mind, equanimity, and faith in my destiny and a spirit guide.

What follows is my story, the account of the first 30 years in the life (not always of his own choosing) of a young American expatriate. The period coincides with a crucial time in European history, stretching from World War I to the end of World War II. First through the eyes of a child, then those of a boy growing to adulthood, I witnessed such dramatic historical events as the painful recovery of a Germany shamefully defeated in a disastrous adventurist war, the runaway postwar inflation of the German mark in the early 1920s, and the deep depression and resulting loss of self-esteem that reigned in the Reich. For the sake of survival, I learned early that one must adjust, going beyond the precept "when in Rome do what the Romans do" by becoming a Roman. Though aware deep within myself of my American nationality, I grew up a German boy.

Economic exigencies and professional considerations caused my father to move the family from pre-Hitler Germany to France in 1930. I recall a Paris that the modern French do not know. Unencumbered by such modern psychological concepts as culture shock, I was compelled to make the almost instantaneous and unimaginable transition to a French youth, simultaneously learning French, Latin, and the English that I had by then entirely forgotten. As another cultural layer was added, I became a product of the exacting, superior French educational system, before finally returning, after more than 13 years, as a virtual foreigner to my homeland.

This is the story of an ordinary man striving to do his very best with the means at his disposal — an innocent taken out of his country at a very young age, who acquired an ability that was to last him all his life — to feel perfectly at home abroad.

Dr. Max Oppenheimer, Jr.

Part
One

Better late than never.

Chapter 1

Conversation Beyond the Grave

EMEMBER, DAD, you always said: "Once I am gone, I want to be excused." Well, normally, I would respect your wish, but we really need to talk. When my time comes, I won't mind one bit if my children want to have a chat, "after hours" so to speak. Besides, I never had a chance to bring you up to date on what happened to me during and after the war. Aren't you interested in hearing what I did with all that education you put me through and how I applied the experience I acquired under your tutelage? You know, we never had a real heart-to-heart talk when we had the opportunity. I guess, being one of thirteen children, you treasured your privacy. I too should have had more talks with my son and daughter, but fathers often just don't think about doing it. Yet, children like to know about their parents. I would have liked to know a great deal more about you, not just events in your life, but how you felt about things that are deep within us and really matter. It would have helped me then and could still guide me now in sorting out stuff in my life. Sorting out can be as frustrating as struggling to disentangle a skein of yarn.

The last time we met, Sunday, December 2, 1945, I had no idea that was going to be it. I would have made much better use of our few hours together. People talk about wasting, losing, killing time, when all one can do is use it, wisely, efficiently, foresightedly. Anyway, the next news I had was on August 24, 1946, about you leaving our world. At least you went on a happy note, with a flush of joy in your heart, buying your weekly carnation in a flower shop in Jackson Heights as you loved to do. I can just see you, enjoying its fragrance and beauty before pinning it on your lapel. Then you excused yourself, fading out of a world you brightened with your presence. I should have learned from you about carnations and purple violets. Always focusing on some abstract idea, I often missed the beauty in front of my nose: the clouds against the sky, the hills, the flowers, a child probing, touching, discovering his or her universe!

Do you realize this talk is not like any we have had before? I have finally caught up with you, even overtaken you. We are on a level playing field with regard to age and life experience. Here you are, still 76, and I nearing 83. You would be surprised how much I remember about our times together. Sometimes it seems every word you ever spoke remains with me to this day. When I was just a little boy, you wanted to teach me "not to cry over spilled milk." Every time I used the German *schade* — too bad, it's a pity, you would say, "*Schade ist tot!*" — "Too bad is dead," meaning "what's done is done, forge ahead." One day you showed me an obituary in the newspaper. There in big black letters framed by a thick black border: "Herr Schade, mourned by relatives and friends, had made his transition." You just said: "See, Mr. 'Toobad' really did die. Just as I told you." It was both funny and sad, and every time I think of the word *schade* I remember you and the late Mr. Schade.

I remember, too, the silly little ditty you taught me for fun when I had a stomach ache:

> A man from Homburg on the Hill,
> loose bowels made him very ill.
> From Dorteweil another guy
> about the opposite would cry.

I suppose that, besides providing me with a lesson in geography, it taught me about humor by antithesis, which, much later, I put to good use in the study of baroque rhetoric in Spain. Once, when we were walking out on the Lüneburg Heath near Hamburg and tissue paper would have come in handy, you told me about the tramp whom a gendarme asked for his papers. "Sorry," the man replied, "I always use grass!"

Don't worry, I have more edifying memories than those: the glorious lines of poetry by Heine, Schiller, and Goethe; the great books you encouraged me to read; the answers to questions about Biblical parables and other writings that puzzled my young mind. I partially owe you my predilection for and appreciation of the classics in world literature. For as I grew up, you kindled my interest in the great books and writers, including Chamisso, Freytag, Lessing, and many others. A thoughtful man and a self-taught humanist, you made it all easily understandable, keeping your illustrations simple, to the point, and applicable to everyday life.

I remember you telling me about your early youth and your father's difficulties in providing adequate support for the family, your struggle to gain an education and apprenticeship in commerce without having any money, and your decision to leave for Spain. I know you lived in Spain for 16 years before coming to the USA. I was fascinated by your travels there, especially the story of how you journeyed on horseback and by train as a salesman and once had yourself rowed across the Strait of Gibraltar with merchandise samples to avoid customs duty. I know that you eventually became a successful businessman with a lumberyard and a maritime salvage business on the side until you lost most of your fortune.

However, in my life with you, three incidents, even you may not recall, are most salient to me and surface at times. The first two brought us very close to each other; in the third, you very perceptively almost hit upon the truth. The first was in Ostende. You had decided to take a short vacation to join mother and me in the beach-front hotel. I knew you were a good swimmer, and I begged you to come with me for a dip into the North Sea. It was the first and last time you and I did something like that together. After our swim, we were getting dressed in one of those small huts on wheels, which a horse had pulled onto the shore, as was the custom in Ostende. Suddenly you felt ill, started breathing in spasms, acting as though you were about to have a stroke or heart attack. I was scared and wanted to help, but did not know how. I was certain I was going to lose you. Fortunately, it passed and you were able to get dressed. It was the closest I had come to facing the loss of someone close and dear to me.

Then there was the time in Paris in 1938. You had been very ill and the doctor prescribed leeches to suck blood from your body. I was scheduled to return to New York. You must have been feeling distraught and confused. You stumbled out onto your bedroom balcony where I had been standing and suddenly clutched me hysterically, babbling words I could not understand. Were you afraid you might never see me again? Did you try to express love for me? *What else could it be?* Whatever flashed through your mind, you were holding on to me for dear life. Even knowing you were not yourself, I was moved and upset by your inarticulate panic.

The third incident took place in 1941, at the time of my graduation from New York University. Conservative by nature, delighted to be enjoying my first-ever senior prom in the ballroom of the Waldorf Astoria, I was content to spend the entire evening there. However, some of my friends, knowing I had your 1939 Buick Super at my disposal, talked me into driving out to Westchester County. I reluctantly agreed. On the way out of the city, on the Sawmill River Parkway — in the middle of nowhere — I hit some sharp object on the road and blew two tires. It was late and help didn't arrive for hours. With only one spare, the car could not be driven away and had to be abandoned on the side of the road.

The next morning I informed you of the catastrophe for which I alone was responsible. I offered to pay for the towing and two new tires. You asked to see my savings account passbook and noticed that I had made frequent withdrawals from it. It was my money, to do with as I pleased, but you insisted on knowing why I had withdrawn the money. At that time you gave me an allowance and paid for all my expenses except incidentals. I remained mum, and very perceptively you suspected that the unexplained withdrawals must conceal some vice. I conceded nothing, but you were right. I had withdrawn money to satisfy my anorexic habit, which tormented me occasionally, especially when I was driving myself to long hours of study and homework. You did not question me further, but you were angry and I felt guilty. I never took your displeasure lightly. You even generously offered to pay for the damage to the car (but you did ground me).

I admired in you that ability, based on the knowledge of foreign languages and cultures, to be at home in many countries and always endeavored to emulate it. You knew how to sound the right chords with words, certain to elicit the right response and establish instant rapport. Everybody liked you, because they never felt you posing a threat to them. Your sense of humor was ever present, subtle, paradoxical, at times the more powerful for purposely escaping the immediate grasp of the person to whom it was directed. I still recall a Sunday afternoon in a Parisian *pâtisserie*, where customers were frantically buying all the pastries. A very formal lady ahead of us had taken every piece from a tray except for one. Knowing full well this was not the sort of humor appreciated by her kind, you impishly, but respectfully, inquired (meaning, of course, to be of service), whether she had overlooked the last one. I also never knew you to enter any deserted restaurant without the comment, "Not one occupied seat available!"

Did you ever reflect on the fact that we take lessons for everything: dancing, improving our golf game, bridge, and so on? When it comes to being a good father to our children, we seek no special training, merely doing, I suppose, what we saw our own fathers do. What they thought was good enough for us, should be good enough for our children. In my case I gave my children considerable leeway. Frequently, if I had misgivings about some measures taken — for my own good — during my childhood, as a father I took the opposite tack. You once punished me for taking a valve stem apart on my new bicycle — I merely wanted to find out how it worked in case I ever needed to repair it. So I allowed my son to take apart the lawnmower, or anything else he cared to, at his own risk. It bore fruit. He is much handier with such things than I ever was. For me, learning foreign languages while a child in Europe was a necessity, a question of survival. Still, disregarding all the free advice from friends and relatives, I never insisted that my children learn them.

I should have spent more time with my son and daughter. Yet, I was too preoccupied with my own affairs: work and research. I occasionally took them with me to the gym and pool but was often a distant parent, frequently away from home. My only excuse is that I was always there for them when they needed my support and still am. I meant well when I did not, as my mother did all through my school years, nag them about their grades and insist on their being at the head of the class. I wanted them to be free to pursue their own interests. I never pushed them into careers or activities they did not select of their own free will.

I wish you and I had talked about dreams, horizons instead of artificial lines drawn before us on the ground as though life was a game of hop-scotch instead of a grand journey. I confess I knew no better than to set for myself but short-term goals: degrees, rank, rungs of ladders that only extend so far, at most a ceiling, never the sky. I aimed for articles, books, but never took that deep breath and persisted in hatching the *magnum opus*. Perhaps I cowered too early on, fearing the disillusionment of a Knight of La Mancha and a Faust, settling instead for the safe and reasonable. I should have looked for role models outside my immediate surroundings. Then again, perhaps I learned patience too late in life.

I am grateful for one very important lesson I learned from you and Mother. You both set for me a laudable example of open-mindedness. You both were scrupulously honest, responsible, democratic human beings, treating everyone equally and fairly. You were true citizens of the world. In our household I never experienced any socially discriminatory sentiments, xenophobic prejudices, or parochial world views. Thanks to you I lived in foreign countries, learned their tongues, communed with their people, savored and absorbed their culture, wholeheartedly opening my mind and heart to their beliefs and passions. It helped me gradually outgrow the narrow, untutored, and inexperienced views I harbored as a child with regard to national and regional borders — allegiances so passionately espoused by so many all over the world.

To paraphrase Shakespeare's Shylock, does not every human being, be he German, French, Russian, Chinese, have eyes, hands, organs, dimensions, senses, affections, passions? I might quibble with his claim of all humans being fed with the same food, but we all do eat and drink. If pricked we all bleed, if tickled we laugh, if poisoned we die! At the risk of being labeled an unrealistic dreamer or a fool, at the end of my life, I cannot see any merit in overindulging in provincial pride. It is naught but arrogance, for any creature on this planet has equal right to claim superiority with as little a chance of proselyting any but the other sheep in his puny flock. Perhaps you did not intend this for me, but I like to think of myself as *ditya planeti* — a child of the planet.

I followed your footsteps along other lines. You gave me life, but never made me feel I was in your debt because of it. You respected my privacy, my freedom, my choices in my adult life, while always standing by me. I adhere to the same code of conduct toward my children, expecting nothing, but enjoying and vicariously participating in their achievements. Unlike all the manufactured goods today, humans do not come into this world with a warranty. Neither did my children. The least I can do is stand behind them after the fact.

Mother was not a complainer, coming from a rather stoic background. Perhaps you were never aware of it, but in letters to her sister, she revealed feelings I never knew her to have. She was quite homesick while in Germany. Worried about your health and overwork, she longed to return to the USA, always staunchly making the best of her situation. However, I have no misgivings about my circumstances. I did the best I could. Knowing how treacherous it is to navigate life's Scylla and Charybdis, I would settle for living mine over again just as I did before, every minute of it, counting my blessings.

You were always special to me, Dad. Though small of stature, you stood tall and higher still in my esteem. I wrote this book for you and for my children. Reading it, you will know more about me than I ever knew about you. If I did things the way you intended me to do them, take the credit. If I did not, place the blame on me for misunderstanding your intentions. I take full responsibility for everything, as I think all of us should always do. As you taught me, I never call on Mr. Schade, for we both know he is dead.

He started traveling from planet to planet
in order to, as they say, form his mind and heart.
— Voltaire, 1694–1778

Chapter 2

Hamburg!

REMOVE A GRAY SPOTTED OWL or some pesky squirrel from its natural habitat and the entire nation will protest and stand up in arms. Take a five-year-old boy, born and raised in New York City, move him 3,000 miles away to some country in Europe, and no one will make much of it. At least no one did in 1922, when concepts like culture shock were not widely known. That year my parents talked to me about a big move we needed to make. It must have sounded mildly exciting to me. I truly do not remember, but I am fairly certain it did not produce any feelings of alarm. Perhaps my curiosity was aroused as to what awaited me. Possibly I started learning that acceptance of whatever fate has in store for us is a constructive way of handling any given situation.

As I presently relate these happenings, I shall make every effort to search my memory for the exact manner in which my childish perception assimilated the impressions made by subsequent events. This is history as seen through the eyes of a child, and the events are those I recall witnessing and experiencing with the intellectual and emotional resources available to me at that time.

Until I was told about this impending move, my world was quite commonplace and the people in my life familiar. There were my parents. My father was short, corpulent, with a mustache. I respected and at times feared him, though over the years I grew to admire and love him very much. He was a thoughtful, intelligent, and self-educated man; he spoke excellent English, French, German, and Spanish. Occasionally, he was given to choleric outbursts. He was 47 years old when I was born. He had practiced sports such as horseback riding and swimming, but when I knew him, his only exercise was an occasional walk. In his younger years, however, he must have been quite a sport. There was a story that when he courted my mother, he climbed a cherry tree to pick some fruit for her. He jumped off a low branch and his lower leg bones broke and went into the ground. Since this happened on a Sunday, there was a long delay in getting him to a hospital. The result was a critically infected leg. He refused amputation, lay in the hospital for many months, and recovered completely. This story made a lasting impression on me.

My father, concerned with his high blood pressure and being 16 years older than my mother, wanted to be sure that we were provided for in the event anything happened to him. Thus he devoted all his thoughts and energy to his business, earning money, and making our lives pleasant. He certainly was the most unselfish man I knew. He was always considerate of everybody and treated everybody with equal respect. I always felt he was at all times very solicitous and protective of my mother.

My mother had beautiful, long black hair; she was very attractive and lovable. She was thin and a little taller than my father. I cried when, years later, she cut her long hair (my father punished me for crying). She was 31 years old when she gave birth to me on Friday, July 27, 1917. When I was older and she reminisced about my birth, she made it very clear to me that she did not care to repeat the experience. I know my mother always wanted what was best for me, but she did not convincingly communicate to me her intent or engender in me immediate enthusiasm for what she had in mind. However, I learned throughout my life to bow to her wishes. She could be stern due to an unbending Calvinist streak that ran in her family.

She was born and raised in Switzerland, had lived in England for two years, and spoke excellent French, German, and English. She also knew English shorthand.

In New York, my maternal grandmother took care of me during the day. She spoke a strange language, which I did not always understand. (I discovered later that she was Swiss from Geneva and spoke French.) She never learned English. I picked up some French from her, as young children readily acquire bits and pieces of the languages to which they are exposed.

My maternal grandfather was a severe-looking man. He had owned a tin-ware factory in Switzerland, which had burned down. So he came to America, but never recovered financially. The last time I saw him he was laid out in a coffin and there were many people in the room. I was encouraged to kiss him good-bye on his forehead. I still remember how cold and stiff he felt to the touch of my lips.

Then there was my aunt, Marguerite, my mother's sister, a lovely affectionate lady. My uncle Charlie had a harsh raspy voice, but was a prince of a man. Both of them were my godparents and were like parents to me years later when I needed moral support. Like many Swiss, Charlie was an excellent cook. He was in the Swiss watch business. I always thought he would have done better as a cook.

We lived in the Bronx, first on Fairmount Place. Then we moved to a larger apartment in a big red-brick building on University Avenue and Fordham Road, facing a park with a nice slope for sledding in the winter. I know there were a few linden trees there, because one night I was permitted to accompany my father as he harvested some of the leaves. My mother used them to make linden tea. She made it sound as though it was a clandestine operation and had me swear a sacred oath never to whisper anything to anyone about it. She was most insistent on this last point.

My father owned a big car with a removable canvas top, and sometimes we would go for a ride with other members of the family. I had the distinct impression that owning a car was special. Maybe this triggered my lifelong love affair with automobiles.

One more incident stands out. Our apartment had been remodeled and the walls in my room were painted white. In some spots the painter had left some white blobs on the wall. For some reason these amorphous little lumps of a sickly white, wrinkled paint produced a nauseating effect on me. From that time on I no longer wanted to drink milk. I would visualize the blobs and feel like throwing up. My mother had to dilute the milk with tea before I would drink it. It took me many years to overcome this queasiness.

My father lost all his money a year or two before we left the United States for Europe, when he had accepted a position as a commercial representative for a large American firm dealing in scrap rubber, H. Muehlstein and Company. When we departed America, my parents did not have much more than $1,000. Doing business in Europe for an American firm was an opportunity for them to regain financial security.

Thinking back, I suppose the move, tantamount to a youthful "exile" to Europe (for even at that age, after my arrival there, I knew full well that I was an American away from my own country), engendered in me the awareness of being an outsider. Yet, I always tried, as hard as I could, to be one with the world I happened to be in. Somewhere in my consciousness sprang up the concept of what the French call *déraciné* — uprooted (it sounds more dramatic in French — at least to me). It initiated henceforth a feeling of exclusion, which endures to this day, concomitant with an almost obsessive desire for social inclusion, no matter how varied the locale and circumstances, as well as the willingness to expend any necessary effort, especially in learning language and culture, to achieve it.

My parents and I traveled to Germany on an American ocean liner. I only remember a single detail about the entire trip. There were long metal objects on the deck that I would constantly trip over and then look for my mother for comfort about my bleeding knees. I kept falling over and over again on these same sore patellas. I am sure I celebrated my birthday on board the ocean liner.

In 1922, we landed in the large port of Hamburg. Upon our arrival, my parents rented a few rooms from a widow. I dimly remember her name as Frau Römhild. She was a friendly lady, but I could not understand anything she said. I no longer had my own bedroom, but had to sleep in the same room with my parents. Apparently, it was very difficult at this time to find anything to rent, and it took many years before we finally had our own five-room apartment. Even when the owner of our second lodging, Fräulein Zimmerman, died, we could not just take over the premises. My parents had to buy another apartment and exchange it for the one we were already occupying. My father rented an office on Valentinskamp, near the two railroad stations, the Dammtor Bahnhof and the Hauptbahnhof, in the downtown business section of the city.

Soon after our arrival in Hamburg, I was riding on the streetcar with my mother. We were conversing in English. I was painfully aware of all the people in the streetcar, with severe faces and eyes, sternly looking me over. I noticed no smiles. I was frightened and could only assume a strong disapproval of something concerning me. Since at that very moment I was doing nothing unusual but talk in English, I decided I would no longer stand out in a crowd or be in any way different from those around me by anything I did or said. I never wanted to feel that uncomfortable again. I made up my mind that I must, as soon as possible, forget English and learn the language spoken by everyone else in Germany — and speak it exactly as it was spoken there.

There was much unrest in Hamburg because of the post–World War I conditions. Losing the war was terribly depressing for the German people, and they suffered from the consequences. There was shooting in the streets, and I could see and hear from the window of my apartment people looting stores, scurrying about with bundles, and shouting, as police tried to keep order. On tumultuous days I was not permitted outside. One afternoon I was taken for a walk along one of many canals in Hamburg. A crowd of passersby was watching and cheering on three men who were stealing a coal barge anchored alongside the canal. The police arrived too late and the boat, propelled by the men pushing down on large poles, disappeared behind a bend in the waterway. They were not out to steal the barge. They merely wanted to take it somewhere and steal some coal — a very precious commodity. Numerous were the poor who could not afford it.

I was given a bundle of German bank notes to play with. My parents explained to me that German money was losing more of its value every day. I was also told that my parents had American dollars and that these did not lose their value. Therefore, my father could exchange his dollars for more and more German marks. Thus, the inflation or "devaluation," as this loss of value was called, did not affect us as much as it did others.

One day, when I was playing with my German marks, Frau Römhild's son, a young man, came in and told me that I could buy something with them. I was delighted. I had no idea I could exchange this paper money for something real. Well, I had been given a flashlight, but it did not work anymore. He told me it needed new batteries. He took some of my money with him and came back with a battery. The flashlight worked. Some time later, when I wished to repeat the procedure, I found out my money was not sufficient to buy anything. I now had a very clear idea of how inflation worked in economics. I was to witness it many more times in Europe as both inflation and devaluation, especially in France, where one dollar bought more and more French francs throughout 1937.

Unfortunately, I cannot explain how I acquired German. It just happened, and I started forgetting the English and very little French I knew. After all, except for my parents, I was constantly in the company of individuals, especially playmates, who spoke nothing but German.

My father was gone all day at the office, and my mother joined him later in the morning to help him as his secretary. Since my parents were absent until about seven or eight o'clock at night, they needed someone to take care of me. The day my mother found her is as clear in my mind as though it had occurred yesterday. But only recently did I realize how much this event was to influence and shape my outlook on life and my entire value system, especially with regard to society, human relations, and ethical behavior.

One morning my mother and I visited a lady to see if we could hire her to live with us as a maid and be a caretaker for me. I was immediately suspicious and experienced a certain degree of anticipatory hostility. Someone was about to intrude into my life and threaten the *status quo*. We rang the bell and a lady greeted us, had us enter a small room, and sit down. I sat on a chair nervously fidgeting with a small toy car. I could not understand the conversation, but I knew it partially concerned me, as the lady kept glancing at me with a somewhat worried look on her face. I don't know why, but the devil was suddenly aroused in me and I began systematically destroying the toy. I remember demolishing it with great gusto so as to make an impression on everyone.

I have had in my life, and still at times have, the unfortunate urge to destroy some utensil I no longer have any use for, either because it does not work anymore and I don't want to be tempted to fix it, or simply to get rid of it. I guess I want to be sure neither I nor anyone else will be tempted to possess it. It is an obsession to get something irretrievably out of my life, and I really have no excuse for it. Even today I occasionally give away or sell a book so that I don't need to read it or because I don't have the right place for it on my bookshelves. But on this occasion it was different. I wanted the lady to know how naughty I could be.

This may have been the first time it happened to me, but I have experienced it again since: I sensed a split in my personality. I was both actor and witness. The witness was guiding the actor's behavior. This dualism of being simultaneously actor and witness allows one to monitor one's behavior and reflect on the situation at hand as it evolves. Here, however, the goal was to deter the lady from wanting to deal with me, and I acted accordingly. I knew that what I was doing would characterize me as a child difficult to handle. I don't know what went through the lady's head. Despite her concerned looks (she may have felt challenged to take me on or perhaps the need for employment overrode all other considerations), she accepted the position. She became an integral part of our household for over seven years. It is hard to believe that destiny did not play a role in providing us with the best possible person on the very first interview.

Fräulein, as I was told to call her, was not to be considered a maid despite the fact that her duties included those normally performed by one. Her name was Elfriede Stettinius, an East Prussian name, and she came from a civil-service family in Silesia, where she lived in a small town, Bernstadt, in the Riesengebirge (Mountains of Giants) region. This entire part of Germany was later ceded to Poland.

Maids usually were addressed by their first name, but we never once called Fräulein "Elfriede." Raised with a fair general education acquired in Breslau, she had, before and during World War I, served as the housekeeper and overseer of a large estate. Her fiancé had been killed in battle. She was now living in Hamburg with a brother, a widower and public school teacher, and his daughter Irmgard, a few years older than I, and keeping house for them. Fräulein was integrity personified.

She was a proud German — serious, totally trustworthy, and very conscientious. She was a fairly big woman with long brown hair done in a knot. She had kind brown eyes. She was mature, self-assured — a presence that commanded respect. One did not argue very long with Fräulein. She always came out on top, and I soon learned that she had my parents' full support. Since my father and mother were gone most of the day, she was the one who taught me much of what I now know. She was a caring woman and took her job very seriously. She treated me as she would have a German boy, which, considering the postwar times we were in, was most appropriate. I did not want to be taken for a foreigner. I wanted to blend with the landscape and the people.

As I write these lines, I am flooded with memories that lay fallow for many years and I try to glean from them lessons which, three-quarters of a century ago, I failed to heed. Perhaps I was too young, too insensitive, too concerned with myself, too busy coping and learning more mundane skills to really understand what was going on. In my mind I had established a hierarchy of the individuals that constituted my immediate family. Fräulein was not in the same class as Mom and Dad. She was not really family. But that is where I was very wrong. I emphasize this, because many of us may at one time or other commit this error when evaluating our relationships with others and at some future time learn to regret the lack of appreciation for the love bestowed upon us by others. *How could I be so blind as not to realize it sooner?* Now I know why she cried when, in 1930, we left for Paris, while I, thoughtless, insensitive, devoid of gratitude, acted as though I was glad to turn a new page in my life and experience new places and friends.

Fräulein knew and spoke only German with me, and I had to catch on to survive. I had to learn about everything, but there was plenty of time since I did not start school until 1924. She taught me all the German holidays and the traditional ways of observing them from Epiphany or the Coming of the Magi until *Silvester,* or New Year's Eve. On this last day of the year, Germans would eat pike for good luck and pour molten lead from a tin spoon into a receptacle of cold water, the so-called *Blei giessen.* The odd shapes that resulted would be interpreted just as one would tell fortunes from tea leaves.

Fräulein introduced me to all the seasonal pastimes children engaged in. In winter, of course, there was sledding. In the fall we would fly kites. We would also gather chestnuts — big, shiny, red ones. I picked hundreds of them and wanted to keep them forever. Some I strung on a string like beads. Then one day I found worms coming out of them and very hastily and gladly parted with my treasure. She taught me about Easter eggs and bunnies, and had me memorize songs and short poems, especially for Christmas Eve. I would proudly recite them to my parents before and during the handing out of presents. I would also recite more and more of them to prove how many I could learn by heart. Fräulein would further explain and reinforce the lessons I learned from other kids on the street about games such as hopscotch, spinning tops, and shooting marbles; she taught me the vocabulary needed to enjoy them. I also learned about life and its ups and downs.

The entrance to the apartment building on Emilienstrasse, where we first rented from Frau Römhild, had two sets of glass doors, staircases, and apartments, one on the left and one on the right. A favorite game with other children living in the building was for one of us to stand behind the glass door on the inside and keep another kid on the outside from pushing his way in by pressing against the glass. Once, when I was trying to push my way in, unfortunately on the opposite side from where I lived, I broke the glass. The other kid, who was holding the door shut, was on home territory, since he lived on that side. Although we were both guilty of breaking the glass, the janitor concluded that I was pushing my way into the side of the building where I did not live, therefore trespassing, and ultimately to blame. My parents had to pay the repair bill and I was grounded. It took some reflection on my part to see the justice in all this. Eventually I understood the janitor's reasoning (not as far as my guilt was concerned, for we were both guilty), but as to my parents being made to pay for the broken glass. I was on the wrong side of the apartment building and, in a sense, guilty of being in the wrong place at the wrong time doing the wrong thing.

In addition to the traditional German childhood delights, Fräulein was a gold mine of information about regional dishes and how they differed, even in name, throughout the land. I found out that in Hamburg a roll is a *Rundstück*, but elsewhere a *Semmel, Brötchen, Wecke,* or *Pamel.* I learned all these words in daily usage, which one can only learn when living in the foreign country — preferably at a young age, when the brain absorbs it all like a sponge.

And every night, after giving me my bath, Fräulein would pour a bucket of ice-cold water over me, *"zum abhärten"* — "to toughen me up," she proclaimed. To this day I end all my showers with a cold dash and think of her when doing it.

Fräulein fashioned me into a German-speaking little German boy, who still always remembered his original identity, silently and proudly clinging, at least in his own mind, to the knowledge that he was from New York. Such is the flimsy stuff from which at an early age may spring feelings of patriotism, at least until enlightenment transforms these emotional flights of fancy into more substantive viewpoints.

Had I been raised in the USA, my child's mind would never have been overwhelmed by the image of war as it was while being brought up during the postwar years in Germany — and later in France. A five-year-old child is mature enough to grasp the horrors wrought by a conflict like World War I, and if raised in a sane, healthy, supportive environment, should be capable of handling these disturbing events. I was told about Kaiser Wilhelm II, as well as Field Marshal Paul von Hindenburg and his famous 1914 victory over the Russians. But it was the first time I realized that I had been born during the war and that my own country had been involved in it. I suddenly understood the hostile glances at my mother and me in the Hamburg streetcar. "Don't be noticed, especially not by how you speak," was the lesson I learned from the experience, and I continued to blend with the environment.

Many Germans I met had lost relatives in the war. Fräulein told me about all the colonies Germany had to give up, such as Cameroon, and I saw many pictures of these places in a big book in my father's library. I was also assured that Germany had done a better and more humane job of colonization than other countries. I accepted this on faith and kept my own counsel.

Living in Europe between two major wars, I, of course, had ideas on armed conflict which were more complex than they might have been without this experience. Neither in Germany nor in France was the specter of war ever out of sight or mind. There were always people I knew or met who bore the marks of war — amputations, scars, illness — that made it difficult to forget the ghastly damage wrought. Medals and accounts of heroism did not seem to provide adequate compensation for the suffering war had caused. In France, certain aspects of war and ceremonies related thereto became even more incomprehensible. Occasionally in Paris, when I visited the *Arc de Triomphe* at the top of the *Champs Elysées*, I would see delegations from a group called the *Gueules Cassées* — the shattered faces — deposit a wreath at the tomb of the Unknown Soldier. They were horribly disfigured veterans without the benefit of present-day cosmetic surgery and amputees without prostheses. I could not fathom how they found comfort for the mutilations suffered in the metal tokens they wore or the ribbons that decorated their chests and with the illusion they had served their country in a worthy cause. I remembered my father explaining to me that the true meaning of the title of Erich Remarque's novel *Im Westen Nichts Neues — All Quiet on the Western Front* was how the headlines of newspapers around the world, were summarily dismissing the daily toll on human lives during World War I.

Fräulein Zimmerman, the spinster from whom we rented our second apartment on Gryphiusstrasse 12, told me how she had lost everything after the war through the devaluation of the mark. All she had left was a living room full of antiques — including a spinning wheel, old furniture, dishes, and knickknacks, her bedroom, and the rent my parents paid her. She and her family had once been well-off and belonged to the patrician families of Hamburg.

The citizens of Hamburg were a proud people. They were not Prussians. Hamburg was one of the free Hanseatic cities, like Bremen, Lübeck, and others. The merchants had formed the *Hansa*, a league for their mutual defense when trading abroad. The German spoken in Hamburg was very pure and free from regional dialect. In purity it was second only to the German spoken in Hanover because of one slight negligible difference: in Hamburg "*st*" was pronounced as written and not "*sht*" as elsewhere. Indeed, should anyone learn that you were from Hamburg, he or she would jokingly say, "*Oh! Ich stolpere über einen spitzen Stein!*" — "I stumble over a pointed stone," emphasizing the "*st's*" pronounced elsewhere in Germany "*sht*." In that part of Germany, between the North Sea and the Baltic, a Low German dialect, Plattdeutsch, was also spoken and even had its own literature. However, it was disappearing fast. At school we had to read some stories written in Plattdeutsch, but when one of our teachers asked the class whether anyone still occasionally spoke it at home, only one student raised his hand. I was proud of the fact that I spoke very pure German, not like that of Frankfurt, Berlin, Bavaria, Swabia, or Silesia.

Fräulein taught me some Silesian words and told me about the legendary giant *Rübezahl,* who haunted the Silesian woods and mountains. I enjoyed learning how people in different parts of Germany spoke and memorized some of their linguistic idiosyncrasies.

Another victim of World War I was Frau Klein. She was an old lady who lived in utter poverty. She would come to our door from time to time and relieve us of some things we had no longer any use for. We would also give her some leftover food. I was told that under no circumstance should I confuse her with the beggars that were seen on the streets. She eked out a meager living by collecting scrap and selling it for pennies. One day Fräulein took me along to visit Frau Klein. We brought her some things and food. She lived outside the residential section of Hamburg in a camp located beyond a wire fence and made up of dilapidated shacks. Her place was neat despite its miserable environment. All I really remember is that I was told that Frau Klein was reduced to this way of life through no fault of her own and that she deserved the same respect that I showed people who were much better off. We conducted ourselves as though we were paying a courtesy visit to a friend. I felt that Frau Klein was a lady like any of the others I knew and, indeed, she had the bearing of one. That habit of not looking down on someone with whom life has dealt harshly has been ingrained in me. The episode taught me sympathy, empathy, and gratitude.

Hearing about the casualties of war and witnessing deprivation did not make me afraid of life, but merely put me on my guard and alerted me to sobering realities. Children do not necessarily expect the worst and may even possess innate faith and optimism, which prevent them from thinking that calamities might befall them. Besides, after reading about all the victorious heroes in Greek and German mythology or in books on Indians, Arabs, and others, I figured that if I must some day fight in a war, I might come out on the winning side. Actually, the only thing I dreaded at that age was the thought of having to undergo an operation for appendicitis or to lose an arm or a leg.

When Marshal von Hindenburg came to Hamburg on a visit, Fräulein and I joined a huge crowd of people so that I could see a living military hero. I was impressed but somewhat disappointed. He looked pretty old to me. Nevertheless, he must have been somebody special for the rigid airship, built around that time, was to be named after him. People were collecting money in the streets for the construction of the zeppelin. Von Hindenburg became president of the Reich in 1925, but from what I remember adults saying, the Germans had little confidence in his ability to solve the economic and social problems besetting the country. He was, after all, a tired old man, hardly up to the task of resurrecting a nation not only vanquished in World War I, but severely subjugated and beaten down thereafter.

The airship zeppelin came to Hamburg on a further fundraising tour of Germany, and Fräulein told me about the great German inventor Graf (Count) Ferdinand von Zeppelin of whom the Germans were so proud. I was very much aware how much the Germans liked to recall their past glories and important historical figures. The loss of the war and of their colonies weighed heavily on the national consciousness. They were constantly on the lookout for national accomplishments glorifying Germany, such as the launching of the SS *Bremen* and SS *Europa*, at that time the two largest ocean liners in the world built in Hamburg by Blohm and Voss shipbuilders. The citizens of Hamburg also boasted that they had the world's highest crane.

With hindsight, I realize that in the 1920s German self-esteem was at the lowest possible level and that anyone able to restore it would be acclaimed a savior. What simpler way to explain the success, rise, and credibility of someone with a physique as un-German and non-Aryan as Adolf Hitler? The economic, social, and psychological conditions prevailing in the 1920s enabled the rise of a Hitler — of which I was hardly aware at that time.

I don't remember ever having been conscious of any prejudice against Jews. During the six years I went to school in Hamburg, students always had a few hours a week of religious instruction on subjects taken from both the Old and New Testaments The only difference I ever noticed was when a young boy moved into one of the apartment houses on Gryphiustrasse, and a few of the kids pointed out that his parents were Romanian and Jewish. However, he was always welcome to join us in our games. Although I was only a child, I can state unequivocally that my first acquaintance with prejudice against Jews was in later readings of books such as the *Golem* and *Jud Süss*, and of course the Bible, but not in my daily life.

Of interest is the fact that some with the name Oppenheimer may be Jewish. I was originally baptized in the Lutheran Evangelical Church. Never during those years in Hamburg did anyone bring up the subject of religious preference in my regard nor did anyone make a reference to my name. It was not until 1936 that my religious preference was questioned — at the YMCA in New York City.

I liked everything about Hamburg except the climate. Located on two rivers, the Alster flowing into the Elbe, in the northern part of Germany between the North Sea and the Baltic, Hamburg suffered from a cold, damp climate with very few sunshiny days and a great deal of rain.

Yet my life there was well balanced, and there was plenty of time for everything. I had many friends, and everyone knew everybody else on Gryphiusstrasse. By the time I went to school, a private elementary school, I was like any other German boy, indistinguishable by language or behavior.

One can teach with a whip, but with
sweetness and love one can do better.
— Spanish Proverb

Chapter 3

Hamburg —
The Carefree Years

I WISH THAT IN those early days in Hamburg someone had told me about Horace's advice: *carpe diem* — enjoy the day. I would have savored with keener awareness the pleasures of the moment to store up a reserve for the future when my days might be less carefree. These were the years when I started school and when, through lessons learned both in the classroom and from everyday experiences, many of my beliefs, habits, likes, dislikes, moral principles, and rules of conduct were shaped. The chronological sequence of the events I recount may not always be accurate, but everything else pertaining to them is just the way it happened.

My parents decided against sending me to kindergarten and waited until I had passed my seventh birthday to enroll me in a private school, the *Wahnschaff Schule*. It was located in downtown Hamburg, at Rabenstrasse 5, a good residential section quite far from my home. I had to commute by streetcar. The school building looked like a huge residence and was flanked by residential homes with large front gardens enclosed in iron fences. In place of a garden there was a spacious fenced courtyard in front of the school. It served as a playground during class breaks and for physical education classes. On the first day of school my mother took time to accompany me and impress upon me how I would commute on my own. Like all the other kids, I was equipped with a *Ranzen* — a school bag with slate, stylus, ruler, and so forth inside. I carried it on my back, rather than under my arm, to keep my posture straight. This was the custom in Germany; carrying books in a briefcase under one's arm was considered bad for the posture of growing children. In a small leather case, hanging from a strap across my shoulders, was a snack for later in the morning. I really looked forward to school — much like a sacrificial lamb ignorant of its fate. Actually, it turned out not to be at all bad. It was fun getting to know all the new kids.

The school's primary function was to teach the first four grades and prepare students for the entrance examination to the *Gymnasium* (Latin and Greek) or the *Realgymnasium* (Latin and modern languages). Our classroom was pleasant, with a large stove on one side to heat the room in the winter. Sometimes, when we were good, our classroom teacher, Fräulein Baecker, allowed us to bake apples on the stove.

Fräulein Baecker remained with us for the next four years. I soon fell in love with her — a very platonic love, I might add. When Fräulein Baecker's mother passed away, she was given a few days off and two students were delegated to take a flower bouquet to her home and offer the class's condolences. I was so nervous that, after we rang her doorbell and she opened the door, I burst out in uncontrollable laughter after handing her the bouquet. At that moment I would have liked to be swallowed up by the earth. Yet her reaction was kind, understanding, and considerate. She knew children and their behavior.

The discipline at school was strict, but the general atmosphere was genial. In German, one would term it *gemütlich*. However we knew that we had better behave, lest we face dire consequences. Indeed, I recall when one of the students had committed some very wicked act, the details of which we never knew despite the flurry of rumors that circulated among us. Classes were dismissed and apparently with his parents' consent, the boy was taken to the school director's office and whipped with a flexible rod. I saw him coming out of the room — blood streaming down the back of his legs. It was a sobering sight and made an indelible impression upon the entire student body. I was an obedient student — I knew that my parents would endorse any punishment handed out by the school — however, I was inclined to talk to my neighbors during class and occasionally was reprimanded for it.

Fräulein Baecker was an excellent teacher and well liked. One day, early in the first grade, we were given some kind of an exercise. I did not take it very seriously and thought it was a game. At that time my entire attitude in school was easygoing. I realized later that it was our very first exam. The teacher returned the tests to us marked with numbers ranging from 1 to 5. Mine was a 4. I did not have the foggiest idea as to the meaning of this number. When I proudly showed it to my mother she became very angry. She explained to me that a 1 meant very good, a 2 good, a 3 satisfactory, a 4 poor, and a 5 fail. She told me in no uncertain terms that on all future tests I would be expected to bring home 1's or 2's. I am now convinced that this scene, staged by a very angry disappointed mom, became forever programmed into my subconscious and governed my school behavior from then on. I became competitive and ambitious with regard to grades. Getting good grades became for me a lifelong obsession and, in a sense, I felt it was my duty to bring home the best possible grades to please my parents, especially my mother.

The only other teacher I remember from those years was the music teacher. He was a short, stocky, very lively man with abundant long black hair swept back like a mane. He looked just as I thought a musician should look. One day he played the piano during our music lesson and asked us all to stand up and pretend we were conducting. We waved our arms and hands as best we knew how, keeping time with the music. Although I was certainly not gifted in that direction and could not even carry a tune, through some strange fluke I must have done well enough to attract the teacher's attention. He singled me out and, as he played the music over again, asked me to repeat my motions of conducting. I felt elated, wondering whether I had some hidden talent that might blossom in the future. Deep inside, though, I knew I would not rise to the occasion. This time, with everyone's attention focused on me, I failed miserably. The teacher, no doubt disappointed not to have discovered a prodigy, went on to something else and my brief vision of becoming a celebrated conductor vanished forever.

One Spring, the school rented a small steamboat to take the entire student body, teachers, and chaperones on an excursion to the *Lühe*, outside Hamburg, to see the cherry trees in blossom. Playing in the countryside, I ran towards a group of my friends, mistook a deep swampy creek for a sunken path, and jumped down on it. I sank up to my neck into a slimy, cold, liquid muddy substance. After my embarrassment was past, I ended up naked, wrapped in a towel in the hot engine room. But instead of being scolded, I became, for the rest of the day, a bedraggled celebrity!

Gryphiusstrasse, the street we lived on, was quite a distance away from one of the next parallel streets, Engelstrasse. Between Gryphiusstrasse and Engelstrasse was an empty lot and the elevated train — *Hochbahn* — which circled Hamburg. Engelstrasse residents were less affluent than those on our street. They were literally on the other side of the track. The kids there, whom we merely glimpsed, but did not know, looked tough and we were afraid of them.

Normally, the kids from Engelstrasse did not venture outside their home territory. But one day they did and came looking for trouble on our street. I was willing to fight one at a time. However, not adhering to a code of honor, several boys ganged up on me. Outnumbered, I ran and sought refuge in one of the tiny fenced-off front-yard gardens of an apartment building. Luckily, the Engelstrasse boys did not dare trespass. A large crowd of kids from our street had also gathered by this time. Spiritually, they were on my side, cheering me along. Physically, they remained strictly neutral, merely agreeing that I had claimed and found sanctuary inside the small yard. They were ready to call parents, should the enemy attempt to trespass. Thus began a long siege reminiscent of Troy, without the wooden horse. I was perched on a stone ledge within the fenced-off lot. My enemies surrounded the fence like hounds cornering a fox at bay. The episode lasted a long time. Eventually the besiegers called it quits and much relieved, I went home.

In general, I was not afraid to fight, assuming I had a chance to win. I recall one day when my friend Franz and I really got mad at each other. We started fighting bitterly, almost savagely, about something. Soon we were out of control, clawing and scratching each other, rolling about in the street, bleeding and covered with dirt. Our clothes were torn. Finally, exhausted, we went home. Fräulein reported the incident to my parents; besides I bore the marks of the fight. My parents grounded me for several weeks during which I could no longer play outside. Franz's parents did not punish him, however, and I thought I had been dealt with quite unfairly.

My parents and Fräulein emphasized ethics in my education and in their counseling. I was never to lie or cheat. If I rendered a service to someone, I was not to accept any compensation. I must at all costs keep a promise. These lessons of integrity were reinforced by my readings of tales about knights who would die rather than allow a blemish on their honor.

This dichotomy of right and wrong led me once to commit an act of monumental stupidity. I was walking with two friends on the sidewalk that ran perpendicular to Gryphiusstrasse. We were approaching, without being aware of them, the iron pillars supporting the bridge on which ran the tracks of the elevated train. One of us suggested a contest to see who could walk the farthest on a straight line, with his eyes closed, without chickening out and opening them again. Off we went and I, the very epitome of integrity — or if you prefer, idiocy — smashed my face full force into the iron pillar. Quite bruised, I was bleeding profusely. My friends had cheated and squinted. They were convinced I would do the same and would stop just short of smashing into the column. When at home I showed my bruised face and sheepishly confessed to my foolish action, my parents again were very angry. I gave a great deal of thought to the subject of keeping promises and learned a lesson about being selectively ethical in the future.

Among the social events we looked forward to were birthday parties. It was customary to invite friends to one's birthday party and in return be invited back. My parents did not socialize at all, but my mother, once we had our own apartment, was very good about having nice birthday parties for me so that I could invite these companions. Because my birthday fell in July, when school was out, she very considerately had the party during the school year. We always had a great time. Presents were opened and many games were played, including contests with prizes.

My mother and Fräulein saw to it that everything went smoothly and served the food.

Some parties were elaborate, however. I remember one where a friend's family had a small collapsible theater with hand puppets. I volunteered to improvise a play, and entered the booth-like contraption, inserted both hands into two hand puppets, and raised them up to the front opening, which represented the stage. I manipulated the puppets, made up a plot, and had them interact with each other. Of course, as is customary in puppet plays, at the end one puppet beats up on the other with a club. My audience, including the adults present, liked the performance and I was very pleased with the applause.

I confess that I liked to show off and occupy center stage, which occasionally caused problems. At one of these parties, I was reprimanded for being too exuberant. I told my father about it in detail and he thought I had been dealt with unfairly. I believe there were some nationalist undertones in the matter and I had been singled out because the parents knew I was American. He advised me, should it ever occur again and were I to feel justifiably wronged, to simply leave the party and come home. Walking out on a party sounded great; I suppose I wanted to show my independence and manhood, and my resolve never to take slights from people. I don't know whether my attitude caused me to look for just such an opportunity, but there was another similar occurrence. Perhaps I willfully encouraged it. I felt on top of the world walking out on the party. God only knows what went through my head. Perhaps this devilish dualism arose again in me: I was both witness and actor and the former prodded the latter.

I liked to read, and I had received many books as presents. My father also had acquired a fairly complete collection of German classics. As I matured, I was gradually given permission to read some of them. I also had the opportunity to read many American classics in translation. I read James Fenimore Cooper's *The Pathfinder* and *The Leatherstocking Tales* in German. Translations of American authors such as Jack London, Mark Twain, Oliver Curwood, Ernest Thompson-Seton, and others were very popular in Germany and, for that matter, all over Europe. It was through Thompson-Seton's tales about bears that I learned about Yellowstone Park. I was fascinated with Harriet Beecher Stowe's *Uncle Tom's Cabin*. I loved reading about Greek, Roman, and Nordic mythology, especially the *Nibelungen* legend about Siegfried slaying the Dragon and later on being murdered by Hagen. Such stories nurtured my imagination, and I attempted to apply some of what I had read to my daily life when I asked one of my friends to join me in pledging our mutual friendship by drawing blood with the point of a knife and mixing the drops of blood.

The citizens of Hamburg were very strait-laced and strict not only with their own children, but with those of others. They felt responsible for enforcing discipline and good morals at large, unconcerned as to whether implementation of the code was within their jurisdiction. One afternoon I was strolling with two friends near our school. We were in our early teens. One of the boys was brazen enough to light a cigarette and smoke it in plain daylight. A gentleman, a complete stranger, crossed the street, snatched the cigarette out of my friend's mouth, slapped him violently across the face, asked for his name and address, and told him he would report him to his parents. This casts some light on the attitude and behavior of the Germans with respect to authority and is consistent with their acquiescence in the political events that occurred a few years later in the country.

The only girl I knew, besides Franz's little sister and Fräulein's niece, was Rita. She was, I thought, a beautiful girl. Much older than I, Rita lived in an apartment diagonally across the street from me. From my bedroom window I could see her window. She lived with relatives and took care of their small children. She walked with them where we played on the street. She could not possibly have had any interest in me, yet she started talking to me. Perhaps she was merely getting acquainted with the neighborhood and looking for boyfriends her age. I learned her name and, despite the big difference in age between us, she encouraged the flirting. No doubt she was amused by this young admirer. Some evenings she would draw back her curtains and wave to me from her window. I fell hopelessly in love with her and spent more and more time watching for her. My parents and Fräulein finally caught on and made me realize the absurdity of it all. Besides, a few weeks later I saw her with a young man. She pretty much ignored me, and I knew what it felt like to have a broken heart.

Eventually, the empty sandlot where the neighborhood kids played was occupied by a neat row of new five- to six-story red-brick apartment buildings. Under the buildings were garages and steep driveways leading downward. They stood out as the most modern sight on our street. People started owning cars, although most garages were unoccupied. (Nobody I knew owned a car.) Hamburg was modernizing. Downtown, the triangular *Chilehaus* was built, possibly the first office building in the world where one could simultaneously view from one point both façades diverging from each other at an acute angle. On our street each new apartment had a balcony and the bricks in line with the corners of the balcony criss-crossed each other at one end so that these ends protruded. Thus they provided a flimsy hold for any would-be daredevil reckless enough to scale the wall from the garage driveway to the first balcony.

Now in those days, children — even chaperoned by their parents — were not permitted in movie theaters. There were few exceptions to this rule. Some movies were open to children, though, and I had seen Harold Lloyd in a movie where he scaled and dangled from skyscrapers. My imagination fired by this movie, my tendency to be a showoff, a group of kids daring me to do it, all drove me to attempt climbing the first floor of one of the buildings. Using the precarious hold provided by the end bricks, with both my fingers and toes, I succeeded in reaching the balcony and with a sigh of relief, vaulted the stone parapet. Standing there I had time to reflect on the forthcoming descent. I suddenly realized that this was scarier than the ascent. I did not have the courage to bang on the windows, reveal my presence to the tenants, and ask for help. And it was too high to jump. In the end, I overcame my fear, climbed down, and never did it again.

During this time, Fräulein had Sunday off. My parents, confined all week long to their office, were accustomed to taking a Sunday morning walk in the nearby city park, the *Stadtpark*. It was huge and in parts resembled a forest with oak and chestnut trees. I did not always care for the walk, but I loved the opportunity to talk to my father about a variety of subjects. As time went on I asked a great many questions about puzzling problems I had encountered at school, in my readings, and in my daily contact with people. My father always had an explanation and would often illustrate his points with amusing stories or jokes. When I inquired whether the stories in the Bible represented real facts, he suggested that parables should not be taken too literally, that sometimes wisdom can be presented and taught more attractively by spinning a captivating yarn that enhances the truth. He might even have quoted the Italian proverb *se non è vero, è bene trovato* — if it is not true, at least it is ingeniously contrived.

At the age of ten I learned to swim. The Germans had a foolproof, quick method to teach swimming. It guaranteed that one would learn in ten lessons to swim at least 100 meters. I learned at an indoor pool, the *Kellinghusen Schwimmanstalt*. The lessons were 15 minutes, and our total stay in the pool, including undressing, showering, and dressing again, was limited to an hour — one was charged extra to stay longer. Lessons, like everything else in Germany, were very disciplined. The first day the swim master made me jump into the pool at the deep end so that I would conquer my fear and see for myself that I naturally came up to the surface again. He fished me out and pulled me to a nearby ladder with a long pole. Then, tied to a rope hanging from a fishing pole-like rod protruding from the pool deck, I would at his direction perform breaststroke movements. During the second, third, and fourth lessons he had me swim with a heavy cork life belt around my waist. By the fifth lesson, I started swimming without any belt, huffing and puffing right behind a pole held beyond my reach by the swim master, as he yelled instructions to me. By the seventh lesson (slow learners would take no more than ten), I could swim twice around the pool, four lengths and four widths, and received a certificate stating I had swum myself free — *frei geschwommen*. I graduated and was allowed unsupervised use of the deep side of the pool. It was a very efficient method and no one dared fail.

My mother did not know how to swim. One day, she offered to accompany me to the pool. I was not thrilled. What would I do with a non-swimming adult? It might prove embarrassing. Besides, I might need to spend valuable time with her instead of swimming. Once in the pool I was about to show her how to perform breaststroke movements, when she cast off from the edge and swam away. I was truly nonplussed, standing at the shallow end with my mouth wide open. My mother had secretly taken lessons to surprise me. I was impressed and proud of her. She became a dedicated swimmer into her middle 80s.

Franz and I would often go swimming together. One day we were supposed to bicycle to the Kellinghusen pool, I on my bike, he on his father's, which was a little big for him. We were going to take a soccer ball along and play with it before swimming. At the very last minute I was unable to go. Had I gone, I would have carried the ball. In my absence Franz carried it. As he rode on Sierichstrasse trying to manage a bike that was too big for him, the ball somehow got between his knee and the bike handle. He fell and a truck right behind him went over him, badly mauling his right arm with its axle. Franz lay in the hospital for a long time. I often visited him in the afternoon. The arm healed, but Franz never really had the full use of it. I believe it may have kept him out of World War II. I briefly saw Franz again in 1955, as I came through Hamburg on official business as an Army Captain. It was a painful meeting. Franz had lost his sister and brother in the war. Like his father, he had become a physician. We sat facing each other, formerly bosom friends, our minds darkened by the memories of a war in which we had been on opposite sides.

*Enjoy the present day, trusting as little as possible
to what the morrow may bring.*
— Horace, 65-8 B.C.

Chapter 4

Make the Best of It!

WHEN I WAS NEARING the end of my fourth school year, a major decision had to be reached: in which school should I enroll next? Although the *Wahnschaff Schule*, a private school, offered instruction beyond the fourth year, it was usually — for educational reasons — advisable to send children, if they were qualified, to a *Gymnasium* or a *Realgymnasium*. Courses offered by these institutions, over the subsequent seven years, would provide the opportunity, but not compel one, to pass the *Abitur* examination and enroll in a university. Public schools were more selective in their admission policy and offered a more competitive environment than private schools. Most fourth-year students at the *Wahnschaff Schule* took a week of exams to qualify for either of the above high schools. To my great relief and joy I passed, although this was expected on the basis of my grades. Not wanting me to study Greek, my parents opted for Latin and the *Realgymnasium des Johanneums*, housed in a large building with a huge courtyard, located in the Armgartstrasse at a good distance from my home. I commuted by streetcar.

Becoming a student of a *Gymnasium* was an achievement of which most of us were quite proud. Being admitted to the first grade, or *Sexta*, was a shot of adrenaline to boost our self-esteem. We now had the right and the distinction of wearing the school service cap. Its color would indicate what class we were in, ranging from *Sexta* to *Oberprima* (second year of the first or highest grade). The color of the ribbon or band circling the lower part of the cap indicated the school colors. The first cap I wore, with immense pride, was a gorgeous blue with a white-red-white band. It was for many of us the beginning of a long preparation to enter a university. There was a special aura about being a student of a university. We knew (although by then prohibited or at least discouraged) about university students fencing with sabers until they could sport the scar of a cut across their cheek. Once, after school, a few of us went walking around the University of Hamburg. Through a basement window visible from the sidewalk we saw some students fencing with sabers in a gymnasium. They wore padding on their chests, but no masks on their faces, obviously striving to acquire this coveted distinguishing scar known as a *Schmarre.*

I entered the *Realgymnasium* in the fall of 1928. The feeling of camaraderie, team spirit, belonging, that prevailed among the students of the same class in the *Realgymnasium,* cannot be overemphasized. We supported each other, observed a certain honor code, would never have snitched on each other, and generally got along well. Discipline was strict, taken for granted by us, but benevolent and fair rather than cruel. A permanent room was assigned to our class and our various teachers would come there to teach. We all would be standing at attention next to our desks at the beginning of a class until the teacher had entered and bid us to be seated.

In my very first Latin class, we were standing waiting for the teacher, Herr Nolda, to enter. He was somewhat late arriving and I started talking to my neighbor. Suddenly, Herr Nolda appeared at the classroom door. I did not stop talking in time, and Herr Nolda's glance sweeping the classroom came to rest on me. I was in the back row. He summoned me, not by name, which he did not as yet know, but by pointing. I stood at attention facing him, my face red. He reached way over to his right with his right arm and applied a very forceful slap against my left cheek. Then he asked my name and sent me back to my seat without a further word. No one ever mentioned the incident again and I became one of his best students. Such actions by teachers produced the desired effect. Few students ever got in trouble. Corporal punishment was rare. When it was administered, it was usually by a teacher in front of the entire class, the culprit bending over and the teacher dealing out a predetermined number of blows with a flexible rod on the buttocks. I only remember one such incident at the *Realgymnasium*.

School, compared to what I was to experience in the not-too-distant future, was relatively easy. In Latin class, we had a reader with very simplified texts. The Latin sentences we had to write were also elementary, illustrating various rules of grammar. Dr. Wrage, the class teacher also taught German. A snappy dresser in a bow tie and horn-rimmed glasses, he looked and acted more like our idea of a Britisher. Perhaps we were impressed by his doctor's title. And somehow, because of his urbane teaching style, it seemed he might be more at home on the faculty of a university. Twice a week we still had to use the now less common vertical writing (*Steilschrift*), rather than the increasingly more popular cursive writing (*Lateinschrift*). Older Germans still used the vertical writing, or at times a mixture of both styles. But vertical writing was a little harder to decipher; it consisted of mostly vertical straight lines connected by slanting straight lines.

A Herr Zander (translated "Mr. Pike Perch" in English) taught religion and natural sciences. Occasionally he would stray off the subject. Once he began to rant and rave about some of the atrocities committed by Americans against the Indians. I guess he still had bitter memories of World War I. Xenophobia manifested itself in many ways.

In German, whenever two synonyms coexisted, one native and one a foreign loan word, we were encouraged to use the pure German word: *Fernsprecher* (long-distance speaker) instead of *Telephon,* or *Verabredung* instead of *rendezvous*. It denoted a certain reluctance to use French terms in post-World War I anti-France Germany. I believe most of us willingly preferred using the purely German terms, thus showing that we took pride in the German we used, especially since, as I mentioned before, the citizens of Hamburg were proud of the phonetic purity of their language.

We enjoyed our class breaks, especially the longer midmorning one during which we had time to buy snacks at a small canteen. We could get some deliciously filling bakery goods for a mere five *Pfennig* (five German cents), such as *Punschtorte*, a moist, bread-pudding-like, sweet cake. We laughed and played often and hard outside of class. We could borrow books from the library to take home and read for fun, not for study. Over a holiday break, especially at Christmas, when my mother often went away with my father on trips to Paris, Budapest, or Algeria, I would take home an entire armful of books and try to read them all. After going to bed, I sometimes attempted to read under the sheets with a flashlight, hoping Fräulein would not catch me, though unfortunately she did every so often.

Most summers my mother chose to travel to her native Switzerland. I was treated to a showing of Schiller's *William Tell* in Altdorf, the more enjoyable as it was performed where the legendary action allegedly took place. We took the cogwheel train to the top of Rigi-Kulm and visited the Lion Monument and the Panorama in Lucerne, touring several times on a small steamer the entire Lake of the Four Cantons. Many years later, after the end of World War II, this annual trip enabled me to serve as guide to a few American officers from the XXI Army Corps general staff on a short tour of Switzerland.

One summer my mother elected to go to Garmisch-Partenkirchen in Bavaria. We stayed in the beautiful Hotel Sonnenbichel. Guests had access to a large forest and a pond suitable for bathing and swimming. (When I saw it again in 1954-1955 it had been converted to a hospital.) My father usually stayed in Hamburg to work, but joined us later for a week or two. During this particular visit, we had rain every day for five weeks with the exception of two. Despite the rain, we managed to take many excursions. Once we took the funicular railway up to the Kreuzeck, a peak near Garmisch. A terrible thunder and lightning storm broke out as we were halfway down on the return trip. The car we rode stopped in midair and we dangled for over an hour from the cable far above the ground in the storm. It was an unforgettable adventure.

Renting a rowboat at the Badersee, a beautifully transparent green-blue lake with the sunken statue of a nymph at its bottom (*Die Nixe im Badersee*), rekindled my imagination which loved to dwell on mythical gods, goddesses, and spirits. We also toured the extravagant castles of the mad Louis II of Bavaria, Neuschwanstein and Hohenschwanstein. I was overwhelmed by the sheer luxury of the castles' contents and learned about the turbulent life and death of Richard Wagner's patron. We visited the violin makers of Mittenwald and eerie ravines near Garmisch, known as *Höllentals Klamm* (Hell's Valley Gorge), and *Pachtnachts Klamm*. We were also treated to a detailed behind-the-scenes conducted visit of the Passion Plays theater in Oberammergau, but did not see the play.

Frustrated by the bad weather, my mother decided to take the bus and travel to St. Moritz. We arrived there one day before my birthday. Our bad luck with the weather held firm. On our arrival it began to snow. I told the person at the reception desk that it was going to be my birthday, a serious mistake on my part. I was presented with a box of chocolates, which I immediately sampled. I shall never know for certain the exact cause of it, but the next morning I lay deathly sick with a temperature of 106 degrees. A doctor was called and I hovered for four days between life and death with, it appeared, acute food poisoning. The chocolate, gracefully aging in a hotel desk, may have been to blame. My father had to go home. Mother and I returned to Hamburg a few days later. I was kept on a strict special diet of porridge and other such tasteless foods for months, without fruit or any of the goodies I normally enjoyed. I suffered from a somewhat delicate stomach for years afterward.

In the summer of 1928, we vacationed in Wiesbaden. We stayed at the Hotel Eden opposite the casino. (In 1945, when I drove by in a jeep, I noticed the hotel had been shut down.) My father came with us, brought all his correspondence files with him, and set up his office in the hotel room. Twice a day he took a walk in the park and went to the *Kurhaus* (Thermal Spa) to drink the awful-tasting, but supposedly healthful, hot mineral water straight from the spring. The rest of the time he worked, communicating by letters or telegrams with his European clients.

Encouraging me toward lucrative employment, my father offered me a job as an errand boy. I would deliver his messages to the local telegraph office and for every trip he would credit me with a small sum of money. I could draw from this account whenever I needed spending money. I ran many errands and saw my net worth increase considerably. Once or twice a week I drew out some of my earnings, rented a wooden kayak, and pad-dled it on the casino's lake. I was a very happy boy. On certain weekends the casino staged impressive fireworks.

In the hotel dining room, where we ate three meals a day, my parents became acquainted with a Dutch couple from Scheveningen. Much later on I found out that in World War II when the Dutch wanted to make sure that a stranger was not a German spy, they asked him to pronounce the name of this beach town. No German, the Dutch claim, can pronounce it correctly. I would not have bet on that.

Every Thursday I walked to the municipal indoor pool. We were allowed to swim until three o'clock in the afternoon, when we had to vacate the pool for members of the British Occupation Army. I remember freely joining the other boys in cursing those unwelcome foreigners who deprived us of a longer swim and who, for the most part, did not under-stand what we shouted at them.

A few times my parents dropped me off at an outdoor "swimming pool" located near Wiesbaden on the left bank of the Rhine River. It consisted of a square pool deck floating in the river. Around it were cabins to dress and undress. Underneath the south and north sides of the deck were gaps, allowing the very strong river current to flow through. Thus we were actu-ally swimming in the Rhine, protected by the four sides of the deck, but fully exposed to the current. Always looking for daredevil stunts, some of us climbed to the top of the cabins facing the Rhine at the south end, jumped 15 feet into the river, and were immediately swept away by the current. The trick was to catch hold of some part of the outside deck struc-ture before being swept past its north end. We squeezed through one of the gaps back into the inside swimming area and safety. Fortunately I never missed. Had I, I might have been swept past Bonn and Cologne.

Another summer was spent in Ostende, a Belgian beach resort on the British Channel. We stayed in a very good hotel with extremely elegant service. The meals consisted of many courses, and the food was served in style. My two favorite pastimes were swimming every day and flying a box kite. Conditions for flying kites from the windy, sandy beach were ideal and the kites did not come crashing down. I even succeeded in send-ing small paper messages, wrapped around the string, all the way up to the kite.

Swimming at Ostende entailed a fairly complicated ritual. We had to wait for low tide. Then we went to the beach to find a vacant cart-like cabin mounted on two wheels. Once we had donned our bathing suits (trunks were not allowed), we called for a driver with a horse. The driver would then harness the horse to the cabin and pull us down to the water. At the end of the swim we had to find our cabin to get dressed. It was there, in the dressing cabin, that I saw my father have the attack that scared me and remains one of my most vivid childhood memories.

In early 1930, my parents asked me to come into the living room to hear some important news. I was not to confide to anyone what they were about to tell me until they said I could. Soon we were all moving to Paris where my father was to open a new office for H. Muehlstein and Company. It would be a more strategic location for his import-export business. He would be closer to many important clients in France, the Netherlands, Belgium, Italy, Spain, Hungary, and North Africa. Of course, I was taken by complete surprise. At that precise moment, I truly believe that my only thought was, "Gee! Wait till my friends, teachers, everyone I know, hear about this! They cannot possibly match this. Paris! Wow!" There is something sad about parting, but there was such a tremendous thrill in starting anew! A whole new life awaited me. Any problems I had (and I don't think I could have thought of a single real one except the next day's homework) would disappear, the slate wiped clean.

Soon our departure became common knowledge. My mother went to the *Realgymnasium* to inform the administration of my departure. I was given a final grade report stating I would be promoted to the next or fourth grade (*Quarta*) and "wishing me well in the future." The director advised my mother to enroll me in a German school upon our arrival in Paris, because, he claimed, French schools could not compare in quality. How wrong he turned out to be! Herr Nolda, the Latin teacher, of whom I had become a favorite student, rightly counseled my mother to attempt to place me in a French school, if somehow I could manage the transition, considering all the catching up I would have to do in French and other subjects. Evidently, Herr Nolda did not allow any national German dislike for the French to taint his good judgment. I gave no thought to what might happen once I was in Paris. I was merely enthralled with my new adventure and the effect it must be producing on all those who knew me.

I am ashamed to admit now, that although dimly aware of the hurt I was causing my Fräulein, I acted most defiantly, brazenly pretending my leaving her — after seven and one-half years — was a routine parting. Had my early years already begun to inure me to what was to become my life's pattern, constantly leaving friends and acquaintances behind, starting fresh among new ones with nary a pang or sigh of regret? Or was I acting in a very insensitive manner, perhaps because I wished to look grownup and virile?

As to Fräulein, we had unfortunately, without any malice on our part, left her without purpose or prospect. I now believe she was devastated. It was like losing an entire family all at once. Since 1922, she had watched over me every single day! Soon afterwards, she wrote us. She had married a widower and had become Frau Elfriede Blümel, which means in German "little flower," a name that hardly fit her. If anything, she was a radiant one of quiet beauty. I have no recollection of saying farewell to anyone, except for my cursory parting with Fräulein. We corresponded with Frau Blümel for a while, but after a year or so we received no reply to our postcards or letters. We assumed that under the Hitler regime she may have deemed it unhealthy to correspond with foreigners.

Better a well formed head than a full one.
— François Rabelais, 1494–1553

Chapter 5

An American Boy in Paris

PON OUR ARRIVAL IN PARIS, around Easter time, we stayed in a centrally located hotel on the Boulevard Haussman until our furniture caught up with us and we could move into our apartment. My parents had rented it on the fifth floor of a new building located at 187 Rue de Courcelles in the 17th *arrondissement* (one of the 20 wards), a residential section in northwestern Paris. We were the first occupants of our brand-new apartment. Actually the building was on the very edge of Paris. The old fortifications of the city had been razed to erect it. The remaining ramparts were still intact, extending to the east in front of our apartment building and perpendicular to it as far as the eye could see along the recently constructed Boulevard Berthier. The broad embankments or mounds behind the defenses, covered with grass and sloping down toward Boulevard Berthier, were an ideal picnic and playground for adults and children alike. Immediately in front of our building was the *octroi* — the tollhouse — where all commercial traffic in and out of Paris, to and from Levallois-Perret, a suburb adjacent to Paris, stopped for a customs check. The traffic procession frequently included (besides automobiles and trucks) livestock herders, traveling with a few goats, peddling milk and cheese; horse carts; and any other colorful means of conveyance one could possibly imagine. I had a prime view of this spectacle from our balconies. Construction crews started razing the remaining ramparts to begin a building frenzy, which continued for years. Eventually, the *octroi* and all the fortifications disappeared.

After our arrival, while still in the hotel, I was granted a short period of grace until life would start in earnest. My father was quite busy setting up his new office and hiring staff. He needed employees fluent in German and English. They were hard to find among the French, and the French government did not readily allow hiring of foreigners. He ended up employing a polyglot Austrian, who, in my perhaps inexpert opinion, seemed to have forgotten his own native German. He turned out to be a disappointment and my father soon let him go.

My mother also had her hands full, settling down in the new apartment and looking for a maid. At that time many maids were from Alsace, which had reverted to France after World War I. Most spoke French as well as a heavily accented, guttural, Alsatian German. Looking for husbands, they would usually quit their positions once their search proved fruitful.

During this period of transition my parents and I ate our evening meals together in restaurants where I was especially intrigued by the many *hors d'oeuvres*, *tartes* (open pies), numerous cheeses, *baguettes* (yard-long French bread), as well as the self-assured professionalism of the waiters. The endless parade of varied cheeses truly astounded me, especially after my father showed me, near the Place Clichy on the Rue d'Amsterdam, the store specializing in, and famous for, an incredible variety of aged cheeses. Imagine my dismay when I saw in the display window one or two particularly awesome specimens and, as living testimonial to their authentic maturity, worms weaving a rhythmic dance on their surfaces. The store exists to this day, and I am certain its products are by now ripe enough to satisfy the most sophisticated tastes of the most demanding clients!

My favorite dish was *sole meunière*, grilled filet of sole served with lemon, and a boiled potato. It replaced my former favorite in Germany, *Wiener Schnitzel*. Unfortunately, eating sole often gave me a nettle rash. I was plagued by this allergy as long as I lived in France. My gastronomic bliss thus came to an abrupt end. Perhaps the pressures I was to be exposed to for the next five years were partly to blame. Luckily for me, a few years later, Paris developed a craze for *choucroute garnie*, a German-Austrian-Bavarian dish consisting of sauerkraut, mashed potatoes, frankfurters, knockwurst, and smoked pork tenderloin. New restaurants like the Tirol and Hungaria sprang up all over Paris, the latter two on the elegant *Champs Elysées*, serving this typically German dish to thousands of eager Parisians.

Of course, everything I saw was new to me and quite different from what I was familiar with in Hamburg. I went around goggle-eyed, observing the differences between the French and Germans. I asked my parents many questions and tried to pick up new French words. At age 13, I had an enormous amount of catching up to do to learn a new language at a level corresponding to that of someone my age. Since in my very early childhood, before age five, my grandmother had spoken French to me and I had heard my parents speak it when they did not want me to understand what they were saying, I had at least been exposed to it. However, for all practical purposes French was like Greek to me.

My parents had their own problems. The rent for our apartment was apparently exorbitant, 30,000 francs ($2,000 a year). Starting a new office in new surroundings was very stressful for my father. I also learned at that time that my father was on a commission, and that H. Muehlstein paid only one-half his office expenses. Besides, he did no business for his own account and represented only Muehlstein. Thus, my family had financial worries. A move like ours required severe adjustments for everyone.

My mother located a potential school, *Lycée Carnot*, for me close to our home. A *lycée* is a public secondary school which offers classes ranging from elementary to the Bachelor of Arts degree. It is a hybrid — between a high school and a junior college. However, the degree is not granted by the *lycée*, but rather, upon arduous written and oral examinations, by the university in which the academic region of the *lycée* is located. In the case of *Carnot*, the degree would be granted by a baccalaureate office of the University of Paris.

One morning, a week or so after our arrival in Paris, my mother and I went to *Lycée Carnot*. Students were still on Easter vacation. We went to see the *proviseur* — the headmaster, who upon learning my age, sent us to the professor in charge of the fourth grade.

Professeur Van Daële looked like someone with a Dutch or Flemish name should: sandy blond hair, blue eyes, crisp in manner, a clipped nasal enunciation, but quite French and very polite in his demeanor. The classroom was lined with bookshelves on which were thousands of volumes. I found out later that Van Daële ran a lending library for his students and that it was not compulsory, but advisable, to become a member thereof.

Professeur Van Daële was not a man to trifle with. He had been gassed during World War I and was often subject to violent asthmatic coughing fits. He would turn crimson and reach for a small air pump, the kind Harpo Marx used in his films, to blow air into his nostrils, as we watched in transfixed anguish. He had a very short fuse and we feared his outbursts. He was, however, as I found out with time, an intelligent, fair, and conscientious teacher, quite progressive in outlook. Some years later, he even opened a private glider school.

All professors at the *lycée* were *Agrégés de l'Université* — meaning they had passed a grueling competitive examination to acquire this designation. Passing this exam assured them of a job, first in the provinces and potentially in Paris, as the number of vacancies in *lycées* at the time of the exam determined the number of candidates awarded the degree.

My mother explained to me later that Van Daële, after learning I had been promoted to the fourth grade in Hamburg, suggested I attend the last trimester of his fourth grade as an auditor. I would flunk in June as, under the circumstances, I would any grade I was placed in, yet automatically reenter in the fall the same fourth grade where I belonged. If I was as good a student as my mother claimed, I might, with extra tutelage in French, Latin, and English during the long summer vacation, possibly be able to follow in class. Van Daële was not promising anything. It was totally up to me. He sent us to the bookstore across the street from *Lycée Carnot*, where we purchased an enormous load of books including two giant dictionaries — one Latin-French, one French-Latin.

When classes reopened after Easter, I walked from 187 Rue de Courcelles up the Rue d'Ampère, then right a few steps on Boulevard

Malesherbes to the entrance of *Lycée Carnot*. Many well-known people attended *Carnot*, among them Jacques-René Chirac, now president of France. A few steps past the entrance was the school building proper: large, oblong, with a huge empty courtyard in the center. Around this courtyard were two stories of classrooms. The ceiling was an iron framework with glass panels protecting the inside from the elements. I did not learn until 60 years later that the ceiling was the work of Gustave Eiffel, the creator of the famous tower — I should have recognized the similarity of these metallic structures.

I went to Van Daële's classroom with enormous apprehension. He must have told the students about my status. I was assigned a seat, from where I simply sat and watched. Most of the time I did not know what was happening around me, understanding nothing or very little. I focused mainly on the French, Latin, and English classes, since the others — history, geography, geology, mathematics — were beyond my comprehension.

In English class I sat next to Baron. He was very big and mature looking for our class and wore a suit and tie with an empty left sleeve stuck into the left pocket of his jacket. He had lost his arm in a car accident. Baron did not like me very much and grew impatient with my constant questions in broken French. I tried desperately to remember whatever English I might have known as a five-year-old child, but it was too simplistic for the English teacher. He gloomily predicted I would never be capable of managing the English curriculum.

Classes ran from Monday through Saturday, morning and afternoon, with Thursday off. We had short breaks between classes and a long break for lunch, which most of us ate at home. A very small number of students (*demi-pensionnaires* — those who were partial boarders) ate lunch at the *lycée*. I always walked to and from home. Thursday was not a day of rest, but rather indispensable, to allow students to catch up on their heavy homework. Thursday mornings were also set aside for two- or four-hour detentions — *retenue,* or in French school slang, *colle* (glue) — assigned for either misbehavior or deficient schoolwork. In my five years at *Carnot* I only received a two-hour *retenue* from the *Surveillant Général* — a non-teaching official in charge of discipline, nicknamed G.D.B., or *gras du bide* (potbelly) — for brawling during a class break in the courtyard.

Then began for me a very demoralizing period. After class I would go home and, with constant recourse to dictionaries, attempt to complete some of my homework. The Latin I had learned in Hamburg was extremely elementary. In France we were reading Caesar's *Commentaries on the Gallic Wars* and Vergil's *Bucolics, Georgics*, and chiefly his *Aeneid* in the original. I would sit at my desk for hours trying to make sense of one of Caesar's prose sentences or a few lines of Vergil's verse, hoping to find the phrase in the voluminous dictionary. There is a European saying: "When learning a foreign language, one must look up a word seven times before mastering it." This is where I learned the discipline of looking up words countless times until they finally stuck, never relying on guesswork, always making sure I knew the precise meaning. This discipline, rarely practiced in the USA, except for physical skills, was to stand me in good stead throughout my life.

My struggle with French literary texts was even worse. We were reading Racine's drama *Athalie* (Athaliah), about the Old Testament queen, daughter of Jezebel, who had murdered 42 princes of the house of David to conquer the throne and was later slaughtered by a mob. I was hoping my parents might help me with the French, but good as their knowledge was, it was insufficient. Nor was there enough time to explicate texts of Shakespearean depth and difficulty. I would spend hours trying to decipher a few alexandrine verses from Racine, with the help of a French-German dictionary, and would be unable to make any sense of it. I was hopelessly frustrated, and looking down from my fifth floor window, could not help but think what a relief jumping out of it would provide. I pleaded with my parents to let me attend another school with no Latin, but my mother was adamant: Latin and English it was to be! The choices in a *lycée* at that time were: A — Greek and Latin; A' — Latin and either English or German; B — Any two of English, German, or Spanish. (This designation is no longer used in the French school system.) I was in A'.

My mother tutored me in English, and I started borrowing books from Van Daële's library — mostly detective and mystery stories. I thought a thrilling plot with a surprise dénouement would keep my interest alive through the entire volume. It gave me the patience and motivation to look up words in the dictionary, and slowly I began to increase my vocabulary. Thus, I read Leblanc's stories of Arsène Lupin, gentleman-thief, who undoubtedly inspired some of the Cary Grant and William Powell impersonations on the big screen. Very popular at that time were the Edgar Wallace novels translated from English into French, some of them dealing with Al Capone. I vaguely remember his *Crimson Circle*.

My classmates behaved pretty decently toward me. A few, knowing I had moved to Paris from Germany, called me "*Boche*," the racist equivalent of *kraut*. It brought on a few brief fights, where I made it very clear I was an American and not a German. Often, when they made fun of me, I failed to grasp their meaning. To this day I try to comprehend why a few of my classmates burst out in wild laughter at what I had said.

One day after school, on the way home, we stopped at a bakery to buy a *croissant*, a *brioche*, or a *petit pain au chocolat*, all standard French bakery items. They asked me how I managed my homework. I replied: "*Ma mère m'aide*" — "My mother helps me." Perhaps I mispronounced the "d" as a "t." The boys immediately started making fun of me and laughingly kept on repeating: "*Ta mère tête*" — "Your mother sucks." I felt quite helpless and embarrassed. At that time I did not know what they were laughing at. I did not know the meaning of *têter*. I am still not certain of the reason for their jeers, but their laughter keeps ringing in my ears.

On one occasion I unwittingly triggered a disaster for myself. This particular incident taught me a lasting lesson about the occasional unforeseeable irascibility of the French under certain circumstances, a trait which might explain the frequent antagonism felt by American tourists toward the French and their behavior. After a class break, we were lined up in front of our classroom awaiting Van Daële's signal to file in. I stood in front of the line. Van Daële, in deep thought, was sitting at his desk on top of the podium. I don't know what possessed me. I meant no harm. I guess I wanted to try out my new, painfully acquired, extremely limited French. Incapable of formulating an intelligent sentence, drawing on recently read words from literary texts, hoping to sound funny, I uttered the rather lame observation: "*Voilà Van Daële sur son trône!*" — "There's Van Daële on his throne!" Van Daële's reaction was apocalyptic. He was aware that I referred to him in whatever I said. He rushed toward me, asked me to repeat it. I did. He turned crimson and acted as though he was ready to kick me out of school. I honestly did not know what the fuss was all about, but I was terror-stricken. What had I done now?

That evening I told my parents about Van Daële's fulminating rage. My father's comment was brief and to the point: "Never ever make remarks about anyone, especially not a teacher." My parents also enlightened me that "throne" in French slang could refer to a toilet seat, a precious bit of information I immediately added to my growing knowledge of the language. Not in my wildest dreams had I imagined the professor perched on a toilet seat. I don't remember whether my mother went to see Van Daële and explained my *faux pas* to him, or whether she wrote him a letter of apology. I begged his forgiveness the next day, and I was reinstated in his majesty's good graces.

Gradually, as the weeks went by, I began to realize the staggering amount of homework French students were expected to do. In Latin alone, of which we had eight hours a week, we had to prepare a major piece of written translation from French into Latin — *thème latin* — and one from Latin into French — *version latine* — each week. In addition, we had to prepare readings from Caesar and Vergil, which we were called on to recite in class. Of course, homework was assigned in all other subjects as well. In French there was a weekly composition — *thème* — on a specific subject.

The volume of memorization assigned was inconceivable and beyond anything I had experienced in German schools. Every week teachers had students memorize some 10 to 15 lines of French, Latin, and English verse and a few paragraphs of prose in French and Latin. During the trimester, a few students were selected at random to recite the material. Then came a surprise revelation, which made me wonder whether I was dreaming. At the end of the trimester, a *composition de récitation* — a recitation test — was given. The class was held responsible for all the material memorized: about 10 pages of French and Latin prose, 200 to 300 lines of French and Latin verse, and a large amount of English verse and prose. The teacher would place slips of paper with the names of all students in a hat and draw them at random. Then, as his name was picked by chance, the student would step up to the podium and recite as flawlessly as possible a portion of the memorized text until stopped by the teacher. The texts would be recited from beginning to end, each student starting where the previous one had left off. All students would be present and listen until called upon to recite. They had to perform at least twice, once in Latin and once in French. English recitation would be conducted in a similar manner by the English teacher. We were graded on all points: perfect memorization, pronunciation, and delivery. Little did I realize that a few months later I would be, in preparation for this test, reciting pages and pages of French, Latin, and English to my mother until I could perform perfectly.

In addition to receiving a grade, French students were also ranked numerically for each exam. I soon discovered that our class ranking in tests was more important than our grade. Each trimester we were given written exams on all subjects: Latin-French and French-Latin translation,

French composition, history, geography, mathematics, sciences, art, physical education, and so forth. Anyone placing first in any of these exams during the fall trimester would be invited to an afternoon collation in January on St. Charlemagne's Day and enjoy hot chocolate and cake.

My ambition to take part in this honor was not fulfilled until two years later. At the end of each trimester the registrar would statistically determine the overall best student. The latter would be awarded the *prix d'excellence* — excellency prize. Other students with good grades would be listed on the *tableau d'honneur* — the honor roll, which we routinely nicknamed *tableau d'horreur*, or "horror roll." A limited number of outstanding students were honored with the *Félicitations du Conseil de Discipline* — Felicitations (Congratulations) of the Disciplinary Council, which might cause one's chest to swell with pride, but brought no material reward. Both distinctions, if awarded, were recorded by a stamp on the bottom of one's grade report. Some time in June, at the end of the school year, the administration and faculty of the *lycée* presided over a distribution of prizes, and any students ranked first and second in any subject received a prize, usually a book. Students who did not expect any were conspicuously absent from this ceremony. Most had already left for the long summer vacation, which lasted until about October 1st.

Discipline at *Carnot* was ironclad. In my five years there I know of only two exceptions. During my first trimester as auditor and the entire year in the fourth grade we had a history and geography professor named Muret. For mysterious reasons, deeply buried in the *lycée's* past, he had been nicknamed Gédéon, a biblical judge of Israel dating back to the 12th-11th centuries B.C. Two students at the time had started a literary masterpiece, unfortunately for posterity never completed, *Voyage en Gédéonie* (*Voyage to Gedeonia*), in which Muret played the principal dazzling role. An elderly man, he was just about stone deaf, had long pointed eyebrows, which he twirled from time to time, and had an execrable habit of speaking in a halting snycopated manner, inserting countless "ugh's" between the words of his sentences.

In French there is an untranslatable term for students "raising Cain" to protest a professor: *chahuter* is the verb, *chahut* the noun. The first time I witnessed this "chahut" against Profesor Muret the noise generated by the students was incredible. Yet, this rather gentle academic would merely twirl one of his eyebrows and repeat: "I hear, ugh, a little, ugh, whisper." The class would burst out laughing.

Lost in the deluge of Merovingian and Carolingian kings, I was dumb-founded. When in geography or history class "Gédéon" showed slides, many students would throw spit balls in the dark at the ceiling and walls. The din would gradually escalate to such a degree that it became audible even to him. Angry and irritated, he would stop the slide show, switch on the lights, draw back the shades, and see the spit balls gradually dropping to the floor. Eventually the noise became so loud that the *proviseur*, whose office was below Muret's class, began to hear it and ordered us to stop. Muret soon retired.

The other exception to *Carnot's* stern discipline was even more unusu-al. One day, in the third grade, two strange students presented themselves to our teacher, Marcel Abraham, who soon after was appointed undersec-retary of the French Ministry of Education under the new minister, de Monzy. The youths introduced themselves as Durendal and Boussu, claiming to be transfer students. They convincingly stated their credentials were being processed and in the meanwhile immediately started misbe-having, creating a major disturbance, and impeding the teacher from car-rying on. They were soon found out to be frauds, operating under false names, and, I believe, suspended from the *lycée* they had come from. We were never enlightened as to their real motives. And I never forgot their pseudonyms, for Durendal was Roland's (Charlemagne's paladin) magic indestructible sword, much like King Arthur's Excalibur.

Strange and disappointing to me were the physical education classes at *Carnot*. The *lycée* had a small basement gym and an outside courtyard. At least one-half the students obtained medical excuses to skip gym. As a result, both gym teachers had lost all interest in their jobs. It was regret-table, since one of them had at one time been kick-boxing champion of France. During the day, both would quite often patronize the bar across from *Carnot* to *boire un coup* — have a drink. The effect thereof was quite discernible: glazed eyes, a stiff hesitant gait, and a lack of interest in com-municating with students. It was thus not uncommon, when gym class came around, for one of them to fetch a chair, turn it around, straddle it, rest arms and head on its back, and tell us to occupy ourselves playing either soccer or handball.

A few of us, eager for exercise, faithfully attended the two one-hour gym classes each week. We played informal soccer or handball. Once in a great while, in good weather after class, an even smaller group of us would take an hour or two before starting homework and go to the *Bois de*

Boulogne, the large Paris park. The rest of the boys would rent a taxi and all pile in like sardines. I had beforehand fetched my bike, and holding on to the taxi would hitch a ride with them. Even if I had to let go of the taxi to avoid a catastrophic fall, we would arrive at our destination pretty much at the same time. We worked up a real sweat and returned home to hit the books until midnight.

Occasionally, on Thursday mornings, my mother and I went swimming at the Danton pool. There I might glimpse Poussard, French springboard diving champion, practicing for the 1932 Olympics, alone and without fanfare. I believe he came in last in Los Angeles. Once, we had to vacate the pool so that Cartonnet could set a 200-meter European record in the breaststroke. We were astounded to see him pass out in the water at the end of his feat. Those were the days when Olympic champions trained without a retinue of coaches, shrinks, financial advisers, agents, and such. They were mere mortals like us!

In the winter some of us might, on a Thursday afternoon, go ice-skating at the indoor artificial ice rink of the Winter Sports Palace (*Vélodrome d'Hiver*) or at the outdoor rink seasonally installed in the outdoor pool of the newly built Molitor Aquatic Complex. Once or twice I managed to go ice-skating at the *Vel d'Hiv* with my mother on a Thursday morning and saw Sonja Henie practicing her figures on a portion of the rink roped off for her personal use. Only once in five years was it cold enough for the ponds in Versailles to freeze over. A friend called me on a Sunday and persuaded me to go skating with him and another classmate. We had so much fun and stayed so long that on our way home we found the giant Versailles gates closed and had to climb over them.

The trimester finally and mercifully came to an end. I only took, and duly flunked, two exams: Math and English. My grade report officially and lugubriously informed me, as expected, that I was "recognized as incapable of being promoted to the third grade and must reenter the fourth grade on October first." At least they did not recommend my starting from *enfantine* — kindergarten! I took it as the school's demonstrating some faint hope in my future ability to follow. After all, had I taken the third trimester in Hamburg, I would have been in exactly the same position in the fall: the beginning of the fourth grade.

It was now time to do, in a methodical and organized manner, whatever was necessary to bring my knowledge to a level allowing me to successfully attend the fourth grade in the fall. Professor Van Daële had given my mother the name of a tutor, Monsieur Lelièvre. An elderly man, he neither held the diploma of *agrégé* nor taught in a *lycée*, but turned out to be an excellent instructor. I commuted to his home in the Passy section of Paris, past the Eiffel Tower and the *Trocadéro* (the latter replaced in 1937 by the *Palais de Chaillot* for the Paris World Fair), every weekday for most of the summer. He taught me Latin and French grammatical analysis in the minutest detail. I translated from and into Latin and analyzed French texts down to their precise morphological and syntactical components. I spent the mornings with him and devoted my afternoons to the homework he assigned me.

Gradually, it all began to come together! It was tedious, but the progress I was making, together with the satisfaction and self-esteem it gave me, provided the needed motivation. It taught me immense discipline and patience, at least in the realm of knowledge acquisition and scholarly research, if not in other more mundane aspects of life. The foundation for discipline in other pursuits had already been laid by my German role models. It, of course, would be reinforced during the next five years in the *lycée*.

The French educational system marked and molded me in this relatively short, but incredibly intense, period into the end product it was designed to achieve: an individual fully prepared to enter and exit by competitive examinations the various university-level French institutions, which inevitably, with few exceptions, lead to his place, often for life, in the French hierarchical system.

My only occasional recreation was to see a movie with my parents on Sundays. This was the time when such French actors as Chevalier, Raimu, Azais, and Fernandel were at the peak of their fame. But there was another unique Parisian event and attraction which, despite my heavy work schedule, I was fortunate enough to witness: the Colonial Exhibition of 1930. Among all the shows of this kind, including several world fairs, I have ever seen, *l'Exposition Coloniale* stands out as unique and unforgettable.

Erected at the *Porte* and *Parc de Vincennes* in the southeastern part of Paris, the exposition consisted of numerous pavilions representing all the French colonies and territorial possessions at that time, with displays of their art, agricultural and industrial products, human resources, and other notable characteristics. All the colonies — Algeria, Morocco, Tunisia, Indochina, Cambodia, Annam, Laos — and many others were included. We could see a life-size replica of the temple of Angkor Vat and one of Washington's White House. It was a wonderland of colonial architecture. There also was a rather complete zoo. I was able to take time out from school work and visit the displays numerous times. Visiting the Exposition was an education in itself and helped me learn many new words and terms.

In a pavilion that had horrifying, graphic photographs of sexually transmitted diseases raging in some of the colonies, my mother availed herself of the opportunity to initiate my education on the subject. At the same time, she inspired me with such a holy terror of possibly catching syphilis or gonorrhea that, at that very moment, a life of sexual abstinence seemed to be not only acceptable, but by far the most prudent and rewarding lifelong behavior to adopt. Her admonitions stamped themselves forever in my brain.

Toward the end of the summer, my mother decided we needed some sort of a change. Paris, during the warm months, is deserted and somewhat depressing. She suggested a few days on the Channel beaches of Normandy, in Trouville. Deauville, adjacent to it, much more elegant and with a casino, was too expensive. However, after a few days, she developed an asthmatic reaction to the salt air. Disenchanted with the extremely low tides and unattractive swimming conditions, she asked me whether I minded returning to Paris. I, of course, saw no reason in prolonging her discomfort. Thus ended a transitory period during which I had accomplished a great deal. I felt I could now face, with a certain equanimity, self-confidence, and increasing faith in my ability to cope, the imminent *rentrée des classes* — reopening of school — with new classmates, but with at least the comfortingly familiar presence of Professeur Van Daële, who could only be pleasantly surprised by my working-summer's results.

My initial experience at *Lycée Carnot* may have had me doubt that the French in their educational methods adhered to the Rabelaisian precept, as quoted at the beginning of this chapter — emphasizing form, style, and quality over quantity of knowledge. However, years later I realized that French teachers placed much significance on developing their students' rational thought, logic, and above all scholarly discipline. As you sow, so you shall reap!

He who strives and toils without rest,
shall gain salvation and be blessed.
— Johann Wolfgang von Goethe,
1749–1832

Chapter 6

The Academic Grind — *Le Bachot*

"*ACHOT*" WAS THE slang term normally used by students and teachers to designate the *Baccalauréat* or Bachelor of Arts exam and diploma, which represented the provisional goal of any student enrolled in a *lycée*. In the days before World War II, a student wishing to obtain the *bachot* had to pass two series of written and oral examinations, one year apart. These examinations were given annually in June and October by the Baccalaureate Office of the Faculty of Letters of every university in France and in the French Colonies. Student anonymity, to prevent discrimination and preferential treatment by those who administered and corrected the tests, was insured by assigning students a number and not having them take the exams under their own names. Furthermore, students took these exams at a *lycée* other than their own.

The written portion, which lasted about a week, covered all subjects learned over the years. A student had to pass the written portion to qualify for the oral, which lasted several days, but was less demanding. If one passed the written, but failed the oral, one was permitted to take just the oral in October. If one failed the written, one had to start again from scratch in the fall. Failure at that time meant waiting a year before being allowed another attempt. It was not uncommon for students to try a frustrating number of times.

In the third grade, we had a rather mature classmate, the son of a wealthy industrialist. He always dressed in suit and tie, had a mustache, had failed the *bachot* five years in a row, had his own apartment, and, the rumor ran, a mistress! He did not remain in our class very long. Either the distractions were too much for him or his parents threw in the towel.

Students took the first part of the *bachot* after completing the first grade, or *première*. If they passed to qualify for taking the second part, they could opt for continuing their studies in either the Mathematics (*Math Elem*) or Philosophy (*Philo*) class of the *lycée*. Their choice depended on whether they planned a career in science or the humanities as well as on personal preferences. Upon completing either *Math Elem* or *Philo*, exams for the second part took place under the same rules and conditions as those of the first part. Only after completing both parts did one earn the coveted degree. Authorities made it clear that only one diploma would be issued and warned against losing it. Since my birth certificate had been issued before my parents had decided on a first name, my diploma for the *bachot* ultimately read: Monsieur Oppenheimer, male.

The *bachot* was actually awarded not for attending school, but for successfully passing the battery of exams. In theory, anyone capable of preparing for them and passing, without attending classes or with private tutors, could have qualified for the diploma. But I know of no one who did. In fact, the percentage of students passing on the first try was low. We were shocked beyond belief when the top student in the class ahead of ours flunked the *bachot* on his first try. He must have panicked, but the very possibility of this happening scared us to death.

When I entered *Carnot*, my mother had been told that, since I was a foreigner, I would be required to pay tuition. Normally, secondary education in France is free. It is indicative of either the essentially democratic nature of the French character or of the ingrained inertness of French bureaucracy that *Carnot* never bothered billing my parents. Initiating the paperwork for processing just one student in the entire *lycée* no doubt appeared too daunting.

As I look at my grade reports from *Carnot*, which I still have, I find it hard to believe what discipline and diligence accomplished for me. I applied myself unreservedly. It was inconceivable for me to miss a class even when indisposed. I remember suffering from a painful boil on a critical part of my buttocks for days, which made sitting down nigh intolerable. Still I never missed a day of class and most certainly never dozed off. The math teacher, Sizaire, and the fourth grade teacher, Van Daële, both offered students — for a fee — homework preparation and tutoring sessions once a week after classes. They were, of course, optional. Not surprisingly, the good students were those who signed up for them. I did too, since I needed all the help I could get. During those sessions we learned valuable and efficient methods for doing our homework in math and Latin.

The work with Professeur Van Daële proved especially fruitful. He put me on the right track for practicing a disciplined method of translation, which I advocate and use to this day. First, one absorbs the entire meaning of the original text, then translates it into the target language, making certain every semantic element and nuance present in the original is accounted for in the translation. After this comes the hardest part: mentally detaching from the original, still imbued with its entire meaning, and reformatting the literal translation into a fluid text that, stylistically and artistically, contains all the meaning of the original, but in its authenticity appears to have been composed in the target language, free of foreign and awkward phrases. If the translator's efforts are successful, the end product in the target language will not, as the Italian proverb cautions, "betray the original." Nor, to borrow a metaphor from Cervantes, will the translation "look like the reverse of a tapestry, with the blurred pattern and all the loose threads showing, thus hardly doing justice to the impeccable front thereof."

Our instructors were in general top-notch. A few had amusing traits, but not enough to encourage breach of discipline on our part. Corlin, the art and drawing teacher, a disciple of Cézanne, good enough to now have some still lifes hanging in Paris museums, had the rather vulgar speech patterns of the *La Villette* district of Paris, which might be compared in its effect to London cockney. We just loved to hear him repeat in his drawn-out slaughterhouse drawl: "Leonardo da Vinci, he was a formidable guy, an extraordinary artist!" Professor Sizaire, whom we nicknamed "Ciseaux" (Scissors), with all his brilliant competence in math, had less attractive mannerisms. He would stand at the blackboard, furiously writing equations or drawing geometrical figures with his right hand, while indelicately inserting his left hand inside his pants right above his backside, and scratch. He also frequently indulged in unfolding a huge white handkerchief, holding it at a goodly distance from his face in front of him. Loudly clearning his throat, he sent the spittle over a considerable distance into its center, and thoughtfully contemplated the results of his marksmanship. This routine, oft repeated, held us spellbound.

Besides meals and sleeping, my activities at this time were limited to attending classes and doing homework. I was still surprised, after less than a year in France, to rank second or third in Latin and in the top ten students in French. By the third trimester of the fourth grade, I gained first place in recitation, which shows what "applying the seat of the pants to the seat of the chair," together with some other attributes, can accomplish. Thus persevering, with continuous application and progress, I obtained the Excellency Prize in both the third grade and philosophy. I even placed third in English in a nationwide competition, *Concours Général de 1934*, as recorded in *The Paris Times — Le Temps —* of Thursday, July 12, 1934.

Though restricted to this academic treadmill and constant grind to please my mother and eventually to appease my own increasingly addictive drive to place first, I still found a great deal to enjoy in life, at least now and then. After class, before reaching home, a few of us sought occasional temporary relief in simple pleasures. Besides playing an hour of soccer in the *Bois de Boulogne*, we might for a modest sum rent a table and paddles to play Ping-Pong. In the early 1930s, table tennis became very popular. At that time, the yo-yo craze also swept France. In a newly opened department store, *Les Magasins Réunis*, a Filipino yo-yo master, engaged by the management, demonstrated his mastery of the toy for customers and a crowd of gapers. The French equivalent of Woolworth's 5 and 10 cent stores opened in France as *Uni Prix*, a novelty for us and worth a visit. One of the grocery stores, *Luce*, on the *Place Péreire*, introduced another novelty, dry ice, to refrigerate ice cream. We found the solidified carbon dioxide fascinating. We tried to get some and experiment with it without suffering burns; if held in one's hand it sticks to the skin.

We never tired of looking at cars, especially limousines and sports cars: Bugattis, Hispano-Suizas, Alfa-Romeos, Delages, Talbots. We learned to recognize the various makes and models. Once a year Paris had its automotive exhibit, *Salon de l'Automobile*, at the *Grand Palais*, at the foot of the *Champs Elysées*. I remember the BMW motorcycle on which, in a prone position, someone had set the world record of 244 kilometers an hour. I started saving for a motorcycle, which in the end, I was never to own.

After we were introduced to chemistry, some of us were obsessed with a desire to experiment. Once, a friend and I plugged in an electrical cord and stuck the other end into a bowl of water. We forgot about alternating current and blew the fuse. Not discouraged, I went to the fuse box that controlled our apartment and replaced the lead fuse with copper wire. This time I blew the apartment fuse. Obstinate, I went to the apartment house fuse box and repeated the procedure. I failed again, blowing all the fuses in the building. No one found out and the concierge of the building, his sinecure temporarily interrupted by complaining tenants, soon repaired the damage. It was an interesting experiment, not to be repeated without a continuous current.

The friend who cooperated with me in this failed experiment was the son of a stomatologist. He was rather forward, a showoff, and somewhat reckless. Once, when we stopped in a bakery for a snack, I witnessed him drinking a glass of beer and eating a *baba au rhum*, a popular French rum-flavored pastry. It was a gustatory exploit I never forgot: beer and *baba*! He liked firearms and had access to some belonging to his father. One afternoon at his home, he suggested firing at a target, behind which he had placed a metal saw to make sure the bullets would not penetrate the wall. He missed. While we were fooling around trying to patch the wall, the reloaded gun discharged accidentally and the bullet whizzed close by my head.

On rare occasions, time and weather permitting, after completing homework, some of us, of a Thursday afternoon, would stroll and browse along the quays of the Seine River, where the book dealers of secondhand and rare books have their stalls. We looked for bargains and for books of a mildly erotic nature, to which in those days social mores would not allow us access: the *Tales* of La Fontaine, the *Memoirs of Casanova*, the *Tales of Boccaccio*. We surreptitiously attempted to catch a few suggestive lines of spicy text, or, better still, hoped for some graphic illustrations. The only other chance peep at bare bosoms was a hasty look at the periodicals in the barbershop, while awaiting one's turn for a haircut.

Another entertaining diversion was the lavish swimming pool at the Lido, a well-known Paris nightclub, which was available to the public during daytime, though at a steep entrance fee. A classmate sometimes had free tickets and would invite me to join him and his younger brother, to enjoy the pool and sample all the amenities: sauna, steam bath, and powerful water hoses, the latter known as "*douche écossaise*." However, the pool staff grew weary of non-paying, non-tipping clients making such extensive use of everything and taking over the place. Today the Lido is one of the world's most sophisticated and extravagant nightclubs, with a budget of over 50 million francs per show.

Also among my classmates was the nephew of the renowned French writer Georges Duhamel, a member of the French Academy. Another, Daydé, rather shy and quiet, was driven in a chauffeured limousine every day to and from *Carnot*. His father, an engineer and contractor, had built the famous *Pont de l'Europe*, the bridge that spans the Saint Lazare railroad station. I recall that in fourth grade, Monsieur Paul Crouzet, Inspector for the Education Department and author of a French literature manual used throughout the country, came to inspect our class. He was probably close to retirement and visibly past his prime, or *gaga*, as we kids might have indelicately put it. Professeur Van Daële treated the distinguished elderly visitor with all the courtesy due his rank and position: "*Monsieur l'Inspecteur Général*" this . . . , "*Monsieur l'Inspecteur Général*" that. . . . Crouzet appeared half asleep in his chair, like a veteran Inspector who had seen it all, was now secure in his position, and no longer had to prove any inspectorial zeal.

Van Daële was very proud of a mimeographed syllabus on Latin syntax, authored by his father, who also had been a professor. He sold it to us as a compulsory text. Explaining to Crouzet everything we did in the fourth grade to achieve the highest possible academic results, Van Daële also presented his treasured syntax to him. Crouzet reluctantly took it, opened it at random, and lethargically glanced at it. Now, in those days, blue mimeographed texts were often faded and hard to read. Crouzet's myopic attempt proved fruitless. Helpless, he looked up at Van Daële. Van Daële, with a "*Permettez-moi, Monsieur l'Inspecteur Général*," leaned over Crouzet's shoulders, grasped the open binder, turned it around 180 degrees, and presented it again to him with a gentle "*Voilà, Monsieur l'Inspecteur!*" The venerable author of one of the best textbooks I have ever seen and still consult today had tried, unsuccessfully, to read the syllabus upside down.

In the summer of 1931, we spent a few weeks on the beach in La Baule, south of Brittany, and took excursions to visit worthwhile sights, especially Carnac with its mysterious prehistoric giant stones, the dolmens and menhirs, reminiscent of the British Stonehenge. In 1932 and 1933, my father offered me a marvelous surprise. He arranged for me to travel to England and spend the summer with the Bernard Chase family so that I could practice and improve my English. A near disaster almost prevented me from going.

On a Sunday, a few days before my keenly anticipated departure for England, my parents and I went out to dinner. On our return to the apartment we were greeted by a horrible smell and the sound of water pouring down from the ceiling. Filthy dark water, inches deep, was almost everywhere. Most of the furniture was ruined, as the varnish had already started peeling away in wet curls with the water dripping and dripping. It was soon discovered that the tenants above us had forgotten to shut off the bathtub faucet and left the premises.

My mother was in shock. I immediately offered to cancel my trip and help in any way I could. After some deliberation, my parents decided I should go as planned. They would move into a hotel and see about insurance and possible legal action. Everything turned out all right, but of course with much inconvenience for my parents. The furniture was repaired and the apartment redone at no expense to us. After everything was settled, they traveled to a spa near Vichy in central France so that my father could take a rest and drink the thermal water.

I took the ferry from Calais to Dover and met my new English friends, Mr. Chase and his son John, at Victoria Station. Bernard Chase represented H. Muehlstein in Great Britain. He and his sweet wife had three children, an older girl and two sons. John, just a little younger than I, was the perfect companion. Bernard Chase's brother, his wife, and three children — an older girl and twins younger than I — joined us and shared in the expenses for food and lodging.

In 1932, we all went to Lands End, the southwestern tip of England in

Cornwall, where we had the good fortune of staying on a farm. The Chases had cars and twice a day drove us to the beach for swimming and surfboarding. We used short surfboards on which we lay from the waist up to catch the incoming waves. We had the best of all worlds. We were permitted to help the farmer, Mr. Dale, with the farm work. We learned to milk cows — sort of — and took part in dyeing sheep. We brought in the hay, stacking the sheaves, then loading them on a cart. In the late afternoon, we looked forward to high tea with crumpets, buns, jams, Devonshire cream, and other goodies. No one even thought of calories in those days. At a fair in Truro I had the opportunity, for five British pounds, to take my first flight in an open cockpit biplane and loop the loop. It was revenge on my mother for not allowing me to fly to London. I had never had so much fun nor such good company in my life.

Once the cows got out and we had to herd them back at night. Mr. Dale's dog, who also watched over the flock of sheep, helped, of course. I was inclined to be willful and a showoff. One evening I incurred Mr. Chase's anger. He had decided not to drive us to a movie and refused my suggestion that John and I go there by bus. I thought Mr. Chase unreasonable and talked John into going with me. Mr. Chase was very angry with me for disobeying his orders, but bore no grudge after I promised not to do it again. Ultimately, as he pointed out, he felt responsible for me while I stayed with them in England.

Before the vacation in Cornwall, John and I had hit golf balls at his father's country club and played billiards at his home. John also played the trumpet and told me about all the great jazz trumpet musicians. After the vacation, John had to return to school, but the Chases drove me back to their home in Broxbourne, Herts, north of Tottenham and London. My friends very generously enabled me to visit London, see the British Museum, eat in Soho, and attend a performance of Shakespeare's *Midsummer Night's Dream* in the open-air theater of Regents Park. It was a moving romantic experience, never to be erased from my psyche, to see this play in an ideal setting, on a beautiful August evening, to the sound of Mendelssohn's music. My father had to phone twice from Paris to remind me I had no choice but to return and resume classes.

I found it almost heartbreaking to leave England. I had never been away from home before, yet not a single day had I felt homesick. It had been so much fun — and a learning experience — for a single child to adjust and fit in with a large family. Both Chase families had taken me in without reservations and treated me as though I was one of them. I realized how much younger they acted than my own parents, suddenly aware of the fact that my father was no longer physically active.

It also was my first prolonged contact with the British. They were decidedly different from the Germans and the French, proudly sure of themselves and their ways. Their food and customs were quite new to me. Never before had I taken a hot-water bottle to bed and awakened to a cup of hot tea. They listened, but remained skeptical, when I described and took for granted the superiority of the French educational system, an assertion which in all fairness I had not researched in depth. The British system, from the way they described it, appeared less disciplined and more informal to me. Daily customs also differed in England. In Paris, we shook hands with each other each time we met or parted. I thought the British would do the same. Not so. They were more economical with physical demonstrations of friendship. The most important fact I learned was that I could survive on my own away from my parents.

In 1933, the Chases extended their friendship once more, inviting me again for the summer. This time, instead of taking the short crossing from Calais to Dover, I chose the longer four-hour trip from Le Havre to Southampton. I boarded the small ship *Versailles* and we started out on a fairly rough sea. The *Versailles* was soon rolling and pitching wildly. Many passengers remained outside, and I was standing on deck with my suitcase next to me. The spray from the waves was being blown right at us by the wind. I was getting wet and could taste the salt. I made up my mind that I would under no circumstances get seasick, although some passengers had already succumbed to the air and the motion of the ship.

Lunch was being served below. The French do not like to miss a meal, even when it might be a good idea to do so. We had covered a good part of the distance to England, and I was eagerly anticipating our arrival, hanging on tight to my resolve to control my stomach. A passenger emerged from the stairway leading from the dining room to the deck. He had evidently indulged his appetite and was now ready for fresh air to help his digestion. The rolling ship tossed him about; he staggered, looked around for support. The *menu complet*, which he had just enjoyed and which indubitably lived up to the highest standards of a French ship's cuisine, rose together with the motion of both the vessel and his stomach. The wretched passenger, unable to act gentlemanly, do the proper thing, and reach the rail, wastefully heaved the rather expensive repast on my suitcase. I had no choice but to wipe it off with my handkerchief. Understandably this proved too much of a challenge for me. The passenger's heaves accomplished what the heaving waves could not. I headed for the rail, did what I had to do, and soon regained my composure and seasoned sailor's footing.

The Chases traveled to Bracklesham Bay, near the old town of Chichester. We rented a cottage, often sailed, weather permitting, and swam. We took a drive to Bournemouth, where I visited Admiral Horatio Nelson's ship *Victory* of the Battle of Trafalgar fame. I again committed a really foolish act, when immediately after a large evening meal, merely to show off, I plunged into the sea and swam out of sight. The water was cold and when I returned to shore I was not feeling too well. A hot bath restored me to a normal state, but I did not regain the Chases' favor quite as fast. This delightful summer was the last time I saw the Chases until the Army shipped me to Great Britain in 1943.

In the fall of 1933, I entered the *première* taught by Professor Druesnes. At the end of the school year, we would all be taking the feared exams for the first part of the *bachot*. Druesnes, an imposing figure of a man, authoritative and deliberate in manner, was a very fine teacher, but very serious and outwardly unemotional. Very strict, he taught French and Latin. By then, I took total dedication to class work, at the exclusion of everything else, as a mode of life. In all these years at *Carnot* I never had a date. In fact, I knew no girls. I do not know about my classmates, but I believe, in general, dating and going with girls started after the *lycée,* at the university, no doubt with gusto to make up for years of abstinence.

This constant academic discipline did not imply a lack of enthusiasm for, a weariness of, or a hostile attitude to the subjects we studied. Looking back, I see that this is where I developed an almost obsessive fascination and consuming love for language, both as spoken in daily usage and as fine-tuned in literature. This passion probably began in Germany, when I wished at all costs to blend linguistically with my environment. It grew in France and remains with me to this very day. My European experiences evidently shaped my views on language. My French teachers relentlessly monitored and corrected our work in French and Latin. I readily fell under the spell that words can exert on the mind. I wanted at all cost to speak French like a Frenchman, a goal I soon achieved. In the third grade, a new student from Chartres, Lucien Bailly, transferred to *Carnot.* (He became and was, until his death in 1997, my best friend.) Another student told him

I was American, and Lucien, after talking to me, was convinced he was pulling his leg.

I am very biased in favor of articulate language. Whenever I acquired a new language, I always wanted to learn to read, speak, and write it with the native fluency of the very best role models. I always aim for correct oral and written speech, untainted by foreign or substandard forms. While fully aware of and allowing for the inherently changing and evolutionary nature of language, I highly value semantic precision, clarity of expression, beauty and artistry of style in their various cultural settings. I well know these are difficult goals to attain. Therefore, I am reasonable in my demands for perfection, but at least expect continuous striving for it. Slovenly language is a regrettable habit to be shunned.

These ideals have also shaped my views regarding the national language problems in the contemporary United States. I believe all nations should establish a firm language policy, especially where necessitated by coexisting languages, and adhere to it. Members of such nations, whether native thereof or recently admitted, should take pride and pleasure in mastering, to the best of their ability and without clamoring for exemptions, the language of their chosen country. Each language must be regarded as a national treasure to be cherished. It is, after all, the essential time-binding tool through which the cultural experience of a people lives, evolves, and is transmitted from generation to generation. History affords us a wealth of examples proving that, while multiple languages in a nation may be enriching to a degree, a common tongue is essential to its cultural unity and future. If one thinks enough of a new country to cast one's lot with it and leave the land of birth, it should be done wholeheartedly, as a full-fledged member, not a half-hearted fellow traveler, with pledged linguistic allegiance.

For reasons that I failed to understand, I seldom wrote a French composition that ranked among the best in the class. I wrote well enough, the style was good, but the contents of my theme — the emotions expressed therein — did not appear to correspond to what teachers expected from a perfect paper. I have often wondered about this. I console myself by remembering that, ultimately, one person's reaction to and judgment of another person's artistic output cannot be entirely based on rigidly objective criteria and is bound to be somewhat weighted by very personal subjective biases. Once in a great while I managed to turn out something that aroused a teacher's full approval and moved him just as the subject of the paper had moved me. The one I recall was a sensitive description of the play and motion of light in the paintings of the Dutch artist Jan Vermeer de Delft, for whose mastery I had an overpowering admiration. The deep feeling in my writing must have touched a chord in the grader. In Latin, on the other hand, my work placed first or second. According to the teacher, I usually managed to catch the feel of the language when translating into it and to capture every nuance of meaning when translating from it. The criteria for correctness here are more precisely defined. In English, once I had caught up, I remained securely at the head of the class.

My undistinguished showing in composition was not due to a lack of interest in literature. I loved it. In Germany I had already been an avid reader of the great writers, at least those accessible to me at my age. I was easily caught up in the pathos and ethos of my literary readings. I also responded with sensitivity to the artistry of the style, the beauty of the language, and the music of the poetry. It was the same with French. I was as always partial to the early epics and to medieval literature. I particularly resonated to the starkly realistic, personally experienced anguish, and black humor of the rogue poet François Villon. The beauty of Ronsard's sonnets, stylized as it might be, was for me irresistible. I admired the lawyer's logic of the Norman playwright Corneille, where duty always reigned supreme over passion, and the passion overriding duty in the characters of Racine. I was literally overwhelmed by the great writers of the 17th century, the period of the "Sun King," the *Roi Soleil*, Louis XIV. The effect of the ever-present 12-syllable alexandrine verse, with its caesura in the middle, perfectly alternating masculine and feminine rhymes, and monotonous cadence, was almost hypnotic. I felt the same way about the somber ring of Shakespeare's sonnets, of which we had to memorize a few. Even the precise, tightly succinct, elegance of Latin writers like Cicero, Caesar, Seneca, Vergil, Ovid, Quintilian, and Livy, stood out as shining examples of the highest stylistic standards. They were the focus of my emotions.

When in my readings I encountered words with meaning I was not sure of, I always consulted the dictionary, a habit I still maintain today. It is the best way to acquire a rich vocabulary and discover the roots of words. A good dictionary which describes a word's etymology, its multiple shades of meaning according to context, is a window into the past. Recorded therein for the perceptive searcher is the history of how mankind perceived its evolving universe and transmitted its interpretation thereof in spoken or written metaphors. Viewed from this perspective language is fossilized poetry.

I discovered I was partial to none when reading literary texts in several languages. Whenever I read either German, French, or English, I assumed a different mind-set, each of which caused me to blend intellectually and emotionally with the text and the language. Thus, I never failed to find in each one its intrinsic natural beauty and music. It never would have dawned on me, nor does it ever now, to compare languages to each other with regard to beauty or sound. They may differ in other features, such as levels of abstraction, wealth of vocabulary, or syntactical mechanism, but any other differentiation is purely subjective — like a preference for one name over another. I began to discover that I loved language *per se* — not merely a particular language — for its own sake and its miraculous nature, potential suggestive power, and endlessly ingenious adaptation to human needs.

There were deeper reasons for my attraction to literature. Because, as I emphasized earlier, my life was almost exclusively confined to classes and homework, my contacts were few, mostly fellow students. I saw my parents at mealtime, slightly more on weekends. There was much less communication between us than in Germany. The conditions were not always ideal for pleasant conversation. Much of the latter consisted of complaints about the difficulties with the business or the ups and downs of the stock market.

My father was somewhat of an insomniac and instead of just waking me up in the morning, once in a while he lay down next to me for a few minutes prior to my getting up. It was innocent enough; he was not under the covers or too close, but still it was not to my liking. He would be breathing heavily and evidently did not feel well. I knew that he had many headaches at the office and some of his clients proved at times to be downright exasperating. Perhaps he felt an occasional urge to be close to his son. The act may have been on his part an attempt to express his paternal feelings, an urge to be close, which a lifelong cultivated reserve did not permit him to communicate in words. In any event I never objected, not wishing to reject him. I felt sorry for him.

I did not have many role models in the persons around me. I had to find them elsewhere. And thus, for want of another source or because of ideas programmed into my subconscious, I turned for guidance to the great writers and the characters they portrayed. It was, at the time, a natural move on my part, since the ethical worth of classical literature and the virtues of the characters depicted therein had always been extolled to me by those I trusted. The lives of the authors, their literary theories, their memorable lines ("what oft was said, but ne'er so well expressed," as Alexander Pope puts it), finally the actions of their heroes, loomed large in my mind as motivation for my behavior.

In this respect I tried to be flexible, be ready to alter previously held views and impressions — to stand corrected, even though this might bring a disillusioning shock. A perfect example of this was a play by Sophocles, *Electra*, presented at the *Comédie-Française* — the National Theater founded in 1680 by Louis XIV for classical productions. The French Minister of Public Education had at his permanent disposal the right-hand loge nearest the stage. Professor Abraham, after becoming the Minister's assistant, offered several of us the loge and the opportunity to see a free performance. It was my first visit to this famous theater. I was ready to be impressed. No wonder I thought the inflated styles of the actors and their pompous deliveries were divine. Suddenly, a gentleman sitting in the orchestra in front of our loge burst out laughing. The acting was too bombastic, and I learned from this episode to be more critical and circumspect in judging theatrical performances in the future. There is a fine line between the sublime and the ridiculous.

Time passed and quite suddenly the dreaded *bachot*, part one, was upon us. A few of us who ranked at the top of the class had qualified for the *Concours Général*, the National Scholastic Contest, to compete with the best students of France in certain subjects. I took part in the Latin-French, French-Latin, mathematics, and English trials. I was the only student at *Carnot* to score, attaining third place in English. I first heard about this success in July, when some classmates told me that my name was on the bulletin board in front of the Administrative Office. I thought they were joshing me and refused to believe them. They insisted. Finally I looked and could not believe my eyes. To win anything in the *Concours Général* was pretty impressive. Four years earlier, the English teacher had declared me beyond any hope.

Our teachers impressed upon us the seriousness and difficulties of the examinations we were facing. The trimester was over for all practical purposes. Their sage advice to all of us was "cram." With Latin, French composition, and math, we had to rely on what we already knew. As to French literature, history, the entire geography of France and all its (at that time) numerous colonies, physics, and chemistry, including not just the material of the past year but most everything we had ever learned, cramming was the order of the day. There were for this purpose small books that very succinctly summarized in a deceptively small space volumes of information. The problem was that nothing therein was superfluous: it all had to be memorized. For one month I sat — for so long I wore a hole in the seat of my pants!

I was sent to *Lycée Fènelon,* a school for girls, to take the week-long tests. Each one lasted three to four hours and was heavily monitored in every detail. We sat miles apart and surveillance was constant. The atmosphere was incredibly tense. Going to the bathroom was unthinkable. After the written exams we had to wait for the results, another breath-holding experience. Those that passed took two days of oral exams. We went from professor to professor, wondering each time which of a thousand possible questions we might be asked, faced a professor, and answered his questions covering — at random — the material for which we were responsible. The ordeal ended with my passing with honorable mention. The sense of relief was indescribable. It was possibly the toughest exam I ever took, considering our age (I was 16 at the time), the tension, the amount of material covered, the fear instilled in us by professors, and wild rumors of spectacular failures of even good students.

In the summer of 1934 we spent a few weeks in Biarritz. My father had many good customers in the south of France, among them *Société Méridionale du Caoutchouc,* based in the old walled city of Carcassonne. Some of his clients were Basques, who bought from him tons of old tire treads, so-called Number One Peelings, from which soles were cut out for espadrilles, the informal footwear common in that region of the Pyrenees. Mr. Herman Muehlstein, the chairman of the company my father represented, had decided to vacation in Biarritz and had booked a suite at the Miramar, the best hotel in this beach resort. Our lodgings were more modest. We were close to the Spanish border and the gorgeous town and bay of San Sebastián. I had a great time swimming, first at the main beach.

When I swam way out into the ocean, the lifeguards grew tired of my shenanigans and banned me from the beach. I had to swim at a much rockier spot, *Vieux Port* — Old Port, where I could pretty much go as far out as I pleased.

Once a British gentleman started talking to me in the hotel lobby and then invited me up to his room to show me jiujitsu tricks. Fortunately that is all he did. When my mother heard of it, she was quite angry and warned me never to do this again, enlightening me on pedophiliac inclinations.

A Basque business friend of my father resided in Biarritz with his wife and son. The latter had been the proud owner of a convertible sports car until a day or so before we met. Unfortunately, even as far back as 1934, the French liked to test themselves and their cars to the limit. This young man was no exception and had taken a curve on the Biarritz-Saint Jean de Luz road at maximum speed, rolled over his car, totaled it, and miraculously survived. I thus missed out on a possibly thrilling ride with him, which, on second thought, may have been a lifesaver for me.

We took excursions to the Pyrenees during this time: Pau and Lourdes in France, and Pamplona, where they let the bulls run loose in the streets every year, in Spain. I was thrilled to learn that, while living in Spain, my father had often visited Pamplona and had met the famous Spanish writer Benito Pérez-Galdós in San Sebastián.

Lourdes was not as mercilessly commercialized as it later became. We were still able to walk to the spring where Bernadette Soubirous first saw the Virgin Mary. The waves of pilgrims seeking to be healed and the collection of crutches and cast-off prostheses was awesomely believable. In San Sebastián, I also saw an eight-bull *corrida* — bullfight, the first and eighth bull being fought from horseback in the old manner. Another novelty for me was the Basque game of *pelota*, in which one uses a hand-held wicker basket to hurl a ball at phenomenal speeds in a three-walled court.

In the fall of 1934, I had to decide which class to enter toward the second part of the *bachot*. Most of the best students, especially those with a penchant for mathematics, chose *Math Elem*. This class prepared students for advanced engineering and business schools. Those who were leaning more toward the humanities selected *Philo*. I automatically registered in *Math Elem*. Then I began to think of the future. I really did not have the faintest idea of what I wanted to do in life, and there had been no family confabulations on the subject. I was somewhat handicapped in my choice, as I did not want to become a French citizen. I had always taken my return to the USA for granted. For lack of any specific plans and mostly by default — though I had no particular vocation for import and export, in general, or the rubber business in particular — it had tentatively been decided that I would join my father in his business. Frankly, I never had had the time to give my future a thought.

As classes resumed, those of us who had elected *Math Elem* gathered in Professor Sizaire's class. In his quite sobering welcoming speech, he made it crystal clear that we were facing a very tough year. Listening to him, I realized how very tired I was of the constant grind and of competing for top rank in the class. To add to the strain, my two greatest competitors in the academic arena were sitting right there in the class with me: Michel Duizend and Tereschenko, a near genius in math. Years later, I was told the latter had graduated first from the prestigious *Ecole Polytechnique*. We had continuously battled for first place since the third grade.

I suggested to my parents that it was an unnecessary academic hardship for me if I had no plans to use advanced mathematics. Then we debated, since I was thinking of a business career, about whether I should forget about the *bachot* and enroll in a private business school. Because of the commercial school's long curriculum, this route proved impractical. I proposed to them that I settle for *Philo*.

Hard-nosed as ever, my mother thought this would be too easy for me. Her vicarious ambitions for me were unlimited! She did not really know much about the course in *Philo*; her opinion was based purely on the fact that Duizend and Tereschenko were enrolled in *Math Elem*. She offered me a deal. "You may take *Philo*, but on the side you must study Spanish." I entered *Philo* a week or so late and enrolled in a private Berlitz-type Spanish-language school. For a few months, I bicycled in the late afternoon to that school, braving Paris evening traffic. After that I convinced my mother that she was wasting her money. Schools of this kind never seemed to deliver what they promised and certainly not one's money's worth. I guaranteed her I could study Spanish just as well on my own, since I had the book.

With less competition from other students, I attained first place more easily and frequently in every subject but philosophy. The latter was divided into psychology, logic, and ethics. We had a fabulous professor,

Lacombe. He had lively penetrating eyes and a bald head with an unusual bump that gave him a highly intelligent look. He treated us like mature students and commanded our attention. Yet I still found much of it boring, except psychology. When my turn came to deliver a lecture to the class, I took advantage of my now fluent English and picked a book on parapsychology published by the British Society for the Study of Psychic Phenomena. Lacombe approved my proposed theme, and I thrilled the class with stories of ghosts, psychic impressions left behind by individuals, feats performed by mediums, and other such goodies from the twilight zone. A skeptical Lacombe very kindly took it in stride. He was a fair person and did not object when, because of my high standing in all subjects besides his, I was awarded the *Prix d'Excellence* at the end of the school term.

The last year was less stressful than the prior one. The famous Henri Bergson, Professor at the *Collège de France* and the Nobel Prize winner in literature in 1927, was president of the Academic Council that made up the examinations for the second part of the *bachot* in philosophy. Lacombe advised us to read Bergson's latest work very carefully. We all had read his book on laughter, *Le Rire*, published in 1901, in my opinion the most convincing book ever on this subject. The professor's advice paid off: one of the three choices in the philosophy examination dealt with Bergson's book. I passed the second part of the *bachot* with honorable mention and heaved a big sigh of relief. A classmate, Lolik, being a below-average student who had given up on taking the *bachot*, wished to bask in my academic success. He accompanied me to the final distribution of prizes and helped me carry home the 13 books awarded to me.

A few of us who had passed the *bachot* tried to celebrate this and Bastille Day on the 14th of July. We attempted to meet girls in the streets, where dancing goes on all night. However, unprepared for such activity because of academically induced shyness, we soon gave up. I looked forward to a free summer and my return to America after 13 years in Europe.

Bless'd who like Ulysses has journeyed far away,
or like the Argonaut, who won the fleece of gold,
then came back the wiser after ventures untold
to live with his people to his very last day.
— Joachim du Bellay, 1522–1560

Chapter 7

New York, New York!

ASSING THE *BACHOT* WAS tantamount to holding my breath for five long years and finally coming up for air. Just imagine the relief! I had a carefree summer to look forward to and in the fall, the long-awaited return to New York City. I had time and again romanticized this return, perhaps too fancifully. Put yourself in my place. An outsider, despite fitting in, I had watched Germans and French glowing with pride in their own country. I had heard them sing their national anthems. I had seen them parade and thank their leaders for affording them the honor to get their bodies bashed in glorious wars. I may have rightly felt it was now my turn to do the same. For me in those days, owing to ignorance subsequently remedied by experience, New York was America. It took a few years and a widening of my horizon to realize that New York City is its own world and New Yorkers a breed to themselves: there is an America beyond the Hudson and there is no toll charge to reach it traveling west over the Washington Bridge.

I was unaware at that time that the years of *lycée* and *bachotage* had left deep marks, if not scars, on my psyche and affected my attitude toward life. Perhaps unjustifiably, but nevertheless firmly programmed into me as a result of this academic grind, was a behavior pattern hardly conducive to meeting life's challenges with composure and equanimity — let alone panache. Deeply buried in my subconscious still festered the painful memory of my initial school experience in France — especially of not being able to handle class assignments. Instead of focusing on the surmounted obstacles and imbuing myself with a well-earned self-confidence, I clung to the negative aspects of the experience. When given any assignments, under the most varied circumstances, I always initially reacted, and still tend to now and then, with an anticipation of failure — not calmly sizing up the situation before panicking. This reaction became a kind of conditioned reflex, although I never failed to prove to myself, without exception, an unfailing ability to cope with whatever problems arose.

The *lycée* had provided me with the best possible academic foundation: considerable knowledge, sound scholarly methods, and above all self-discipline. It had also accustomed me to gaining the approval of my teachers and parents, the only ones I had to satisfy, by merely doing good homework and placing among the first in class. However, the French system and my own family situation did not prepare me for other aspects of life where dealing with people, not merely with books and paper, is of vital consequence and where other types of achievement are equally valued.

The French, generally speaking, are not team players, a shortcoming they recognize in themselves. In sports, French teams excel far less often than individual French athletes. Examples of this stubborn individualism abound. Years later, in World War II, American Commanders were told to allow, for symbolic and diplomatic reasons, the French 1st Armored Division of General Philippe Leclerc to arrive in Paris first. Leclerc was warned by General Lawton "Lightning Joe" Collins of VII Corps to take a designated route to avoid becoming entangled with American armored troops. With utter disregard for the instructions, Leclerc did as he pleased, causing a spectacular traffic jam of tanks and armored vehicles and raising General Collins's blood pressure beyond the recommended level. In fact, some of the French soldiers en route to Paris, finding themselves in the vicinity of their home villages, gave themselves permission to take leave of their vehicles right there and then. It was thus not uncommon to see empty tanks strewn along the road, in unexpected locations, another example of French individualism.

At the *lycée* we had practiced no team sports where I might have learned some people skills. I was an only child and at home had to get along only with my parents, which was easily achieved by being a good student. Thus my Paris school experience led me to believe that problems in life could always be solved in two simple steps. First, one relies on one's own skills, know-how, and hard work to create problem-free conditions. Second, once the boat is on the right course, one avoids at all cost allowing it to drift off course again. What the *lycée* never prepared me for is the endless supply of boat rockers and off-the-straight-path drifters provided for by society. Most of my life I relied on my ability to create a stable situation where, no matter the circumstances, smooth sailing was guaranteed forever. Worse yet, after the *bachot*, for a fleeting ephemeral time span, I deliriously thought that I had cleared my very last hurdle. Would that someone had then whispered to me, "Hello! Wake up!" I could have spared myself countless moments of irritability and frustration, and presented a more executive image to those around me.

I had never dated girls while at the *lycée* and had not even known any. One occasion on which I enjoyed some feminine company was during the 1934 Christmas vacation. Two classmates, Lartigue and Paul Ozanne, asked me to join them on a skiing trip to Galtür in the Austrian Vorarlberg. Paul's older sister, a married woman in the process of getting a divorce, would come with and serve as an adult chaperone. We were 17 years old, but our parents would be more inclined to acquiesce to the trip if she was going along. Lartigue aggressively pursued the idea until we finally decided to go. My mother gave her permission provided I used the money I had saved toward a motorbike. She had never shared my dream of such a contraption.

The hotel was filled with young people, including many young girls, but we were shy and kept to ourselves. (Besides, we had Paul's sister.) A very pretty dark-haired girl attracted my particular attention. I watched her and saw her go off with some young man. The next morning we found her crying on the hotel stairway. We tried to calm her, but she kept sobbing. I sat with her for a while, put my arms over her shoulder, talked to her, but was unable to bring her out of her disconsolate mood. She was incoherent and I hardly qualified as a father confessor. I more or less gathered that she had been seduced by her date and now bitterly regretted her irretrievable error in judgment. I still remember how protective I felt toward her in my naive indignation, principally nurtured by my literary models and romantic readings. My emotions were a mixture of jealousy of the cad's success and outrage at his taking such unchivalrous advantage of her. Paul's sister wisely advised me to let the girl sort it out on her own.

My parents were most helpful and generous in outfitting me for my return to America, glad perhaps — or relieved — to see me vacate the nest. My mother enjoyed shopping with me for a complete new adult wardrobe. Paris stores did not have a large selection of ready-made clothes for men, thus I was thrilled to find her willing to order my very first tailor-made suits: a casual sport suit of cheviot wool, a business suit, a dark blue suit for dress, and even a tuxedo, which the French incomprehensibly call "un smoking," borrowing an English term never used for that purpose in either England or America. Very fashionable at that time for men in Paris were dress shirts with stiff shirtfronts — some with separate collars. I bought a few only to find them impractical when in New York where I had to have them laundered commercially.

With my own money I bought a few Sulka ties. This New York firm had a branch near Place Vendôme in Paris. Their ties were among the most expensive and the most beautiful I had ever seen. My father had once told me that Herman Muehlstein bought his ties and shirts from Sulka, and I had received one from him as a present during his visit to France. Although brought up not to splurge, I was unable to resist the neckwear after walking the long distance from my home to the shop and staring at them several times through the show window. I kept my purchase secret, fearing parental disapproval for buying such luxury items beyond my means. I wore them with pride and pleasure for years.

We decided not to take any summer vacation, to give me ample time to remedy a few gaps in my nonacademic education. Thus my parents very thoughtfully suggested dancing lessons. I enrolled in the Luxembourg Dancing Academy near the gardens and museum in the Latin Quarter. I learned the fox trot, waltz, tango, and rumba from a very serious lady dance instructor. I was not exactly a Fred Astaire, but approached dancing rather like an academic subject, memorizing the steps and dance patterns. At least it was a beginning. I also spent some time with my father at the office, where he introduced me to some aspects of the business, showing me various samples of rubber, business correspondence, the coding of cables, and banking procedures.

During this time H. Muehlstein made the news. Paris has had since time immemorial a political newspaper known as *Le Canard Enchaîné*, literally "The Chained Duck," but in this case, the "Chained Newspaper." *Canard* in slang means either a newspaper or a piece of false news. One of the items of scrap rubber closest in quality to pure natural latex rubber that my father imported was "pure gum covers." These actually were factory rejects of condoms. Somehow, the *Canard* got wind of this and spread all over Paris the news that H. Muehlstein and Company was selling used condoms to the French.

My father had become acquainted with a businessman whose office adjoined his, a Sephardic Jew, of Spanish origin. He owned a Citroën, which had attracted my attention. Few of my acquaintances owned cars. (The only reason I knew he was Jewish was that my father explained to me the history of the expulsion of the Jews from Spain in 1492, and I was struck by the fact that many still spoke 15th-century Spanish.) He told my father that his niece from Salonika, Greece, was spending the summer with an aunt in St.-Germain-en-Laye, a Paris suburb. She was lonely, bored, and without any young companions. He wondered whether I might visit her and cheer her up. I was shy and embarrassed, but finally mustered enough courage and bicycled to St. Germain to meet her. At least, I said to myself, I would enjoy the exercise.

St. Germain is at about 20 kilometers from Paris and famous for its castle, museum, gorgeous park with English gardens, and a breathtaking view of the Seine Valley. I feared the worst, but found, on arrival, a beautiful — in fact — stunning girl, Lydia. With dark curly hair, a little on the plump side, and an attractive somewhat foreign manner and accent, she appeared delighted to meet me. A young date at last! I immediately turned very shy, but she seemed to be a good sport. To my surprise she even agreed, in a show of true camaraderie, to ride on my bicycle. She squeezed in with me and sat on the cross bar in front of the saddle. I could feel her soft hair against my face.

St. Germain is situated on an elevation. I recklessly took the curving road down to the Seine River and the bridge and with her weight added to mine, gained considerable speed. At the bottom of the hill where, in the main intersection, a *flic* — policeman — was trying to direct traffic, I was unable to slow down and whizzed straight by him. Fortunately, we avoided a possibly serious accident and were able to laugh at the outcome of our wild ride.

Lydia and I saw each other a few more times. I was never relaxed in her presence, always wondering whether she liked me. As a souvenir, she gave me a silver ring with the morbid Latin inscription *Memento mori* — remember that you must die. Lydia returned home and married. I learned later that she perished during a bombing raid on Salonika.

Toward the end of the summer, my father had second thoughts about a vacation for us. A short break away from a deserted Paris might be appreciated. He suggested I stay a week in St. Germain, since I was going there frequently anyway. I was fortunate to find an inexpensive attic room in the best hotel. The owner had a young, tall, good-looking son, a little older than I. There also were two families spending the summer in the hotel, each with a daughter. After I ate my first meal alone in the dining room, one family invited me to sit at their table. Undoubtedly their daughter, Jacqueline, some five or six years older than I, was bored stiff watching elderly guests spending their days resting or taking short walks in the park. The owner's son may have had something to do with the invitation and suggested me as a suitable escort for Jacqueline. As a matter of fact, he must have been behind the scheme. He was courting the other conservatively brought up young girl who, when on a date with him, always insisted upon Jacqueline tagging after them. By pairing me off with the latter when double-dating, he could isolate his prey while I distracted the unwelcome chaperone.

Jacqueline was not beautiful, but very attractive. She had black hair, beautiful black eyes, long eyelashes, and was small, vivacious, and intelligent. The family appeared to be comfortable financially. Her father was a broker on the Paris Stock Exchange, her mother a pleasant, quiet lady. They evidently approved of me, a reserved young man who had just finished his *bachot*. When the hotel owner's son did not have chores to do, all four of us went out together. The son knew many people in St.

Germain, among them the Delage family, who had owned the famous Delage automobile company. The latter was now bankrupt, but the Delages lived in affluent splendor, apparently unaffected by the bankruptcy. They had a beautiful estate in St. Germain, where we spent one afternoon swimming in their pond and eating ripe greengages as they burst on the tree in the summer sun — my definition of paradise on earth.

Jacqueline encouraged me; she was the first girl I ever kissed, at least on the mouth. Under the circumstances and not to my credit, I neglected Lydia. I was hardly up to juggling two girls at once, and I felt more at ease with Jacqueline. Still my bad conscience made me invite Lydia to a dance. She had apparently missed me and acted a little hurt. In any event, she was going back to Greece and I was about to start a new phase of life in my homeland. We were not fated to see each other again. I can still see her as she was, not too content with the prospects of her future life, a trace of sadness in her demeanor.

Meanwhile, since I was obviously enjoying myself, my mother, perhaps a little envious, thought she and my father also needed a change. I could not get them a room at my hotel and they had to settle for one of lesser quality. My mother was very much irritated by this and did not hide her displeasure. She even wanted me to give up my room and move in with them. My father tried to pacify her, advising her not to spoil my fun.

One afternoon my friends and I decided to go to Paris with Jacqueline to retrieve items from her apartment. The owner's son took me aside and asked me to keep Jacqueline at bay when in her apartment, so that he could attempt to make love to his girl. He even urged me to try the same with Jacqueline. It was, of course, out of the question for me to do anything of the sort in view of my fears about the consequences of sex. Besides I had not as yet been initiated to the use of "pure gum covers."

I don't know what really happened at Jacqueline's apartment that afternoon. Though we did separate into couples for a while, Jacqueline and I just necked passionately.

My parents went home to Paris, and my mother indicated she would be very pleased if I did the same. I obliged and made her doubly happy by obeying her wishes and taking the bike with me on the train instead of riding it back to the city. In Paris I began saying good-bye to a few of my friends — actually, under the circumstances, a fairly momentous occasion. In the 1930s, it was quite an event to have one of your classmates cross *la grande mare* — the big pond. The saddest good-bye was from my best friend, Lucien, who had dropped out of the *lycée* to enroll in an art school and prepare for *Les Beaux Arts* (*Ecole Nationale Supérieure des Beaux Arts*), the top French school for graphic artists. After Lucien left *Lycée Carnot* we had kept in touch, meeting occasionally in the evening to walk from the Place Péreire near both of our homes on the right bank of the Seine. We sat and talked for hours in a café like the Dôme, on the left bank, until neither buses nor the metro ran any longer and we had to walk back across Paris, arriving home in the wee hours of the morning.

The time to leave Paris had come. Since the crossing of the Atlantic was not for me an everyday event, I wanted to make the most of it. My parents and I had, at length, discussed which steamship line would afford me the most comfortable journey and good meals for the money. In those days, an Atlantic crossing was a vacation to be enjoyed to the fullest. My father had recommended the Holland America Line and had booked for me a single outside cabin in tourist class on the SS *Statendam*, which was later sunk by the Germans during World War II. Many ships still had first, second (or tourist), and third class. Such an arrangement was soon to be replaced, in a display of democratic spirit, by ships offering almost exclusively tourist class with just a few cabins in cabin class, thus eliminating third class altogether. My father had alerted some of his relatives in New York of my return, and we had also asked my uncle Charlie in New Jersey to spot a conveniently located, inexpensive room for me.

While living and working in Europe, my parents had been depositing most of my father's commissions in an American bank, The Hanover Bank and Trust Company, to which they gave me a letter of introduction. H. Muehlstein and Company had graciously acceded to my father's request and offered to train me and give me a job.

My father also enlightened me about the background and character of Herman Muehlstein, the head of the company. He was a reclusive bachelor who had originally worked for a Boston rubber firm. Once he had acquired a good knowledge of the business and dealt with all its clients, he had struck out for himself and taken the latter with him. Julius Muehlstein, Herman's brother and a bachelor also, was the opposite of his sibling, a complete extrovert and the prototype of the jovial, but sharp, salesman. A third brother and a family man, Charles, ran their Chicago office. My father also told me I could trust Meyerhoff, an old friend of his, who ran the scrap-rubber buying department for the firm.

I sailed on the SS *Statendam* from Le Havre in early October 1935. I suppose I felt slightly apprehensive leaving, at the age of 18, to live my own life in a new world with my first job, but on the whole I was delighted and relieved to depart the parental nest. The journey turned out to be one of the best vacations I ever enjoyed. I could eat what I wanted and stay up as late as I wished. I could hardly believe all the meals that were being served on a conveyor-belt-like basis. Back then, everyone ate the three main meals in the dining room at either of two sittings. Bouillon was served midmorning on deck, tea in the afternoon, and sandwiches at midnight. One could order anything from a generous menu.

In addition to the aforementioned delicate stomach and sensitivity to sole, I had also been plagued with and suffered mentally from acne. My mother and I, after seeing other physicians, had finally consulted a specialist in dermatology. I had been very much impressed with the way he handled the consultation.

The dermatologist was an elderly man. He sat in a darkened room furnished with antique furniture. I kept expecting him to rise from behind his large desk and examine my face. He apparently preferred to exercise his profession at a distance. He exuded an incredible air of authority and medical experience, gathered, I supposed, from watching during his lifetime an endless parade of pimply faces and blotched skins. Glancing at me from afar, he told us I should avoid white bread, eat bananas instead, and gently massage the acne after meals. He assured us it would all disappear by the time I was 18 years old. In those days words like allergy or psychosomatics were unknown, at least to me. I only know that, as soon as the SS *Statendam* had departed for the open sea, any trace of acne and unpleasant reactions to eating fish were a thing of my past.

I continued to overcome my shyness and had a boisterous good time on board. Among the passengers were many young people who had spent part of the summer in Europe and now provided me with plenty of good company. Many took me for a foreigner because of my partially British accent. (British English was taught in European schools at that time.) But I always set them straight — explaining I was an American returning home after 13 years. This aroused their interest in me, and word soon got around about the boy coming home to be a stranger in his own land.

During the day, we played deck tennis with a kind of badminton net and rubber rings, shuffleboard, and used the swimming pool, which unfortunately was preferentially open to first-class passengers. Every night I dressed up in my tuxedo and enjoyed dancing. With the young ladies, perhaps to their disappointment, I was a complete gentleman and cavalier. I never would have even dreamed of flirting with them. We shared a large table in the dining room and ordered as though we never expected to see food again after leaving the ship. At breakfast I even sampled such items as finnan haddie, and once, but never again, bloaters (kippers). I was tempted for adventure's sake to order steak and kidney pie, but the sight of it on an adjoining table drove me to a cowardly change of mind. I never gave a thought to gaining weight, although my mother, who was extremely thin, had occasionally warned me about overeating and appearing plump.

Toward the end of the trip, the weather changed and the ocean became very choppy. The steamer rolled and pitched and many passengers became seasick. The weather grew worse by the hour, and one night we were compelled to stop for repairs in mid-ocean. The dining room grew emptier each night, except for our table; we flaunted our seaworthiness by ordering quite generous meals. At last we resumed normal sailing and drew near to our destination. I knew we were close when the crew started heaving crates of food overboard. I was told that the Captain preferred reaching New York with an empty larder, thus insuring a copious resupply for the trip back, which his company might deny him if too much food was left over.

As we passed the Statue of Liberty, some of my new shipboard acquaintances wanted to know how it felt to return after such a long time. To tell the truth, I was becoming more excited by the minute. I wondered who would be there to meet me on the pier. How would I know them? Suddenly stark reality overcame me. But then I remembered arriving at Victoria Station in 1932 and having no problem at all meeting the Chases. Things usually work themselves out. Helpful in this case was customs inspection, where passengers lined up in front of a letter, corresponding to their last name, that was prominently displayed on the wall.

I remember being mobbed by a bunch of people I did not know and to the best of my knowledge, had never seen before. My father had apparently sent them a picture of me. Uncle Charlie, once he had identified himself to me in his raucous voice, prudently stood aside in what I later learned was his normal reserved manner. He had come alone. Aunt Marguerite and their children were expecting us in New Jersey.

People were introducing themselves like mad — as if I could possibly remember their names or faces. There was Aunt Ida, Aunt Gutta, uncles whose names I have partially forgotten since then for lack of contact. Easier to remember was a cousin my own age, Harold. Impossible to forget was a girl, Gertrude, possibly 14 years old, who most embarrassingly for me, acted as though I was the most unexpected, yet most welcome, male toy she could ever have expected to turn up in her life. Later I learned the term for her behavior: boy crazy. Everyone was delighted to discover I spoke the local tongue. Somehow my father's side of the family seemed to understand that Uncle Charlie had first dibs on me. Maybe they had drawn lots for me prior to the SS *Statendam*'s docking. In any event, I left with Uncle Charlie, bound for River Edge, New Jersey, unhindered, but with countless invitations and promises of family gatherings and free meals in my future. Not quite up to the standards of Julius Caesar's "*Veni, vidi, vici,*" I had arrived and started seeing, but not yet vanquished.

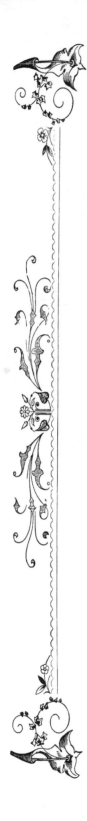

All thinking beings are different,
yet all are basically similar
because of having the gift of thought and desires.
— Voltaire, 1694–1778

Chapter 8

Metamorphosis

ONCE AGAIN, the third time and counting, in my 18 years on earth I was a foreigner, this time in my own country. I was anxious to begin my Americanization. I had a great deal to learn (fortunately without the pressure of exams). Except for knowing English rather well, I was pretty much a greenhorn from the old country. While in Europe I had been registered on my parents' passport, but on my 18th birthday was issued my very own by the new American Embassy. Had it not been for my passport, I might have had to pass through Ellis Island where an immigration official could have, on a whim, changed or shortened my name. Of course, I was highly motivated to assimilate and absorb all that was required to become the proud New Yorker my birthplace had originally destined me to be. Little did I suspect that decades later I might occasionally be tempted to disavow any bonding with this city of infinite egocentricity and, despite its size, parochial viewpoints. I soon realized that in New York City I might stand out even more once I got rid of my foreign accent.

Everything I saw filled me with enthusiasm. I loved the cafeterias where I could eat three meals entirely to my satisfaction for as little as $1.00 a day. A machine at the cafeteria entrance dispensed tickets as patrons entered, and for each ticket a bell was rung, to prevent customers from taking more than one. The ticket displayed prices ranging from 5¢ to over $1 in nickel increments. Each time customers picked a food item — the array of which, especially desserts, boggled the mind — the server punched a hole at the corresponding amount on the ticket. One paid upon leaving. I am ashamed to admit that every once in a while the thought crossed my mind to try and grab two tickets, charge a minimal sum on one, a large meal on the other, and get away with almost a free meal. However, I soon observed that in New York those who deal with the public are much too sharp to fall for such trickery. At busy mealtime hours, a cafeteria employee often stood at the door supervising the process or handing out tickets, insuring that no such devious schemes succeeded.

The difference between Paris and New York was much greater than I had expected. Life in America seemed simpler and more efficient. The clichés and expected images, such as the "time is money" attitude, the gum-chewing public, the skyscrapers, the flaunted wealth and opulence, the directness as opposed to old-country circuitous politeness, now became for me a concrete reality observable in action. To an 18-year-old youth — even one familiar with the centuries-old sightseeing marvels of Europe — the Empire State, Chrysler, and Woolworth Buildings; Rockefeller Center; Times Square; 5th Avenue; and the 3,000-seat, sumptuous Roxy Theater seemed pretty impressive. I missed sidewalk cafés, fancy candy, and pastry stores to which I was accustomed in Paris, but found ample compensation in the ubiquitous candy counters with countless large-size Nestlé, Mounds, Babe Ruth, O'Henry, and other candy bars available for a nickel each.

My father's relatives, especially Harold and his parents, were very helpful in giving me guidance on where to eat, bank, and go for entertainment. Shortly after my arrival, they even saw to it that I bought from Prudential, in a laudable display of financial maturity, an insurance policy for $1,000 with a double indemnity accident clause. My untimely death would now recompense my parents for all they had done for me and temporarily distract their grief.

It came to me as somewhat of a shock that the tailored suits of which I was so proud looked foreign. The jackets were a little short and the trousers flared too much at the bottom. Later I discovered a store on lower 5th Avenue where I could buy tailor-made suits and silk shirts for about $40 and $8, respectively.

Only once was I seized with a sudden feeling of homesickness and passing panic. Uncle Charlie reserved a room for me at the 23rd Street YMCA. It was a run-down building, the rooms were small and shabby, and all wash basins, showers, and restrooms were down the hall. Furthermore, living there would have compelled me to commute to my workplace on the 49th floor of the Chanin Building on the southwest corner of Lexington Avenue and 42nd Street. I was not enticed by or pacified at the thought of the gymnasium and the pool, which were not first-rate either. I wanted as convenient and cheap a room as possible. Fortunately, I found it on 46th Street off Lexington Avenue, four blocks from my office and close to the subways and Grand Central Station. In exchange for a weekly rent of only $5, I was happy to share the bathroom and overlook the bizarre shape of the room (it was very long, and I could almost touch both walls with my outstretched arms). On my way to the office was a cafeteria where every morning, maternal advice and concern for my health firmly in mind, I had a breakfast of cereal and prunes. I was especially fond of all the different kinds of cereals that were not common or available in Europe and to which I had just recently become addicted aboard ship.

The Muehlsteins, very generously for those days, started me off at a $20 a week salary. My parents had no idea how much, or even whether, I would be paid and when apprised of my pay, thoughtfully agreed to send me an additional $50 a month pocket money. I felt rich and immediately opened an account with the Bowery Savings Bank, frugally depositing my parents' gift upon receipt.

At work, I was assigned to a wiry, intense man, quite true to his Scandinavian ancestry. As traffic manager he was in charge of securing the cheapest rates for shipping crude rubber goods by truck or rail, spending eight-hour days on the phone, dickering with steely authoritative finality with his counterparts at competing shipping firms. My first task was to learn the different types of crude rubber and prepare samples to go out to prospective buyers. Besides the most common ribbed smoked sheets and latex rubber samples, occasionally exotic and smelly ones from Africa or South America arrived — some of them even crawling with bugs and red ants.

I witnessed in an adjoining office a high-powered American business tycoon in action. A large, blond, blue-eyed Irishman in charge of buying and selling crude rubber was juggling three or four phones simultaneously, incessantly quoting rubber prices at lightning speed, evidently in full control. It was an impressive sight of intense concentration and split-second decision making involving thousands of dollars. He mirrored the image Europeans had gathered of American businessmen from movies of that period.

For the first time I worked an eight-hour day and was a free man after five o'clock and on Saturdays and Sundays. With no homework, no immediate ambitions for my future, enough money to satisfy my modest tastes, and a financial reserve building up monthly at the bank, I enjoyed a happy, laid-back existence. I was often invited for supper by my relatives and spent many weekends with Aunt Marguerite and Uncle Charlie. Besides my relatives, my only acquaintances were my fellow workers at the office. A few of us, mostly belonging to the lower office hierarchy such as errand boy, mail clerk, and male office workers, had lunch together daily.

A developing masculinity, the memory of Lydia and Jacqueline, and the presence of pretty young secretaries stirred up vague desires of feminine companionship. Shyness, plain lack of know-how, and — more than anything — maternal warnings about premature commitments, rash engagements, disastrous sanitary and financially adverse consequences of out-of-wedlock sex kept me from seeking relationships. (The graphic photographs of syphilitic individuals seen at the Paris Colonial Exhibition in the summer of 1930 had never been erased from my memory.) My aunt Ida, with a less forbidding outlook on such matters, acted as a kind of go-between and introduced me to the daughter of a neighborhood family, originally from Hungary, who belonged to their weekly pinochle circle.

Ethel was a ravishing redhead. Most probably to her astonishment and in contrast to her previous experience with American boyfriends, I initiated my acquaintance with her by sending flowers. We dated for quite a while on Saturday evenings, went to movies, and danced at the Child's Restaurant on Times Square. I never even tried to kiss her. I must not have lived up to her expectations of a red-blooded boyfriend, perhaps I even inspired doubts about my sexual preferences, for she cooled considerably toward me. I knew her parents approved of me, but in the end it was Ethel's opinion that mattered. On one Sunday afternoon date, I sat on a park bench with her for a fairly long while, my arm over her shoulder, without attempting any necking. Such abstinence must have clinched my fate with her. She turned me down for further dates and from what I heard started seeing other boys. Henceforth, I decided to date different girls, enjoy their company, and not worry about unsustainable, dangerous liaisons for which I was not ready.

My parents and I corresponded regularly, and my mother soon decided that I had too much free time. She encouraged me to enroll in night school. I registered for an evening course in business at the Washington Square campus of New York University. The instructor was excellent, and I vividly recall his telling us that it mattered not whether there was any gold in Fort Knox, as long as everyone believed it was there. I also learned much about contracts and other general business matters.

At the office I began to wonder about the training I was receiving. Cutting up rubber samples and keeping them organized in the sample room did not seem to lead to much of a future besides dirty hands. Inspecting incoming shipments at Staten Island piers and bringing back samples proved slightly more interesting, especially since it got me out of the office, away from my boss's watchful eye, and made the day go by faster.

Once Herman Muehlstein invited me to dinner at his penthouse on Central Park West. A butler served us avocado, hard as rock, and at that time an unknown and rare delicacy, which few people in the eastern U.S. had either seen or tasted. (With knowledge gained six years later in California, I could have explained to him that they taste much better ripe.) His brother Julius took me to lunch at Reuben's Restaurant, where the famous sandwich of the same name was created and the menu was comprised of

100 different sandwiches. He also offered to pay the bill should I take a date to the Rainbow Room on top of Rockefeller Center. I was sorely tempted, but my upbringing did not allow me to take advantage of his generous offer — unless he had consented to come along and treat us. On New Year's Eve, we all received bonuses in our pay envelopes and Julius gave us sparkling new dollar bills he had signed with a "Happy New Year" and his name.

After a few months, I began thinking that I was not learning anything useful that would help me to work with my father in Paris, since so far we had only dealt in scrap — not crude — rubber in Europe. I asked for an interview with Herman who, a few days later, transferred me to the scrap rubber and metal department under Mayerhoff. He saw to it that I became acquainted with all the client files and learned to draft business letters. A young man in his office constantly traveled, mostly to buy large shipments of old tires and metal valves from scrap dealers in New York, New Jersey, and Pennsylvania. Mayerhoff planned to have me accompany him so that I would learn the business firsthand. He attempted to secure Muehlstein's approval, but to his and my disappointment, was turned down. I was pretty much relegated to file clerk and letter drafter. In other respects he treated me well, gradually raising my salary to about $27 a week over a period of a year and a half.

Before leaving for Hamburg on July 24th, 1922, I had been baptized by Paul D. Elsesser, pastor of the French Evangelical Church of New York, at 126 West 16th Street, New York City. No doubt my parents did not wish to bring a heathen to Germany or have me perish a nonChristian at sea. Thereafter, my religious education had been acquired in German schools, where we had regular classes in the Old and New Testaments. My parents did not seem to have time to attend services, and I went to church with Fräulein only on rare occasions. Upon our arrival in Paris, where public schools would not think of giving religious instruction, my mother, who had been raised a Lutheran in Calvinist Geneva, began to think of my immortal soul and the possibilities of my confirmation. Together we went to see the pastor of a Lutheran church in Paris. My mother expressed to him her desire to have me receive the Apostolic Rite of Laying on of Hands at a Confirmation, simultaneously emphasizing how immensely busy I was with schoolwork in view of my recent arrival from Germany and my staggering deficiencies in French, Latin, and English. The pastor showed little sympathy for my schedule in the lay world, sternly stating that there were no shortcuts to salvation. My mother, always certain of her priorities, decided on the spot that this would mean Christianity's and the pastor's loss and my passing up Confirmation.

In 1936, after living a few months in my small, dingy room and following suggestions from friends that I might enjoy staying in nicer quarters with a few amenities, I began to consider moving to a YMCA. I checked out several and finally decided on the West Side YMCA. It had a splendid location on 5 West 63rd Street — right off Central Park near the rich and famous, and only three blocks from Columbus Circle, where the Lincoln Center was later situated. I went to the membership office and was treated to a tour of the building, which itself looked like an elegant modern castle. I was immediately mesmerized by the two gymnasiums, two swimming pools, the lounges, library, cafeteria, lunch counter, and other facilities, the likes of which I had never seen. The membership secretary implied that my admission should not be taken for granted, a tone of foreboding in his voice. The weekly standard room rate was about $9. I waited a few weeks and, not hearing from the Y, went to see the secretary. I was told that my application had been rejected.

It was an unexpected disappointment, the first of this kind I had ever suffered in my life. After all, I considered myself a clean-cut young man of model habits. I inquired about the reason for the adverse decision. The secretary hemmed and hawed a long while, but finally suggested I try the YMHA — the Young Man's Hebrew Association. I was speechless. Never before had my religious faith been questioned. Nor had it played any role in decisions affecting my participation in anything. I told him I was Lutheran Evangelical. He brought up my name, which he thought was Jewish. Almost in tears, I explained that I was not Jewish and that I had once been admitted to the 23rd Street YMCA. Why on earth would I wish to join a YMHA, where I had no business whatsoever? He remained adamant.

Very depressed, I told my boss, Mr. Meyerhoff, about it. Although Jewish himself, he offered to help, but I doubted the efficacy of any intervention by him on my behalf. I tried other YMCAs, although the West Side was my first choice. The Railroad YMCA near my present domicile admitted only railroad personnel. The Sloan House YMCA on 34th Street, near the Pennsylvania Station, was only for short stays by transients. Finally, I looked at my few personal documents and took out my baptism certificate. Armed therewith I went back to see the West Side YMCA secretary, a Mr. Glenn Hudson, and showed him the certificate lavishly illustrated with a white dove, the divine light (which evidently had not touched the minds of the Y staff), a baptismal basin, numerous flowers, an official stamp, the pastor's signature, and those of my godparents Marguerite and Charles Frisch. Overwhelmed by this evidence and perhaps moved by my persistence, he promised to resubmit my application, hinting at a prompt favorable action. Shortly thereafter I moved into the Y, starting a relationship which partly because of the difficulty I had experienced establishing it, I never have relinquished to this very day. (In 1999 I expect to receive my Half-Century Club gold membership card testifying to 64 years of continuous membership in the Y.) As a contributor to and now firmly accepted pillar of the YMCA, I have on occasion related at Y meetings this hard-won victory and discriminatory incident. I have little patience with religious or racial prejudice.

I was very happy with my new living arrangements. Every day I walked to and from work along Broadway to Times Square and across town on 42nd Street. I witnessed the opening of many new Horn and Hardart automats along this route and felt at peace with the world and myself. I began a routine of swimming 1,000 yards every evening after work. I made a few friends at the Y, and had no problems besides having to, at times, successfully fight off the unwelcome advances of my boy-crazy cousin Gertrude.

The winter of 1936-1937 was especially ferocious, with snow piled up in the streets well into Easter time. During that winter my right shoe became caught in a trolley track as I crossed Lexington Avenue. I fell, spraining my ankle. Since I carried Traveler's Accident Insurance I spent two weeks on crutches doing nothing besides collecting $25 a week in addition to my regular salary. I even started taking riding lessons in Central Park, as I found a stable run by an ex-British Cavalry Sergeant willing to give me lessons for $5. My life was perfectly serene; I had no problems and maintained very regular habits. Little did I suspect that this would soon change drastically.

I should have realized that this carefree existence could not last for-ever. I never gave my future any thought, merely did my job, drew my pay, and took another course, this time Business Law, at the Sawyer Business Institute, which was very conveniently located on the second floor of the West Side YMCA. I always had invitations for holidays and never felt lonely on weekends.

One of my main preoccupations was to be well dressed. Herman Muehlstein, who seemed to never wear the same suit twice, contributed somewhat to such juvenile sense of values. The errand boy, Johnny O'Connor was, despite his unglamorous job, just about the second best dressed man in the office after Herman. (Julius could not be bothered and wore expensive, but rumpled suits.)

Interestingly enough, back then, two stores, Crawford's and Howard's offered ready-made suits, even tuxedos and tails, for prices ranging from $19 to $22. However, I was aiming higher: for tailor-made clothing. My uncle, a cutter for 5th Avenue tailors who charged $200 for a suit, steered me to a large shop where suits were made using not individual, but a few general and adjustable patterns. This and a large volume of sales allowed them to offer at highly reduced prices suits essentially made to measure. I ordered three double-breasted suits, one of them in white serge with an extra pair of trousers. To wear with the white suit I splurged on four shirts in dark blue, dark red, dark green, and black. A dream, highly influenced by Hollywood films, come true!

On July 4, 1937, H. Muehlstein and Company held a picnic and dance for all employees. It was very hot and there was much dancing, in which I took an enthusiastic part. I perspired profusely. Suddenly someone shouted: "Max, your suit!" My dark maroon shirt, not colorfast, had stained my white suit, through and through — a horrible blotchy red. The realization of the disaster cooled me off instantly. Fortunately, the reliable and highly advertised dry-cleaner, French, Shriner and Urner (often back then irreverently referred to as French, Shriner and Uriner), having se-cured my waiver for any liability, boiled the dickens out of the suit, and miraculously restored it without shrinkage to its original pristine white.

Herman Muehlstein, I was fully aware, had provided me with a job and salary as a good will gesture toward my father, not because of any contri-bution I might make to the company (although I made myself as useful as possible). Sparing in speech and reserved in manner, Mr. Muehlstein had never discussed with me my future or any career possibilities. I had no idea what he thought of me, although I am certain that nothing going on in the office ever escaped his attention. Like all absolute rulers, I am certain he was kept informed of everything. In May of 1937, my father, as a surprise gift, sent me a ticket to France on the SS *Normandie*, at that time the largest and fastest ship crossing the Atlantic. It was the pride of the French Line fleet and had been built in the early 1930s, triggering endless erudite debates among grammarians as to whether it should be feminine *la*, as all ships in English, or a masculine *le Normandie*. (The debate was never resolved during the ship's useful life, but appears to have been discontinued, and rightly so, after it was scrapped.) My father fully intended this to be a vacation for me. However, when I asked Herman Muehlstein for time off, he told me that I was not expected back and should plan to work, henceforth, in the Paris office as my father's eventual successor.

My father had chosen to have my return to France coincide with the Paris World's Fair. For the moment I did not look beyond the coming thrill of crossing the ocean in record time. I bought a large radio for my parents as a gift, since they had never indulged themselves with one. After a grand journey, I arrived at Le Havre and proceeded by train to the very familiar Saint Lazare station, near which my father had his office on the *Pont de l'Europe*. Not unexpectedly, French customs did not spare us the usual red tape to import the radio, but eventually it was safely and satisfactorily installed in my parents' apartment for their never-before-experienced enjoyment.

The Paris World's Fair proved to be a magnificent event. The French had gone all out, razing the old *Trocadéro*, across the Seine River from the Eiffel Tower, because of its abominable acoustics and replacing it with the much improved *Palais de Chaillot*. A new Museum of Modern Art had been built on the right bank of the Seine River, not far from the Eiffel Tower, partly replacing the old Museum of Luxembourg on the left bank near the Panthéon. It now housed many of the paintings formerly shown in the *Musée du Luxembourg*, as well as a Gauguin and Van Gogh exhibit. The fair brought many foreign tourists, including a convention of American Legionnaires. Many of the latter came with their girlfriends; their at times conspicuously gross behavior managed to raise even French eyebrows and call for comments in the French Press. (The French are not so much concerned about what people do as they are about the degree of discretion, or lack thereof, with which it is done.) A giant exhibit in a five-story building of extremely artistic interior designs and tasteful modern furniture attracted many visitors and favorable comments.

My father's business was not very good. One reason for having me return was the slightly declining state of his health. Inflationary pressures on the French franc and the uncertainty of Europe's fate due to the rise of Hitler made the import and export business much more difficult and less remunerative than it had been before. When my father sold rubber to other countries — such as Germany, Italy, or Hungary — procedures established all over Europe meant he would not receive payment directly from his buyer, but from an international clearing account into which a French buyer of foreign goods had paid for his purchase. This caused painful delays that could prove costly because of inflation. Assuming a sale was contracted when the French franc was worth 6.67¢ (U.S.) and was to be paid 90 days later, when the invoice was actually paid, the franc was worth only 4¢ (U.S.). Thus my father would lose heavily on the exchange — in extreme cases unable even to recover the original cost of the goods sold.

My return to Paris coincided with this adverse economic situation, which my father was taking pretty hard. One of his clients, a powerful French tire manufacturer, took years off my father's life. The client was one of those Frenchmen who, under cover of outward politeness and cour-tesy, could prove lethal in his unflinching demands, unreasonable com-plaints, and unwillingness to yield an inch.

I started assisting with the office routine, the business correspondence and the coding of cables, but my father was not good at breaking in help, and I was not really getting the feel of the business — for which, besides, I had but scant interest. I felt I was getting nowhere.

We had no social life. I had no friends. I saw Jacqueline once or twice on a mutually unenthusiastic date. In fairness to her, I was no fun to be with. Paul and his sister, who had skied with me in 1934, invited me to a cocktail party, but I did not drink. Lucien and I occasionally met for an evening walk and a soft drink on the terrace of an outdoor café. Most evenings I spent reading a borrowed economics course syllabus. Then, as they still do now, economic theories frustrated me with their inability to arrive at any consensus or definitive conclusions. With no really mean-ingful routine to engage my full attention and energy, with no real goal or purpose, my state of mind began to deteriorate. I wish I could remember exactly how or why it happened, so that this knowledge might benefit others, but I cannot recall the reasons for my gradually oncoming anorexia.

Anorexia, 60 years ago, was hardly a common concept, if even a known term. My mother, thin as a rail, had always been extremely concerned with her weight. She was a finicky eater, who picked at her food and rarely cleared her plate. My father was heavy and my mother was concerned about his weight, his chain-smoking, and his high blood pressure. He enjoyed eating and liked to talk about it; he had earlier in life been a gourmet, but later had to follow a stricter diet, which he was at times tempted to break. I had never been heavy, but had a tendency to put on weight, and my mother would make remarks about this, urging me to cut down on fattening food and desserts.

Meat, except for veal, did not tempt me unless chopped, hashed, or in the form of cold cuts or sausage. My bout with stomach poisoning in Germany, my allergy to fish, and my pimples, as well as chronic constipation had made me conscious of what I ate. Living in the United States on my own, limiting my budget for meals in order to economize, being at last free from pimples and food allergies, and finally exercising good common sense not to indulge myself to excess in any foods, including candy and rich pastries, had changed me into a well-balanced, carefree person as far as food was concerned. I was trim, did not bother weighing myself, felt comfortable in my clothes, and ate reasonably — perhaps just a little more heartily when I was invited to a free meal. I emphasize these facts to show that whatever triggered an imbalance in my formerly very natural instincts and psychological makeup, I started with a clean slate.

While I had no financial concerns at this time, I was not actually earning a salary, and felt that with regard to my future I was making no progress. Conditions in France and my father's health made it seem increasingly more likely that he might have to give up the representation of H. Muehlstein and retire. He became seriously ill. His somewhat old-fashioned, yet knowledgeable, doctor recommended blood letting to lower his blood pressure and prescribed leeches. Seeing this courageous human being lying in bed, with nary a whimper or complaint, the black slimy wiggling leeches sucking themselves full of his blood and then sliding satiated off his chest, was not for me a morale-raising sight. It strengthened forever my respect and admiration for my father and his display of manhood. Whenever I feel weak, overwhelmed, or am about to know pain, I think of my Dad and try to emulate his stoicism and sheer guts.

My father recovered, but my situation did not become any clearer. France was restless, too, and ministers had difficulty forming stable and lasting governments. Not infrequently one might hear voiced the opinion that France could use a firm hand like that of Hitler — thoughtless words to say the least. I began to feel a loss of control over my destiny. My sense of perfection, which I had hitherto been able to maintain on a modest level, first by excelling in school and then by holding a job in New York, abandoned me. Very possibly, with a misguided personal adventurism to gain self-esteem, I sought control and perfection of a sort by straying into the quicksand of anorexia. Like many afflictions of this nature, it tends to be addictive, self-fulfilling, and cumulative, as though feeding on its own success.

At first it revealed itself as a mere obsession with exercise and slimming down. I became overly conscious of fattening food, abstaining from all starches, eating as little as possible at breakfast and lunch, making up for any "shortcomings" at supper. I would walk rather than take a bus or subway to get as much exercise as possible. Every Sunday morning I walked the long stretch from our house up to the *Arc de Triomphe*, down the *Champs Elysées* to the Louvre Museum to visit the gallery featuring the Flemish School of painters: Jan Vermeer de Delft, Franz Hals, the Breughels, and others. I lost weight, my cheeks became sunken. I grew morose, always on the defensive about my weight. My parents and a few acquaintances became quite concerned, incapable of fathoming what was going on.

We had many deliberations as to what my father and I should do. My father, 68, but older than his years, tentatively decided to think about retiring and discontinuing the representation of H. Muehlstein. It meant that I had to decide what to do with my own future. We agreed I should return to New York and look for a job, anticipating no difficulties with such a plan. The winter of 1937-1938 had been fairly rigorous and refused to yield to spring. My father needed a rest in a better climate than Paris could offer. Therefore, we decided to go to Italy. My father would rest at Bellaggio on the Lake of Como and my mother and I would tour Italy, which we had never before visited.

Italy was awaiting and making preparations for the arrival of Adolf Hitler, who was to visit Mussolini at Easter. In Rome a special road was built for Hitler from the airport to the center of the city. However, we planned to terminate our month-long stay in Italy before Hitler's arrival, to avoid inordinately large crowds. It was a magnificent trip marred only by the unseasonably cold weather. We visited Milan and Pisa. I remember walking miles along a very long esplanade bordered by trees to reach a building in which one of its large walls displayed the famous Last Supper by Leonardo da Vinci. Even in 1938 much of this splendid and famous fresco had disappeared and was barely visible, the paint having been absorbed by the underlying plaster. In Pisa we saw the leaning tower. From there we traveled to Naples. A ship took us to Capri, where we transferred to small boats to visit the Blue Grotto. We also visited Pompeii and Herculaneum, the destruction of which by the eruption of Mount Vesuvius I had read in the original Latin text of Pliny the Elder. Near the top of Mount Vesuvius a guide, a giant of a man, showed us how to pierce the lava on the ground with a steel-spiked stick to see it glow red hot underneath. We visited Florence and Venice, after which we rejoined my father. He met us in Como, where I visited the famous Borsalino hat factory, from which, I believe, Al Capone and other gangsters purchased their fedoras. I bought one, too, to wear on special dressy occasions. We stayed a while in beautiful Bellaggio before returning to Paris.

I booked a cabin on the maiden voyage of the *New Amsterdam* of the Holland America Line. The famous singer Hildegarde was on board and, on a dare, I asked her to dance one evening, which she graciously did. I had a pretty dance partner, an American college girl, for a few nights. After that she suddenly dropped me and I saw her in the constant company of another young man. My guess was that, since I had a single accomodation, she had expected me to be more aggressive and invite her to my cabin.

On arrival in New York, I made the mistake of telling the customs official, before being asked, that I had nothing to declare. The result was that I had to open every single one of my suitcases. I had written the West Side YMCA of my return, and two young members met me at the pier. It was a heartier welcome than the one I had encountered when I first attempted to join. This time, a room had been reserved for me, and I looked forward to finding a job and resuming a normal life.

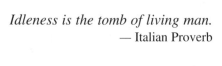

Idleness is the tomb of living man.
— Italian Proverb

Chapter 9

Hard Times

HE YEAR 1938 STANDS OUT — in many ways — as one of the most destabilizing in my life, not so much because it presented me with disproportionately more difficult problems than I had ever confronted before, but because I could not rise to the occasion and be equal to the different kind of challenge they posed. Faced with trying circumstances, perhaps not entirely of my own making, I proved weak and failed. I not only failed to cope, I ended up resorting to a crutch which may, to a large degree, have influenced the direction of the rest of my life. Owing to the good moral example set by my parents, my solid upbringing, a firm grounding in the great books, and a natural instinct for knowing right from wrong and for survival, this crutch did not prove fatal. It was nonetheless adversely significant. I trust some readers may learn from my mistakes.

I had saved $1,000 while working for Muehlstein, and my parents could afford to send me a modest monthly check. This enabled me to live at the Y and pay for my meals. Thus, I was not in dire straits. However, we have, beyond our physical needs, immense psychic needs. In my case, over and above the need for finding a job providing a steady salary, there was the even more urgent need to find employment in order to bolster my self-esteem. I needed reassurance that society had a place for me and my productive services.

Before starting the disheartening daily search for employment, I turned to friends and relatives for advice. I knew I could not count on Herman Muehlstein, since he was most likely disappointed that my father had discontinued the representation. I turned to a French chemist in Muehlstein's New York office. My father had rendered him a significant favor in the past. A Belgian inventor, Bemelmans, had developed a patent for "softened rubber," a method for devulcanizing scrap rubber to recover its original plastic properties. Before the invention of synthetic rubber, this was a critical product. The chemist had been charged with obtaining the patent for Muehlstein from Bemelmans, but had bungled the mission by antagonizing the Belgian. My father, with his talent for dealing with people, had come to his rescue, allowing the chemist to take credit for closing the deal.

The chemist sent me to the New York branch of the French perfume giant Houbigant. The interview did not progress too well, but swayed by the fact that I was American, a product of the French educational system, and willing to start at the very bottom to learn the perfume business, the director tentatively promised to give me a try. I was elated, never suspecting any negative input by Muehlstein during a routine employment check. Some time later, when I checked back with Houbigant, I was informed they had no opening for me. My chemist friend, when informed of this, was fairly certain that Herman Muehlstein had torpedoed my chances with negative comments about me. Bitter as this pill was to swallow, I could understand Muehlstein's action — he had wanted me to work for him in Paris — but not without anger and resentment.

None of my relatives could offer any help. My own cousin, Harold, was in desperate need for a job which he, after much struggling and a long search, obtained at Nedick's, the hot dog and orange drink chain. Envious of his success more than his job, I often watched him in the evening, in white cap and frock, catering with growing ease and dexterity to the hungry crowd.

I began my daily visits to employment agencies. Every night I would buy an early edition of *The New York Times* and scan the ads in the Help Wanted columns, marking them as I read. Early the next morning, I would take the subway to Wall Street and start looking, working my way uptown. A number of ads appeared in those days stating "blond Aryan types preferred." These were hard times!

I had much company in my search for employment. Unemployed acquaintances at the West Side YMCA and I would compare notes and derive little comfort therefrom. One fat Italian tenor, who did not live at the Y, but sought daily refuge there from his small bachelor pad nearby, failed to place in the Metropolitan Opera auditions, finally finding a job at the WPA radio station in City Hall. With no musical talents I could hardly have vied for that position. Another young man, prone to cataleptic fits, which were so common we learned to ignore them in the Y cafeteria or lounge — merely making sure his tongue was not sticking out between his teeth, enlisted in the Civil Conservation Corps. Either it proved too demanding for him or he for it, but after a few weeks he was back at the Y lounge and, during fits, on its floor. There also was the middle-aged medical doctor from Lima, Peru. He was in no need of a job. Subsidized by his wealthy family, he lived at the Y, taking some postgraduate medical courses at Columbia University and lifting weights two to three hours a day in the gym. I cultivated his acquaintance mainly to practice my Spanish. We often ate together and once or twice went to the movies. He was a pleasant man and liked to practice his English on me, especially after he found out that I had a solid humanistic European background. He always ate dessert first, before the main part of his meal, claiming that this insured a better digestive process. Many years later, when I revisited the Y, I found out from a member of its staff and to my utter surprise, that he had been kicked out of the Y for homosexual behavior. He had never once tried any inappropriate actions toward me. I was belatedly grateful not to have been his type.

One Sunday evening, after spending a pleasant weekend in New Jersey, I had dismounted the bus at 181st Street in Washington Heights and decided to walk down Broadway the 118 blocks to the Y. (In those days one could walk day or night through any part of New York City without the slightest danger of being mugged.) Upon arriving at the Y, I encountered pandemonium. Everyone in the downstairs lounge, where the radio stood, was talking about a Martian invasion reported by some broadcaster named Orson Welles. I had missed the now famous broadcast, but reacted very skeptically to its contents. Of course, it turned out to be a hoax.

For a long time I observed a very ascetic lifestyle, having promised myself I would not indulge in any entertainment, such as movies or dances, until I had landed a job. As time passed, my resolve soon evaporated and I occasionally visited the cheap movie theaters on 42nd Street, where admission was a quarter. Once I even went to Minsky's Burlesque. I walked out on the latter, unable to stomach the depressing spectacle of the sorrowful stripteasers and the frequent lengthy intermissions during which hucksters endeavored to sell a variety of goods, such as cigarettes and candies, to the audience.

Every day I continued to haunt employment agencies without the slightest success. The problem, as I soon realized, was that my B.A. from the University of Paris was not a dazzling, irresistible qualification in the eyes of future employers, especially not when I applied for menial jobs. I even went to the unattractive employment agencies on 6th Avenue (Avenue of the Americas), between 42nd and 57th Streets. Crowds of unemployed would be jostling each other there, scanning the handwritten posters advertising scarce odd jobs for low pay. Every so often someone came out of the agency to take down a poster as the job had been filled, and the crowd heaved a sigh of disappointment. These places specialized in kitchen help and ultimately I had neither the motivation nor the nerve to apply for such jobs. In any event, a French B.A. and a fluent knowledge of three languages was not essential for cleaning pots and pans. (As I was to find out later, the Army is much more inclined to seek such highly qualified manpower to fill these kinds of positions.) Meanwhile, my morale was sinking and my despair growing by the day.

One aunt of mine, through an acquaintance, secured for me an opening with a group of men who sold eggs daily from door to door in Harlem — not exactly the opportunity of a lifetime. We met in the dark at the ungodly hour of four o'clock in the morning, possibly with the intention of surprising clients before they had poured their morning coffee, were fully awake, and were in possession of their wits. The man in charge handed each one of us a basket with egg cartons, gave us last-minute instructions, and assigned us an exact time and place for meeting again to critique the operation. Like assault troops invading a beachhead, we scattered over a neighborhood not exactly reminiscent of Park Avenue splendor, with the determined mission of selling as many eggs as possible to Harlem tenants.

With a defeatist disbelief in my selling abilities I began climbing stairs and ringing doorbells. Almost every ring was greeted by loud barking. The tenants of those run-down buildings hardly had the means of feeding themselves, but every apartment seemed to enjoy the protective presence of a canine, often a mastiff, fiercely barking, perhaps from hunger, at the unwelcome intruder. Not a born salesman — rather a hapless Willy Loman — I always took no for an answer. I was incapable of breaking down any prospective egg buyers' sales resistance, more because of timidity and compassion for the poverty of their condition than out of concern for their high cholesterol level, which in those days had not yet been recognized as a threat to health. When, at the end of the morning, we gathered for a bite to eat and to compare notes on our sales performance, I ranked very low — in fact, lowest. I was astounded by the success of a few others and ashamed of my inability to even sell one carton. The man in charge offered to pay me, but I refused and decided door-to-door selling was not my forte. Years later, just for fun, I took a general aptitude test that claimed to discover in me hidden talents for aggressive salesmanship!

During this, for me so painful, period from about May 1938 to the summer of 1939, I managed to find three temporary jobs. They deserve mention only because they reflect the severity of conditions and the, at times, bizarre nature of some of the positions offered.

I was offered a clerical job with a recent immigrant of East European descent who ran a correspondence school for would-be customs agents. The gentleman, with a thick foreign accent, seemed to be almost illiterate. My hours were from about 5 p.m. to 2 a.m., during which time I corrected papers and tests sent in by correspondence students and performed general office work. When I was not busy, my boss had me draft personal letters to his relatives in Europe. He claimed that he was not good at writing letters and since I appeared educated, I could use my imagination and do it for him. It was bizarre to be making polite epistolary small talk with correspondents I did not know, yet were close to him. He, of course, signed the letters as though he had written them. The office was located right above the 42nd Street Cafeteria, between 6th Avenue and Times Square, which gave me at least the opportunity to eat in one of New York City's better restaurants of this type. But the below-minimum-wage salary I was being paid, about $8 per week, could barely pay for my many meals there. He soon discharged me, blaming slow business.

The second, as it first appeared, "once in a lifetime opportunity," offered because of my *bachot* and excellent knowledge of English and French, was with the French Motion Picture Corporation, a French husband and wife team, who hired me at $8 a week. The husband was a fuss-budget who always looked morose and serious, as though consumed with insurmountable worries. He sat in his large office alone — any other arrangement would have been *lèse majesté*, an insult to his authority — idolized, fussed over, and screened from any outside threatening elements by his protective and solicitous wife. She occupied a modest desk in the second smaller office, taking all phone calls and acting as though her husband's every physical need had to be attended to with the utmost care and his mental and emotional balance constantly safeguarded. This empowered him to exercise, in meditative isolation and insulation, his intellectual powers to the fullest, attempting to cope with the demands presented to him by the corporation's mission, objectives, and problems.

The nitpicking lady taught me the filing system, which was unnecessarily complex, and I fulfilled the various clerical tasks assigned to me to her satisfaction. Shortly after I had started on the job, the lady told me I could earn extra money for translating into English the scripts or subtitles of the French movies they imported for distribution in the USA. These scripts had to be submitted to the censorship office for approval. I was delighted, since this task was perfectly suited to my training and abilities. She encouraged me to proceed with the work any time I was not busy with something else. In the meantime, I could not help but observe that business was not flourishing. The wife would cloister herself with her husband in his office for long periods and their worry about the business was obvious.

I had the first inkling that something was really wrong when the wife told me I would not receive extra pay for my translations as long as I did them on company time. This was in direct contradiction to our original agreement. A few days later the ax fell. In view of the dire economic straits in which the French Motion Picture Corporation found itself, my budget-straining salary could no longer be justified. My employers were apologetic about letting me go and found me another job. They convinced the World Theater on 48th Street east of 7th Avenue to hire me. This theater specialized in foreign films. I was hired as an usher, and my hours were from about 5:30 p.m. until a little after 2:00 a.m. My main tasks were to usher clients to their seats, attend to the needs of the projectionist, and help lock up after the last performance.

The job was better than none at all and still afforded me ample time during the day to look for other employment. I would get to bed by four o'clock in the morning and be up and about no later than ten o'clock. The moving picture that showed at the theater for the longest time was the French masterpiece *Un Carnet de Bal* — A Dance Program. The film deals with several different episodes featuring the personalities that have signed on the same lady's dance program. After seeing it another 40 or 50 times, I could have qualified as a stand-in for any of the parts.

Whenever the projectionist rang for assistance, I would be dispatched to attend to his needs. He was a pleasant young man who reclined in a lounge chair in an upstairs cubby hole, which served as projection room. He looked perfectly relaxed, reading or resting, merely watching from time to time so that he would not miss the marks on the film announcing the end of a reel. Then he sprang into action, on the ready, at the end of one reel on one projector, to switch to a second projector and start the next reel. We talked, and he would self-contentedly explain to me — nay, rub in — the security he enjoyed as a member of the projectionists' union, guaranteeing him a salary and job. I would fetch him a sandwich and drink or whatever he desired from the cafeteria across the street from the theater. The work did not hold much promise, but nonetheless I was dejected when the owners told me that the slow business no longer warranted my services. For years after, whenever I passed the theater, I had flashbacks of scenes in French films.

During all this time I was getting thinner and thinner. My relatives, especially my Aunt Marguerite, harassed me constantly with their concerns about my weight, even thinking I suffered from tuberculosis. I had a negative chest x-ray to satisfy them. One evening, aware of my low weight — which I could check on scales in the Y locker room and which was ominously close to 100 pounds — I stopped at a Horn and Hardart's on 8th Avenue just north of 42nd Street. Succumbing either to fear or plain hunger, I wolfed three to four bowls of cereal followed by ice cream. It felt incredibly good to let go and stuff myself, producing both a mental — almost voluptuous — high and an immensely satisfying physical fullness. I had picked bland food, as I could never have done the same with meat, vegetables, and potatoes. Still plagued by anorexia, I calculated — "miscalculated" might be a better term — that with my low weight I could repeat this gluttonous behavior many times before my body would show any effects therefrom.

By the time I had walked the 20 blocks to the Y, I felt very uncomfortable, the results of my action were sloshing around in my stomach. On impulse I walked behind some bushes in Central Park, bent over, and vomited, aiding myself somewhat by sticking my fingers down my throat. Thereby I started an insidious habit that was to last off and on for some 40 years, progressing with increasing refinements or ingenious perfection and calling for ever more inventive subterfuges to dissemble it. To some degree, my entire lifestyle was affected, and it may even have influenced major career decisions. An unending nightmarish and psychologically confusing cycle of weight fluctuations was triggered that made vampire-like demands on my physical and mental energies. I am writing this today not to alleviate my conscience by a belated confession, but to warn and enlighten some readers about a harmful — in some cases even lethal — addiction, caused by the social pressures often exerted on susceptible individuals during trying times. Not to invoke this as an excuse, but none of this would ever have occurred had my life not presented me with challenges I was not prepared to meet.

Two factors saved me from disaster. First, I had a fundamentally healthy body to begin with. Second, contradictory as this may seem at first, a basic preoccupation with personal fitness cautioned me to cultivate a vice and addiction with a certain degree of damage control, limited precautionary measures, and without altogether abandoning an iron discipline in all matters — outside of food — vital to my professional and social obligations. Nevertheless, I immensely regret the energy and attention I wasted over the years, which could have been so much more productively diverted to the undistracted pursuit of worthy goals.

I continued halfheartedly looking for work, but even I knew that my mental state and negative defeatist attitude were my own worst enemies. I blamed economic conditions and society instead of myself. My Uncle Charlie's brother, Edmund Frisch, a wealthy and prominent Park Avenue jeweler, could have with his many connections easily extended a helping hand, but told me that because of my poor attitude he would not help me, even if he could. I knew there was a measure of truth in what he said, although I hated and never forgave him for it. His thoughts could have been conveyed with more compassion and useful advice.

I had an interview with the man who started Linguaphone, which, I believe, became a very successful enterprise. He merely offered me an opportunity to sell his language-learning records on a commission basis. I neither believed in the efficacy of his method nor my ability to sell it to the public and refused. I also followed up on an ad soliciting prospective guides for New York City in view of the expected rush of tourists during the soon-to-open 1939 World's Fair in Queens. I memorized a sightseeing guide of New York, passed the test, and secured a New York Chauffeur's license. (I had obtained my first driver's license in Paris before returning to New York in 1938. However, with no driving experience at all, I believed it wiser to take another course to pass the Chauffeur's test.) Despite the expense incurred, I was not hired.

I also applied for a job pushing jinrikishas — "rickshaws" — two-wheeled passenger vehicles, for World's Fair visitors, but my emaciated looks undoubtedly dissuaded my would-be employer from considering me. More and more discouraged, when idle and depressed, I often failed to resist the sick urge of gorging myself on candy or cheap food, which was available in various locations during those hard times. There still were some bars along Broadway, between 63rd and 72nd Streets, offering free lunch, mostly salty snacks, with a drink. I imbibed no alcoholic beverages, but would sometimes sneak a few free bites with a soft drink. On 14th Street, east of 5th Avenue near Bloomingdale's department store, dingy eating places sold pies, sandwiches, hamburgers, and hot dogs for as little as a dime or a nickel.

There were two movie theaters nearby, where admission was a nickel. Inside, wooden benches — disposed without any apparent order — replaced the usual seats, and hoboes were sitting, lying, or sleeping on them. I went in once, but left almost immediately, ashamed I had been tempted to enter; I wasn't so poor that I had to associate with bums.

I remember that New York City, at this time was feeling the influx of Jewish refugees who were able to escape from the Nazis and emigrate to the USA. Some of them, around Broadway and 96th Street, would gather in local cafeterias, occupying tables and consuming nothing but glasses of water sweetened with free sugar. They sat, deeply immersed in their conversations, until the manager would ask them to leave to make room for paying clients.

Because of my neurotic food habits, my weight fluctuated from 130 to 165 pounds, frightening those who knew me. I looked either bloated or emaciated. To hide my vice, I hinted I might be suffering from an inactive thyroid; but deep inside, I knew that my eating disorder was entirely my fault. Eventually, quite distraught and confused, I began to believe I had a metabolic disorder, going so far as to write my parents about it. I went to see a masseur-therapist on 42nd Street and underwent colon irrigation. He gave me several treatments, prescribing an extreme three-week diet: a full bottle of Pluto water to purge my system every morning and six Temple oranges a day, nothing else. No plumber equipped with a "Roto-Rooter" could have accomplished a more thorough job of cleaning my insides. I felt as pure as a newborn child and lost about 35 pounds. I was right back at an unnaturally low weight and emaciated appearance, looking more and more like a refugee from a Nazi concentration camp.

This dull, depressing routine was enlivened by a few incidents. One evening, a young man dove down on top of me while I was swimming at the Y, twisting my left hand rearward and breaking it. Since I was still insured with Traveler's, the accident produced some financial benefits.

I kept swimming every day, holding my bandaged left hand up above water and paddling with my right. Another time, I felt faint after finishing my swim. I had to sit down on the floor of the shower room to avoid passing out. After recovering somewhat, I managed to get dressed and walk to the emergency room of the hospital. The examining physician discovered a dark blue streak running down my leg from the groin and diagnosed blood poisoning, the cause of which remained unsolved. He surmised I had stepped on a rusty nail, but there were no puncture wounds. I had also developed a very high temperature, about 105°F. The hospital staff asked me how much money I had and took the little I carried with me. I don't recall the name of the hospital, but I am fairly certain it was not the Good Samaritan.

I was assigned to a ward with from 20 to 30 people. The weather was very hot and we were sweltering in our beds. Outside, every few minutes, the 9th Avenue Elevated Train rattled by, shaking the building, the windows, and our beds, making an infernal racket. It was like a scene out of *A Streetcar Named Desire*. No physician made rounds, no medication for my fever was prescribed. The evening meal consisted exclusively of starches: potatoes, macaroni and cheese, bread, pudding — not exactly the ideal fare for someone burning up with a high fever and in pain from a dull ache throbbing in his groin. Lights went out very early, and we all lay there, sweating, unable to sleep or read, the awful trains rolling by with unnerving regularity, keeping anyone awake who might otherwise have passed out from sheer exhaustion. One man started screaming and apparently threatened to jump out of the window, driven to thoughts of suicide by the unbearable noise and heat. Another day passed with the same lack of medical attention and the same fever-stoking starchy food. Every lesson my mother had ever taught me about treating a temperature was being ignored. The third day I rebelled. I clamored to see a doctor, requesting to be released immediately, as I could take better care of myself on my own.

The doctor finally appeared, accusing me of being incoherent and delirious. He held up his hand and asked me how many fingers I saw. He also asked me the day of the week and other questions to make sure I was in full possession of my faculties. It was like a page from Orwell's *1984*. I insisted on signing myself out of the inferno. They did finally spring me from this hellish place, prophesying I would soon rue my willful, rash action. I went home, had the cafeteria and soda fountain send me juices when needed, and was up and around without a temperature in two days.

Every now and then I would succumb to an irresistible temptation to stuff myself with food. Fearful of gaining weight, I followed this up by eating or drinking things that would make me sick and facilitate vomiting. The problems brought on by anorexia, depending on the addict's circumstances, can prove manifold. First of all, throwing up is a noisy process, attracting attention, especially when occurring in public restrooms. With no private bathroom facilities at my disposal, I had to find other suitable locales to attend to this deplorable task. The communal restrooms in the Y were not ideal. Soon someone from the staff, alerted by other concerned members, asked me whether I was sick and using a stomach pump. Using public men's rooms in cafeterias was even more awkward, since it was imperative to do so without attracting undue attention. In cities like New York, managers are especially alert to and suspicious of strange restroom behavior. Therefore, I had to limit their use, bank on no one else being there, and if there was, wait until they left, or cut short my unnatural routine. All of this secret action lead to stressful situations and energy-sapping anxiety.

With no income and little money, I also had to gorge on relatively cheap food. Just as a wealthy drunk can afford four-star liquor while a bum may have to swill bay rum, I could not do my thing with caviar and filet mignon. In cases where I overate and had no opportunity to rid myself of the food, I would, of course, put on poundage and start the frustrating anorectic merry-go-round all over again. It is evident that such abnormal behavior requires stealth, ingenuity, and distracting nervous and physical energy expenditures. Strangely enough, such bulimic sessions acted like a drug, suffusing me with feelings of immense relief when successful, and an ensuing pleasant relaxation. They also often appeared to provide a remarkable flow of adrenaline and surge of energy, in later years, intermittently firing my creative imagination, thus helping me in my professional research and writing. But in the end, the sessions invariably resulted in feelings of guilt and the addict's continuing resolve and soon-to-be broken promise, "This will be the last time."

Over the years, still paradoxically concerned with my health and endeavoring to do as little damage as possible to my body, I devised evermore subtle tricks to rid myself of as much harmful food as possible, maintain an even body weight, and refine the bulimic process to its own perfection. Since fingers down one's throat are not an efficient device, I thought of a gadget to facilitate vomiting: a paper towel wrapped around two sheets of tightly rolled writing paper, the whole forming a long pointed tube. Furthermore, I learned to use my stomach muscles, previously highly developed through multiple sit-ups and gymnastics, to eliminate the food. I also very adroitly assumed body positions that would produce the least possible strain during this violent procedure by allowing a downward flow.

Many years later, still suffering from and periodically succumbing to this addiction, I had to find time to engage therein. This compelled me to find excuses for at times hard-to-explain absences, again exerting a nervous strain on me and depriving me of time that could have been better spent on more beneficial pursuits or more relaxing entertainment. This vice no doubt affected my relationship with my family, causing them to wonder about some of my behavior. Although I made every effort never to allow this weakness to interfere with my responsibilities, doing my utmost to adjust it to changing circumstances, always assigning top priority to professional considerations, I may, at times, have vacillated. Thinking back, some of my decisions were influenced by my subservience to this festering disorder. What may have ultimately saved me is that, while caught in this nigh uncontrollable cycle, I did, nevertheless, exercise some caution and adhered to as many safeguards as possible. One saving grace is that I never drank liquor.

In the end, the stress and guilt became unbearable and potentially too self-destructive. Realizing the number of times I had been engaging in this behavior, with no end in sight but a bad one, I made up my mind to quit cold turkey. Surprisingly, a reasonable, healthy, nutritious diet has kept me fit, regular, and without weight fluctuations — except for a tendency to be too thin. Regrets at this point are futile, the main objective being to warn others of the dangers of anorexia and bulimia and forge ahead free of the affliction.

What might cause this pernicious and addictive eating disorder? Based on my own experience, it would not be likely to occur to an individual whose attention is not unduly focused on food beyond its primary purpose as a nutrient and fuel. However, in our society the emphasis on food is far too strong and contradictory. On the one hand we preach a certain abstinence to achieve fitness and ideal body weight; on the other, fortunes are made advertising the multiple bizarre ways of preparing an ever-diversified array of exotic dishes to tempt jaded palates. Furthermore, our social mores encourage the use of food and the stuffing of individuals from the cradle to the wake. We stuff babies to pacify them, children to reward them, adults to recognize and celebrate achievement, happy occasions, the memory of one laid to rest — programming ourselves to identify the intake of food and a feeling of satiety with a soothing sense of contentment. Once an individual loses the virtue of moderation in anything, in this case food, the results are often negative.

Bulimia goes back at least as far as the Romans, who tickled their throats with feathers to disgorge what they had eaten and resume their orgies. It represents the succumbing to a vice, gluttony, the recognition of one's limitation to indulge it to the fullest, and a consequent artificial and unnatural procedure to override this safeguard bestowed upon us by a provident Mother Nature.

For me, the onset of this disorder appears complex. There was initially the feeling that I was losing control of my life and destiny, the lack of employment and work routinely engaging my interest and energy, the absence of stimulating physical exercise and well-deserved recreation. There was, besides, an idea implanted by my mother that being fat was to be avoided. My bulimia was also a crutch, replacing other habits such as tobacco, drink, sex, which some still healthy instinct in me fortunately rejected. I knew it was a prop, but I lacked the strength to discard it. I often thought of God's words to Satan in the Heavenly Prologue of Goethe's *Faust*: "A good man, despite his dark cravings, is well aware of the right path."

During this long period of unemployment, because of lack of spending money, I had few dates. I did attend YMCA dances, but had only platonic relationships. Recalling isolated incidents, I believe I could have had sexual liaisons, but I was fearful of the consequences and made no attempts in that direction. Once, one of the girls in our dance group, a veritable nymphomaniac, pulled me aside and into a dark corridor at a Y dance. Trembling with sexual excitement, she propositioned me on the spot. I dismissed the idea as too dangerous and complicated and did not follow up on it. In those days it was not as simple to register in hotels, and crossing state borders for illicit purposes was regulated by the strictest of laws.

When I was unable to find employment at the World's Fair, I decided I could no longer go on as I had. I wrote my parents of my intention to use my savings and travel to Paris to consult with them. My mother immediately replied that under no circumstances was I to stop looking for work. Ignoring her command, I booked passage on the return maiden voyage of the *New Mauritania*. My father met me at the Saint Lazare Station. When we arrived home, my mother opened the door and without so much as a greeting turned away, saying: "So you insisted on coming back in spite of my wish." We discussed several possibilities, including my taking a culinary course in France to qualify as a chef. In the end, we decided I should return to school, acquire a second B.A. degree, and try for a high school teaching position. I returned almost immediately to New York and enrolled at New York University.

I moved from the West Side YMCA to the much less attractive 23rd Street YMCA to spend less money on rent and be closer to school. A few weeks later, World War II threatening Europe, the American Consulate in Paris advised all Americans there to go home. My parents took a taxi to Bordeaux, from which they came to the USA on an overloaded ship. One of their fellow passengers was Arturo Toscanini. To save my parents money, I left the Y and we all moved into new apartments in Elmhurst, Queens.

The university gave me credit for two years, actually the junior and senior years, demanding I take the normally required freshman and sophomore courses. I was also granted a full major in French. By July 1941, I had completed all work and managed to use my elective courses to earn a second major in Spanish, skipping the elementary and intermediate Spanish courses, making up the deficiency on my own, and taking all upper-division courses. I received my second B.A. that month. My mother refused to attend graduation ceremonies because it was my second B.A. I enrolled in the summer session at Columbia University, but simultaneously received notice in the mail that I was being offered a teaching assistantship in Spanish at the University of California at Los Angeles. Finally I was truly back on track, doing what I seemed to do best: going to school.

Max and his father and mother, Max, Sr., and Louise Oppenheimer, *circa* 1920, in New York, with their new Chevrolet.

Far right, top: Aunt Margaret. Back row, left to right: Anna Koehler, wife of photographer and friend of the family, and Uncle Charlie. Front row, left to right: Louise, Max, Sr., and Max, Jr. — about four years old — just before they went to Europe.

Otto Koehler

Max Oppenheimer on the beach at Ostende, Belgium, *circa* 1928.

Max and his parents, May 28, 1929, in Hamburg. The sailor suit was typical attire for young men at the time.

Louise Oppenheimer and Max at Versailles, 1930.

Max Oppenheimer in Paris, June 14, 1931, at 187 Rue de Cour-celles.

At the *Lycée Carnot*, Paris, 1931-1932, with Professor Marcel Abraham (front row center). Max is in the second row, second from left; Lucien Bailly is in the top row, fourth from left.

Max, Sr.,   and Louise Oppenheimer in France, 1932.

Max and his father in France, 1932.

Max holding his cousin Edmund, River Edge, New Jersey, 1936.

Aunt Margaret and Max, River Edge, New Jersey, 1936.

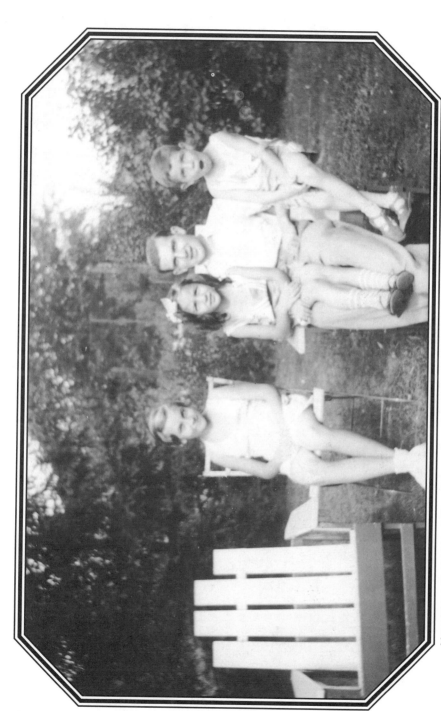

Max sitting with Beatrice (left) and the twins, Yvette and Edmund, *circa* 1938.

Part
Two

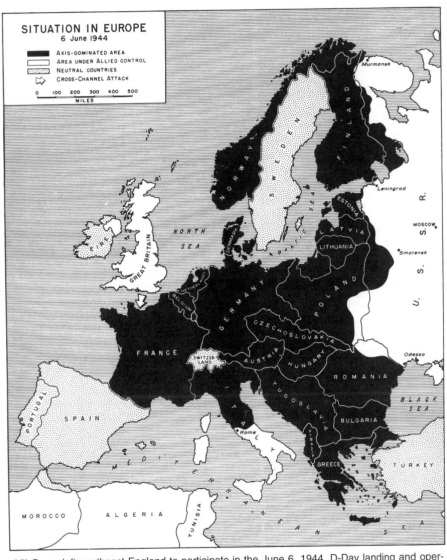

VII Corps left southeast England to participate in the June 6, 1944, D-Day landing and operated in France, Belgium, and Germany through May 8, 1945, when it met with USSR forces.
From *United States Army in World War II: The European Theater of Operations
— Cross Channel Attack*, by Gordon A. Harrison (Washington, D.C.: Office
of the Chief of Military History, U.S. Army, 1951)

All hope abandon, ye who enter here.
— Dante Alighieri, 1265–1321

Chapter 10

World War II — SNAFU

O N SUNDAY, DECEMBER 7, 1941, I was a graduate teaching assistant working on a Master of Arts degree in Spanish at UCLA. I had studied all day and had walked to Westwood Village to have my supper. Of course, I immediately heard the momentous news: the Japanese had attacked Pearl Harbor. My emotional reaction, as befits a patriotic young man of 24 years, was instantaneous: *Enlist!* I decided to first acquire my M.A. degree, which I expected to receive in the fall of 1942.

At that time I had no knowledge of any of the Services and their miles of red tape. I had duly registered for the draft lottery while still a student at New York University.

True to form, since I never win door prizes, my draft number was among the last drawn, somewhere in the 8,000 range. Anyone shirking military service might have considered this a winner! Actually, I did not give the matter much thought, figuring everything would work out as it was supposed to.

However, we were at war! Figuring I might qualify for a commission in Naval Intelligence, I went to the Marine Barracks Recruiting Station to inquire about the possibility of enlisting in the Navy for a direct commission. I emphasized my academic credentials, my fluency in three foreign languages, and caught the immediate attention of the person to whom I spoke. German was of special interest to the interviewer. He took me to a gruff elderly Marine Colonel, who expressed great interest in me, and ordered an immediate physical examination, consisting mainly of an eye test. As expected, I did not score 20/20 on both eyes. In those days, the Navy's eyesight requirements were fairly rigid. The Colonel, clearly disappointed, barked at me, "Man, do you realize you're almost blind?" Then he dismissed me ill-humoredly. Since I had been getting along so far without glasses and expected to pass my driver's license without them for many years to come, I did not immediately go shopping for a white cane. Still, I was disappointed.

Like many others ignorant of the Services' physical requirements, I began to worry I might be classified 4-F, unfit to serve, and prove a dishonor to my family. How little I knew about the Army! Once, during the second semester, I sought advice from the Colonel in charge of ROTC at UCLA. As he listened to me reciting my educational credentials and foreign-language background, this high-ranking beribboned and credible officer leaned back in his chair exclaiming most convincingly, "You don't have a thing to worry about! You'll be immediately sent to Officer Candidate School." More untrue words were never spoken! I remembered them later and understood why this Colonel had been assigned to a cushy desk job in sunny California. With his blind faith in the infallibility of the Army and its procedures, he might have proven disastrous to troops entrusted to his unbridled optimism in combat.

After meeting with him, I let military matters rest and concentrated on graduate work. I passed the M.A. comprehensive exam, and the degree was practically in my pocket, merely subject to completing one more two-semester hour course in the summer. Following the course, I again awoke to reality beyond academia's ivy walls. No longer drawing the skimpy stipend of a teaching assistant, I had to earn money and think of the future.

During my last year in New York, I had dated a Jewish student of whom my parents, especially my mother, did not approve — though even I had grown weary of her continual demands on me and was concerned about the foreseeable difficulties this relationship augured for the future. I took advantage of my departure for Los Angeles to break it off. Indoctrinated by my mother about the seriousness of marriage, entirely inexperienced with women, and financially unable to even think about a serious binding relationship, I still felt the need for a woman's support, company, and love. During the entire school year, I had taken time off my studies for only one miserable double date. A fellow teaching assistant and I had taken two young ladies, both Spanish graduate students, out to dinner and dancing. No doubt we were at fault. We probably kindled no flames in the hearts of two females steeped in the romantic flights of Spanish poetry. In any event, we declared the evening a disaster and promised ourselves not to repeat it.

My father had once surprised me in one of his letters by specifically expressing the hope I might some day meet a clergyman's daughter and when the time was right, marry her. Inducted into Pi Delta Phi, the National French Honor Society, I met the treasurer, Christine, and certainly not because of her financial control over the society's meager funds, but rather because of her charm and qualities, fell in love with her. As though fate (and my father) had planned it, she was the daughter of a deceased Episcopal clergyman.

Professor Zeitlin, Chairman of the Spanish Department, had offered me a much better-paying teaching job than my previous one and suggested I continue toward my Ph.D., but I needed a long rest from school. Besides, I wished to contribute, whatever it might be, to the war effort. I had both hopes and illusions about the worthwhile role I might play in Military Intelligence in view of my knowledge of Europe and foreign languages. In the meantime, I had inquired about enlisting in the Army. To my surprise,

I was told that I was untouchable as I was under the jurisdiction of my
New York draft board. With my high draft number, it looked as though I
was safe, unless the war was to be a long one. No draft dodger in history
could have found a safer haven!

I wrote my father about it. He repeatedly approached the New York
draft authorities until they released me to a Los Angeles draft board. Now
I could waive my draft status and enlist. Christine was fully aware of my
actions. She was planning to attend another year at UCLA to earn her high
school teaching credentials. She was not overly happy at home, as her
mother controlled her life. On impulse, encouraged by and taking advantage of the uncertainty that the war held over our fate, I suggested we
become secretly engaged. Her mother unfortunately heard about it from a
friend who read it in the newspaper's public notices. The resulting bitter
remonstrations from her mother and Christine's desire to leave home and
live at Hershey Hall, a UCLA women's dormitory, gave me the courage to
intervene and urge her to elope. Perhaps it was rash on my part, but the
fearful thought uppermost in my mind was losing Christine. At that very
moment I thought she was the only one for me.

A good friend, Professor Templin, in a selfless gesture for those days of
gasoline and tire shortages, offered his car so that we could drive to Nevada and get married. However, Christine preferred to have a private church
ceremony conducted by the Episcopal chaplain of UCLA, in his home.
We were secretly married on October 14, 1942. We spent the night in a
motel where the clerk asked me if this was "quickie." (The breakdown of American Puritan morality was already looming.) It was not a
"quickie"; over 50 years later we are still married! Strengthened by the
knowledge of our marriage, which was unknown to all but the Templins
and one witness, I helped my wife out of her mother's house to Hershey
Hall. We had little time together. I spent the night of the 23rd alone in a
cheap hotel near the Los Angeles railroad station. At 6:00 a.m., on October 24, 1942, I reported to the Army Recruiting Station in downtown Los
Angeles. The fun was about to begin.

Induction into the Army was a dehumanizing process. Experience has
taught the Services that the transition for new recruits from civilian life to
the military must be absolute. As in all military operations, the element of

surprise is paramount. We handed in our personal effects, our last physical link to civilian life, to be shipped back to relatives or friends. Our fears of failing the physical proved quite unfounded. With the Army in dire need of bodies, a vertical corpse pushed along the recruit line would have had a fair chance of passing. There was a psychological exam, but I should guess only a flagrant deviate would have flunked that. By early evening we had taken the oath and been supplied with a Service record and Form 20, detailing our biographical data and civilian qualifications. As enlisted wards of the Army we had been issued our new olive-drab uniforms and personal effects free of charge. We now were OD from the skin outward. This standardization, together with the new title of Private indiscriminately granted to all, should at least have inspired in us a feeling of *esprit de corps.* What keeps up morale under such circumstances is that everyone is in the same, shall we say, to reflect the general mental state of most, leaky ship.

We were sent to Fort MacArthur, outside of Los Angeles, in itself an electrifying morale-raising name, and arrived rather late at night. We handed the envelope containing our records irretrievably to a Sergeant (henceforth our personal data would remain confidential even to us), who scanned them casually, as though he were thinking, "What are they unloading on us today?" Glancing at my record, he raised his head with these ominous words, "You got more degrees than a barometer, ain't you?"

The Army travels on its stomach, preferably a full one. We were invited to a late supper, our first encounter with an Army mess hall. Then came the important lesson of how to make up a bunk bed with blankets so tight that a dime, dropped on it, will rebound at attention and the ensemble pass a First Sergeant's inspection, removing the scowl from his face. The next event was to be a surprise. Deemed refreshed after 17 hours of energizing initiation into a new lifestyle, we were informed that we would now take the two-hour Army General Classification test, an IQ test determining our future in the Army and our chances of becoming an officer. Despite the late hour, I achieved a safe score somewhere in the high 120s or low 130s, sufficient for OCS. It had been a very long day.

In the morning, rather early, we were informed that the high scorers would go to the Army Air Corps. As we discovered subsequently, this preliminary triage was not perfect. A few illiterates managed to slip through the cracks. In any event, I was now the proud wearer of insignia with wings and could thrust out my chest to the "Off We Go Into the Wild Blue Yonder" song. All of a sudden, I had this passing, but sinking, feeling that this was the point of no return. I could see Uncle Sam pointing his finger at me: "You're in the Army now!"

We had no idea of our ultimate destination. We ended up in Camp Kearns, Utah, a new Air Corps Replacement and Training Center, otherwise known as a "repple depple." It was located approximately 20 miles from Salt Lake City in the desolate salt flats and was to be my home for the next four months.

We soon found out that Camp Kearns was very new, indeed, and very much at the end of the line, like some distant Siberian outpost. Although winter was fast approaching, no cold weather clothing was as yet available. It was an almost Spartan camp with unattractive Quonset barracks and few resources. Not even clothing hangers were available. A Texan and fellow recruit, clever with his hands, immediately started a small cottage industry, adroitly fashioning hangers with nothing but a pocketknife, wire, and scraps of wood. He made a beauty of one for me and refused to charge for it, possibly out of pity for my present financial straits. The Air Corps Finance Department, taken into the secret of my marriage, was sending my wife $38 a month and paying me $22. I schlepped the hanger with me through the entire war.

Most of us, we were told in several briefings, would be out of there in no time, assigned to various schools — such as tail gunner, airplane mechanic, engineering and operations, clerical, possibly even OCS and pilot, navigator, bombardier, or Air Corps administration — depending on our preference and qualifications. Our Basic Training spread over 21 days, but some were not there long enough to complete it. It took me three months to complete basic, for it was continually interspersed with the much less popular, even distasteful, KP and guard duty. Actually, Camp Kearns turned out to be a mild form of hell.

Basic Training was relatively unexacting, KP long and tiring but indoors, guard duty outdoors and a true challenge to one's fortitude. We learned to march in field and parade formation, run an obstacle course, perform calisthenics, and close-order drill with and without rifles. Air Corps Basic Training turned out to be much less rigorous than I had expected, certainly less demanding than the daily duty details. As a matter of fact, having entered the Service in perfect physical shape after a strenuous summer in the UCLA botanical garden where I had worked for extra cash, within a few weeks I had put on weight and was out of shape. When we had KP detail, we stumbled off in the dark, at 0430 hours and slaved under the watchful eyes of the regular mess personnel until 2000 or 2100 hours. Once on KP, the Lieutenant in charge of the mess hall, perhaps detecting in my bearing a vestige of academic training, or more likely, equating my awkwardness with pots, pans, and mop with a clerical background, picked me out of the herd and took me to his office.

His problem was that he had too much money, which he was compelled to spend. Military budgets, or rather the corresponding appropriations, must, by definition, be spent by the end of the period they cover, lest the government suspect your ability to draw them up correctly and frugally. Because of the nationwide war effort, mess and food supplies were scarce. *Did I have any suggestions?*

I was not much help, having no experience with good sources for food supplies in the Utah backwoods. However, from our conversation I finally learned why, in addition to all the unattractive food we were served, there always was an overabundance of frozen fruit. The Lieutenant, in a desperate attempt to spend the money allotted to him, had pounced on the idea of buying the most expensive items he could find. Frozen peaches, pears, and fruit cocktail were pricey, though not enough to exhaust his budget. I tried to hint that such delicacies might be more appreciated if defrosted before being served. So far we had been consistently treated to unmanageable and not very delectable blocks of ice with fruit preserved inside, like fossils of insects captured in amber. Then again, Army mess halls do not take advance reservations and food is not prepared to individual tastes. I left the Lieutenant to his worries, for which OCS had not prepared him, and, grateful for the short break from less pleasant duties, returned to my kitchen chores.

Guard duty was physically and mentally demanding. We always served 24 hours at a time, 4 hours on and 4 hours off. We were warned that being caught asleep on guard duty meant an immediate court-martial and hard labor. The nights on the salt flats were quite cold. We were taken from the guard room in an open truck all over Camp Kearns to the various guard posts, where we stood, with a wooden rifle, for four hours until relieved. The eagerly awaited truck took us back to the guard room, where we tried to catch a few winks. While on duty we stood in the open, freezing in the icy wind. Winter underwear was still unavailable, although overcoats had finally been issued. A few times I lucked out and was assigned a station with a small wooden guard booth, which protected me from the wind. On those occasions, although grateful for the protection against the cold, I feared I would fall asleep. At least once during the night, the OD (Officer of the Day) came by our station to make sure we were at our post, awake, and sufficiently alert to challenge him and ask for the password. I often pondered the sad truth that there was nothing worth guarding in Camp Kearns, Utah.

The First Sergeant of our squadron was a mean-spirited son of a bitch. I gave him lots of space. Some of my buddies were not as fortunate. I don't remember the details, but one soldier in our group, a meek older man, returned one day from Squadron Headquarters, having incurred the First Sergeant's wrath. He was in tears. Apparently the NCO (noncommissioned officer) had coerced him to go down on his knees and apologize. My anger and indignation aroused, I took it upon myself to ask for an interview with the CO (Commanding Officer), a "shavetail" or "90-day wonder" as we called the recent graduates from OCS. I pointed out that I was not pleading for myself, but merely complaining about the degrading treatment of a fellow soldier. Was he, the Commanding Officer, condoning this abuse of authority? The officer chickened out, pretexting his impotence and delicate position *vis-à-vis* a seasoned old Army First Sergeant, for whom he admitted being no match.

Our Basic Training days became increasingly rare, while the other details occurred more and more often. Cleaning our barracks and the latrine for inspection were, of course, a mere housekeeping duty in addition to the KP detail, which alternated in perfect harmony with the more exacting guard duty. By-and-by, most of my companions shipped out to various schools and few men remained from our original Fort MacArthur contingent. I was prepared for this, since in one of the early briefings with personnel I was told that my special qualifications and potential usefulness in Intelligence work required a relatively long background search. In the meantime, I was continuing to learn lessons in humility. Those of us who are articulate and have the advantage of a good general education may benefit from temporarily setting such qualifications aside and collaborating with — or even serving under — less advantaged individuals, many of whom earned their stripes serving long periods on the job. It was my turn to eat dirt.

There was no recreation on the post, no movie theater. On a free evening, the only refuge was the PX (Post Exchange), where the shelves, in perfect harmony with the entire camp, were bare except for a few essentials. Still it was warm inside and there was a free telephone. I often tried calling my wife, but seldom succeeded to make a connection. Her dormitory phone was public. Any resident answering it would have to find my wife, who might not be there. I bought her some cheap jewelry featuring Air Corps wings and spent much time leafing through the *Commissioned Officer's Handbook*, dreaming of a better life, with pink trousers, a green blouse, and wings on my lapels. I looked up other branch insignia, especially fascinated with the sphinx of the Military Intelligence Reserve (which was never worn on active duty).

The deadly routine of KP and guard duty continued without respite. We were told there would be no six-hour passes until Basic Training was completed; most men in our group left for school without ever finishing it. Looking over those who remained, I realized something had gone radically wrong with my records or processing.

We finally finished Basic Training and were promised afternoon passes to Salt Lake City. The next morning we were awakened at 0400 hours and informed we were going on KP duty. We objected. "Tough shit!" KP took precedence over passes. As consolation, I was frequently granted the honor of marching at the head of the KP detail, in full command, barking "Hot, two, three, four," and "March." I would have much preferred to command "to the rear march" and gone back to sleep.

One morning I arrived with my KP detail and was told we had been sent to the wrong mess hall. It was located in an area quarantined because of spinal meningitis. Taking advantage of the resulting brouhaha, I took off for my barracks, leaving our hapless detail without my precious self to the chilling prospect of at least four weeks of quarantine. Fortunately, on my return, no one thought of asking me how I had managed to escape. Evidently, I was beginning to catch on! We spent a delightful Christmas and New Year's Eve and Day at Kearns, being served the obligatory turkey with trimmings and the optional blocks of ice with fruit inside.

By now, the few of us left of the MacArthur contingent had been moved in with newer arrivals. Out of my original group I was the only one with an education still expected to be sent to school. The others were, for the most part, Hispanics either illiterate or very deficient in English, resigned to stay at Kearns until shipped to the Pacific. After Kearns, they might welcome the change.

As I needed a great deal of dental work, every time I sought a break from the constant duty details, now no longer relieved by Basic, I went on sick call and got fillings at the dental clinic. The number of human teeth is at most 32, and not all of mine were in need of repair. Thus my situation became critical and my chances for relief by these extreme means grew more limited with each tooth filled.

After four months at Kearns, finding myself almost competing in length of stay and seniority with the permanent cadre, I requested to see someone in Personnel. Even they had to admit my departure was long overdue. After some deliberations, I was assured I would, with the shortest possible delay, be sent to the Air Corps Engineering and Operations Clerical Course. Now I really grew excited. A seasoned Air Corps veteran by this time, I knew there were only two of these schools — one at Lowry Field in Colorado, one in Los Angeles.

I left Kearns without regret with the next shipment. I couldn't believe it! I was being sent to Los Angeles and would be able to see my wife.

We were assigned to the Anderson School, to which the Air Corps had subcontracted the six-week course. The school had a civilian director and teaching staff, as well as a Commanding Officer, Captain Davis H. Ward, who turned out to be a hard-nosed disciplinarian. We lived in rooming houses, ate in a civilian cafeteria, now requisitioned by the Air Corps, and attended classes from late afternoon to early morning (we were on the second or late shift) in an office building. Everything was located near the Biltmore Hotel and Union Square in the heart of downtown Los Angeles. After Camp Kearns, it seemed like paradise.

Probably because of my education and my four months of training, Captain Ward appointed me Acting Corporal with two stripes, but only for the duration of the course. After February 20, 1943, upon graduating, I would remove the Corporal's stripes from my uniforms and revert to the lowly grade of Private, consoling myself with the sublime words of the Roman Emperor Augustus, "Having reached the pinnacle, one aspires to descend."

The course consisted of 384 hours of combat orders, engineering and operations, military correspondence, military organization and publications, and typewriting. Captain Ward and the Assistant Supervisor, Captain Glenn H. Adkins, warned us that despite our civilian lodgings,

eating facilities, and classrooms, we were in the Air Corps and had better not forget it. We marched in formation through the streets of downtown Los Angeles to and from school, cafeteria, and hotel. We were
also told that those graduating at the top of the class might be appointed
to the school staff and remain in Los Angeles. It certainly was a worthy
goal.

As Acting Corporal, I was accountable for all men in our group and
responsible for marching them everywhere on time: to school, to chow, to
bed. I also had to conduct the bed check every night. The OD came to our
hotel. I had previously checked that all men were in their respective rooms
and reported them present to the officer. Then I returned to my own room,
which I shared with a lanky private, a really nice guy to have as a roommate. We attended classes six days a week and had Sundays off. There
were to be absolutely no overnight passes under any pretext.

My main concerns were to do well in school, thereby earning an assignment in Los Angeles, and to convince my wife to muster the courage
and tell her mother about our marriage. She would not hear of it, afraid
to admit to her mother we had eloped and in a sense lied to her. I then
asked her to at least tell her we were going to get married soon. We would
merely pretend we had done so in a civil ceremony on our own. However, this backfired. Christine's mother finally and reluctantly agreed to
a wedding, but insisted it be a formal one, in the Hollywood Episcopal church, where her late husband had been pastor. But how could we
have a wedding if we were already married? I grew frantic. Time was flying by and I really wanted our marital situation clarified for everyone concerned.

On a Sunday, after the service, we told the pastor of the Hollywood
Church about our elopement. I took the entire matter lightly, since I had
married Christine in good faith. Would he be willing to perform a fake ceremony? No harm would be done and Christine's mother would never
know about any of it. The Father did not agree. His business was to look
for and undo the work of Satan. Inflexible to the end, he could never lie to
Christine's mother, her sister, all the guests, and even the parish. With
priests like him, Martin Luther would not have been in business.

Finally, I called Father Gilbert Parker Prince, who had performed the
original ceremony at his home in Westwood. He immediately thought of
the perfect solution, where no one would lie and no one be the wiser. I
would insist that Father Prince, as a personal friend of mine, conduct the

ceremony together with the objecting pastor from the Hollywood Church. Christine's mother could not complain: two priests are better than one and the wedding that much more binding. Then came the really clever find! Instead of performing a wedding ceremony, it would be a renewal of the vows, often celebrated by couples after 25 years of blissful marriage. Ours had only lasted five months so far, but with our mounting problems, why not play it safe and simultaneously solve the impasse?

Christine's mother agreed, and the date was set for Sunday, January 31, 1943. She never found out about the first marriage (Christine's sister never did either, until 40 years later when my daughter let it slip out.) However, to satisfy Christine's family, I agreed to be confirmed an Episcopalian before the wedding. Fortunately, Suffragan Bishop Gooden was a friend of the family and, when times and circumstances warranted, not entirely adverse to granting dispensations in the old Jesuit tradition. He excused me from all catechism and met with me for two short morning sessions, bowing to my strict military schedule. I was painlessly confirmed, and the bishop could chalk one more saved soul to his credit.

I reserved a room in a hotel one-half block from my own quarters. Then I asked to speak to Captain Ward, certain to be granted an overnight pass on this special occasion. Listed as married on my records, I had to confess my complicated marital situation to the Captain. *Would it be all right, just for my wedding night, to obtain an overnight pass and sleep with my wife?* Captain Ward, impervious to any romantic notions, could see no reason why it would. I would not have been surprised if, a few centuries earlier, he had insisted on his seigniorial first night right on my wedding night, confined me to barracks, and personally attended in my stead to what was expected from the husband. This created a situation where I recklessly exposed myself to certain court-martial if caught.

Every night at 0100 hours, after the last class, I led our group back to our sleeping quarters. My roommate, who was my best man at the wedding and knew the situation, and I conducted the bed check, and I reported to the OD in the hotel lobby that all were in their rooms. I had given my roommate the telephone and room numbers of the hotel where my wife was staying. No sooner had the OD left to check on other groups, than I ran along the second floor corridor to the rear of our hotel and climbed down the fire escape, joining my wife less than a short block away. My roommate had instructions to phone me if my presence was needed. Until the end of the course, however, this happened only once, when everyone had to leave unexpectedly early, before breakfast, for some official formation. Alerted by him, I managed in a wild panic to join my group with some delay, but otherwise unnoticed. However, these illicit absences took their toll on my nerves, which even staying with my wife could not entirely soothe. I was almost relieved when school ended, and I did not have to complete my conjugal duties at such risk.

Despite my poor typing skills, I graduated among the top students of the class with an average grade of 95.9 and a rating of superior. Nevertheless, the Commanding Officer's earlier promise of top graduates being rewarded with assignments in Los Angeles was hot air. The entire class was shipped out on one order, alphabetically, and to various air bases throughout the U.S. We traveled on the same military train, soldiers being dropped off en route according to their destination. Three of us ended up at the New Bedford Air Base in Massachusetts. The CO was a 90-day wonder. A sub-base of Westover Field, Bedford was too new to have any planes; we could not be used to process any of the paperwork related to flights. At the very beginning of my assignment I had asked to apply for OCS, choosing a recently opened Censorship School under the Office of the Adjutant General (AG). I had picked this school for three reasons: it still accepted applications, it appeared to fit my qualifications, and I liked the AG's Branch insignia with its blue, white, and red shield. I was given time off and transportation to and from Westover Field to fill out the application.

Our routine at the base was relatively easy and the treatment humane. We had little KP duty, and we performed mostly clerical work. In addition to the CO, there was a chemical warfare officer on the base, who took his job very seriously. Partly because chemical warfare was his passion, partly to justify his existence, the diminutive, chubby Southerner placed the highest priority on chemical warfare training. He had us wear gas masks routinely on certain days, ambushing us on our way to and from work with tear gas, and measuring the speed with which we donned the masks. A few of us might be walking innocently along, when he gleefully jumped out of his hiding place, and with his assistant, bombarded us with tear gas. I found it hard to begrudge him his childlike delight at the effect this produced on us. He also converted a Quonset hut into a gas chamber and had us cavort inside of it while being subjected to an assortment of noxious fumes.

After being assigned to a regular unit, I was eligible for my quota of weekend passes. Missing my wife very much, I merely used them to get away from the base, enjoy a taste of civilian life, and feel sorry for myself about being a lowly Private and not using my qualifications to better advantage. Unjustified as my frustrations and impatience may have been so early in my military career, they still lay darkly on my mind. I rented a hotel room, enjoyed some privacy, visited the USO club for a snack, roamed the streets of New Bedford, read, wrote letters, and thought. I was obsessed with the desire of becoming an officer and, if possible, serving in Military Intelligence. Fueling my bad mood was also the memory of my disastrous 1938 employment-search experiences, as well as being power- less amidst the inextricable labyrinthine red tape of Service personnel processing. Still, I should have had enough self-control to perceive the futility of fretting and thought of a way to circumvent the obstacles in my way.

One weekend I met my parents, whom I had not seen in over 18 months, and we spent a day together in Providence, Rhode Island. Regret- tably, my depressed mood prompted me, while on pass and enjoying pri- vacy, to succumb once again to bulimic sessions. Evidently overeating and vomiting acted like a drug, both causing guilt and overriding momentary suffering from the impasse of my military progress.

Back at New Bedford, we witnessed some excitement when a pilot from Westover Field landed a P-38 fighter plane on the runway of our base — the first, I believe, to use our facilities. The young officer proudly strut- ted about as we gathered around gawking. He conferred with the CO, and after a while prepared to leave. Excited, again, we all stood watching the takeoff. The plane rolled down the runway, gathered speed, lifted off, climbed straight up, banked sharply, lost its lift, and plummeted straight to the ground, killing the pilot in a flaming crash. Shocked back into the grim reality of the uncertainty of war and much subdued, we returned to our duties.

After a few weeks at the base, the CO decided I might be better em- ployed helping the personnel Corporal keep the enlisted soldiers' records. My natural impulse, of course, was to look at my own Service record. I noticed immediately that stapled to the inside front page of the document, right in back of my vaccination record, was a tightly folded paper. It was a red-bordered urgent letter from the Department of the Army addressed to whoever it concerned. It instructed my first unit of permanent assignment to inform the Department of the Army of my station address so that orders could be cut for my transfer to Military Intelligence.

Along the way, most probably in the Personnel Branch at Camp Kearns, a bright clerk had secreted this valuable piece of paper where it could not be readily seen. Overwhelmed with joy, certain that my quest for the right assignment was at an end, I showed the letter to the CO. Had I known what was to follow, I might have been tempted to destroy the letter and await my pending promotion to Corporal or possible admission to the Censorship Branch of OCS. Everyone, however, was convinced that I would fare much better in both duty and rank in the cloak-and-dagger assignment awaiting me. *L'ultima che si perde è la speranza* — hope springs eternal to the very end.

But the Lord came down to see the city and the tower that the men were building. The Lord said, "If as one people speaking the same language they have begun to do this, then nothing they plan to do will be impossible for them. Come, let us go down and confuse their language so they will not understand each other." So the Lord scattered them from there over all the earth and they stopped building the city.
— Genesis 11:5-7

Chapter 11

Camp Ritchie — The Military Intelligence Training Center

HE CONCEPT OF, as well as the need for, Military Intelligence has most probably existed since man fought man. It has been jokingly referred to as the world's second oldest profession. (On occasion the second oldest is not unrelated to the first.) When one army engages in battle with another, it is best to know as much as possible about the enemy: his strength, his weapons, his morale, and what he knows of your capabilities. However, while the collection of information on the enemy has always been practiced in the American military, Intelligence did not become a full-fledged branch of the Army until 1956. U.S. troops have, since the earliest days, utilized scouts and reconnaissance units to gather data on hostile forces. Nevertheless, a systematized Military Intelligence organization, comprising special units with specific tasks and missions, Tables of Organization and Equipment, and personnel trained by specialized schools with a coordinated plan for assigning them to the various combat units, did not exist before World War II. Most people inside and outside the Army had a very vague notion, mostly fueled by spy novels, movies, and their own imagination, of the reality (or even the actual existence) of Military Intelligence. Early in the war, the OSS (Office of Strategic Services) was created under General "Wild" Bill Donovan, but its *modus operandi* on spying and research activities was highly classified.

With our ignorance of the subject, it is quite understandable that both my colleagues and I at the air base had erroneously inflated ideas about my future career as a spy. Everyone was convinced I could look forward to quick promotions and fascinating secret assignments. Naive, unrealistic, impatient as ever, I too thought that the Army had recognized in me a uniquely suited candidate for this kind of work and would treat and reward me accordingly. A more modest self-appraisal of my qualifications might have proven a wiser and mentally more healthful attitude. My application for OCS and my envisaged promotion to Corporal were quickly forgotten. *Why bother? I'll be an officer before you know it!* What a difference it would have made in my life had the promotion been implemented by the CO before my departure. Instead, secret orders were immediately cut to send me to the Military Intelligence Training Center (MITC) at Camp Ritchie, Maryland — equidistant from Washington and Baltimore in the Blue Ridge Mountains.

In April 1943, full of hope, stealthily as though on a clandestine mission, I traveled by train to Blue Ridge Summit. I was enjoying the landscape as the train slowly climbed to our destination. I could not help daydreaming, wondering what was ahead of me: additional training, special projects, perhaps a direct commission? The first bombshell disrupting my fantasies came when the train conductor, glancing at my uniform and military ticket, asked casually, "What foreign language do you speak?" My "cover" had been blown! Later I learned that, far from being the classified installation I expected, Camp Ritchie was publicly listed in the Hagerstown phone book!

Full of apprehension, I got off the train at Blue Ridge Summit, a mere whistle-stop. With my barracks bag, containing all my equipment and possessions, on my back, I passed the gate which, in large letters, openly advertised the camp as the Military Intelligence Training Center (MITC). No cloak-and-dagger operation there! The MP at the gate directed me to camp headquarters. Ritchie did not look like a tightly run military installation. Commissioned officers and NCOs were in evidence everywhere, with no apparent purpose. No one seemed to be in mortal fear of failing to render the mandatory snappy salute initiated by enlisted personnel and acknowledged by officers. I entered Camp Headquarters and was received — well — like a Private. They knew not, nor cared, that I was coming. No cake was baking in the oven.

An NCO looked at my records and noting I was listed as fluent in German, laconically informed me that I would be in the next Intelligence course and assigned as a Private to an IPW (Interrogation of Prisoners of War) team. Most probably, I thought, I would be sent to North Africa. I was assigned to a barracks and ordered to get settled. My attempts to ask a few questions were met curtly and unsympathetically. *No, there was absolutely no chance of applying for OCS from Ritchie!* I was definitely not qualified for special treatment. One thought flashed through my mind: *Why had they thought it unnecessary to promote me to corporal at the New Bedford air base?*

One of the first privates I met in the barracks was surprisingly eager to further deflate my sinking morale. He gloated over the fact that he was expecting a medical discharge. His was a spectacularly unique case: allergic to olive drab wool. As soon as he donned his issued shirts or jackets, his skin broke out all over his body. "See!" he said, rolling up one of his sleeves, as though he wished to ascertain that the free ticket home had not mysteriously and disastrously vanished. There was no cause for alarm. The rash was very much in evidence. He was quite solicitous of his affliction, as he had no particular love for either Ritchie or the Service in general.

I learned from him and others that Ritchie was a relatively new camp, having been activated in June 1942 to provide specialized Military Intelligence training for interrogators, military foreign language interpreters, translators, and aerial photo interpreters. Later, I learned that in 1944 all Counterintelligence personnel were trained at Ritchie. Formerly the

Max Oppenheimer in Los Angeles, January 31, 1943, when he was an Acting Corporal in charge of a platoon at the Air Corps Engineering and Operations School.

Max and his wife, Christine, in 1943.

Maryland Army National Guard Summer Training Camp, it was converted into a year-round installation capable of housing 3,000 men. Construction of 165 buildings, including barracks, classrooms, theater, chapel,
and a new headquarters was completed at a cost of $5 million.

Surprisingly, military historians seem to have paid scant attention to
this important and innovative landmark in Military Intelligence training
and development. A few local newspaper articles have briefly mentioned
the composite school unit that was formed in Camp Ritchie as a training
cadre for the MITC.

Before closing in late 1945, Camp Ritchie graduated 10,000 soldiers
from its two-month course. However, bare facts do not offer the slightest
insight into the ambiance of the camp, the morale of the students, nor do
they emphasize its lasting influence on and contribution to the future organization of Military Intelligence teams, the crucial role these teams played
in World War II, and their ultimate integration into U.S. Army tactical
units. Without Camp Ritchie, Americans would not have today's Military
Intelligence Service Organization. Only those of us who participated in
the Ritchie experience and witnessed its successful fruition can judge it
fairly, and by doing so, discard all negative memories, retaining only the
proud feeling of having been a part of it.

Whoever conceived the idea of the Camp Ritchie MITC and planned its
mission demonstrated genius and an unerring flair for the creation of a
professional and efficient combat Intelligence Service. However, the leadership of Camp Ritchie, despite its good intentions and brilliant ideas, at
times committed acts that defied all logic and rules of good military organization. We must remember, in this respect, however, that it was all new
and there was little time to meet the Intelligence organization and personnel requirements for the military operations then already in progress in
Africa and expected to materialize in the very near future.

The Commanding Officer at Ritchie was Colonel Charles Y. Banfill,
Air Corps — invisible to us. In charge of training was Colonel Shipley
Thomas, a former Cavalry officer, who had served in World War I and had
authored a small book, *S-2 in Action*, about reconnaissance platoons at the
regimental level. Very much visible, he was now basking in his glory,
dressed in a riding outfit, swagger stick under his arm, escorting guests

around camp, leaving the daily training routine to enlisted personnel. Allegedly Banfill, through his brother-in-law General Strong in the Department of the Army, had been given *carte blanche* to transfer any personnel possessing foreign language skills throughout the Army and Air Corps to Ritchie.

As a result of this priority, Camp Ritchie was teeming with personnel of various ranks and grades more or less fluent in some foreign language ranging from French, German, Italian, Greek, and Armenian, to Hungarian, Russian, and others. Ritchie was merely hoarding language talent, creating a large pool of personnel with varied backgrounds and qualifications but had no specific employment for their abilities. Of course, according to a long-established Army tradition, the officers and NCOs were unavailable for details, and in the biased view of the Privates, were leading the "life of Riley."

Before long, I gathered the distinct impression that MITC should have stood for Military Institution for Total Confusion. In the beginning, Ritchie did not appear able to keep track of everybody in camp. I spent the first week or two, together with another new recruit, staying out of sight. Many empty tents had been set up for training purposes along the main road through camp, and my buddy and I made ourselves scarce after breakfast, huddling in one of the tents, until a curious or psychically gifted officer lifted the flap and found us one unfortunate rainy morning. Scared out of my wits, I jumped up to attention, but he merely made us report to the First Sergeant, and my days as a truant at Ritchie were over. I found myself permanently employed, usually on KP for a week at a time, no doubt to preserve the Sergeant from the strenuous task of thinking up different distasteful assignments on a daily basis. KP duty had first priority over all other activities, and not relieving Privates from KP relieved the First Sergeant from issuing passes. This unassailable military logic — if you have KP you cannot get a pass, if you cannot get a pass you might as well be on KP — later was known as a "Catch 22."

With by now habitual lack of self-restraint, I allowed my disappointment and frustration at being a Private to be shared by anyone who cared to lend a willing ear. In an effort to help, some soldier told me there was an outfit housed in a large railroad car that might still be handing out commissions. One evening after KP, I headed for the railroad car. I was greeted by a Lieutenant Hans Habbe, a fairly well-known Hungarian writer. He had been placed in charge of one of the first psychological warfare units in the U.S. Army. Their mission was to draft and drop leaflets in North Africa to persuade German troops to surrender. They were on the point of leaving Ritchie for overseas. He wanted a man with my academic qualifications and ability to write German on his team, but could at best offer me the rank of Sergeant; he occupied the only officer's slot in the unit and was not ready to vacate it for my benefit. However, something held me back from joining them. I wanted Intelligence, not psychological warfare.

I don't really know why I was so resentful of KP detail. It was a toasty inside job and the food was an all-you-can-eat buffet, but somehow it rankled me to be in a menial position, bossed about by cooks, for which my three university degrees had inadequately prepared me. In the meantime, I gathered more information about the MITC. So far Ritchie was preparing its students to serve on IPW teams, each one of which comprised two officers up to the rank of Captain and Lieutenant, and four enlisted men. Everyone started in the rank with which he had arrived at the camp. I foresaw being incorporated into one of these teams as low man on the totem pole and shipped overseas. Promotion, I guessed, could only occur by attrition. Someone on the team would have to die or be wounded for me to move up, and even this path to advancement was not guaranteed. Another Corporal or Sergeant might be transferred from somewhere else to fill the vacant slot.

So far, I had not thought much about serving in combat. However, I missed my wife, and one's imagination has a way of running amok in such a situation. Some of us began to worry about being wounded in the wrong place. I would have hated to earn a Purple Heart in exchange for the loss of my male attribute.

A railroad track ran along one side of the camp and an occasional train came chugging by. Some evenings after completing KP chores, as spring blossomed and the weather was fair, I might take a stroll along the tracks in the countryside. Pondering ways to leave the Army and rejoin my wife, but mainly out of frustration with my status in the Service, I began to wonder if I could sustain an injury that would set me free. I even thought of sticking my hand on the rail as a train rolled by. But that course seemed rather drastic. It might even backfire and, if poorly executed, lead to a court-martial for self-inflicted wounds. Soon dismissing such sickly thoughts from my mind, I tried to face the future like a man.

Several unexpected developments gave me new hope. The next school course started and much to my surprise and contrary to the original promise from Headquarters, I was not in it. Could my records have been lost once again? I kept my mouth shut because my wife was contemplating spending a few weeks during her summer vacation near Camp Ritchie. I reasoned that the only way for me to be eligible for passes and free weekends would be as a student. A Private not attending school could not count on passes or anything else — except details. I needed to synchronize my attendance at school with her stay in Blue Ridge Summit. (Camp Ritchie did not observe the regular week and the Lord's day. School ran seven days, followed by a free day called "Banfill Day." After all, *he* was God in those parts, and it was fitting to have a day of rest named after him.)

Another event that brought some relief was the arrival in camp of a German-Jewish refugee. With very wealthy parents, his rank caused him no inferiority complex. The cash at his disposal made up for his lack of rank. He arrived in a white convertible Packard, which he had to park outside the camp. Wise to the ways of a now flourishing underground economy, he had pockets full of rationed gasoline coupons, which he most selectively used to exchange for passes from a corruptible First Sergeant. We became good friends. He went through life Teflon-coated, lighthearted, harboring no ambitions in regard to promotions. At the end of the war I heard, through the grapevine, that he suddenly felt strong regrets about not accomplishing some heroic feat, did something really stupid, and was seriously wounded.

Occasionally, some officer thought it a good idea to give Privates in one day the amount of exercise we had missed for a month. We were called out of barracks, had to check out and load a full infantry pack on our unaccustomed backs, then start off halfheartedly on a five- to ten-mile hike, enlivened every now and then by a few hundred paces in double time. The physical condition of this hastily assembled troop of patriotic recruits varied greatly from dismal to fair. The tight exemplary formation we started in was soon metamorphosed into a pitiful bunch of stragglers limping at varying distances from each other along the road. Any passerby, glimpsing this mock-heroic scene, would have sworn we were in a disgraceful retreat (more like many a rout this beautiful Blue Ridge scenery and nearby Gettysburg had witnessed during the Civil War). By the time we returned to camp, most of us were in dire need of R and R (rest and relaxation), not thirsting for battle.

There were infrequent assemblies of all the personnel stationed at the camp. The purpose was never quite clear. At least it provided us with an opportunity to joke about the oxymoron coyly concealed in the phrase "Military Intelligence." I was reminded of the old "Keystone Cops" and Laurel and Hardy movies. However, here I was not watching them, but playing a role therein — unfortunately one more like that of an extra.

New arrivals reached camp almost every day, many of them recent refugees from Nazi Germany shipped to Ritchie because of their knowledge of German. Among them I found some kindred spirits, enlisted men with whom I had something in common, such as an education, a desire to use our special language skills for a useful purpose, and hope for advancement during our temporary, yet at that time indefinite, stay in the Army.

As the time for Christine's arrival neared, I went to Headquarters. In the best diplomatic manner I could muster I reminded them of their original intention, expressed to me quite forcefully on my arrival at Ritchie, to enroll me in the very next IPW course. The clerk took some time to rummage about in his files before continuing the interview. Without ever admitting any mistakes, a good way for the military to inspire confidence in its procedures, he announced that I would be in the 9th Military Intelligence Training Course. At that moment my timing looked excellent.

I began the course before Christine's arrival. With no promotion to look forward to I was not highly motivated and even thought of flunking out, a difficult goal to attain in most military schools. We studied German and Italian army organization, maps, German military terms, interrogation techniques, Morse code, and related subjects. The course was good and the map problems in the field excellent. We would be taken out somewhere in the region on trucks and dumped with a local map and a compass. The idea was to orient ourselves by means of the map and, through significant visible landmarks, determine our location. Then, with the aid of the compass, we had to find our way to an agreed-upon meeting place. This practice was always conducted at night, so I made it my business to reach my destination as quickly as possible, return to barracks, and go to bed. Some of the guys preferred to get lost on purpose and end up in some village bar. A married man, I was not inclined toward such extracurricular activities. The greater portion of the course took place inside the classroom, and our physical condition was stationary at best.

My wife arrived on the train from Baltimore a few weeks later. It was a wonderfully emotional reunion. She liked her rooming house and the landlady. We had many opportunities to be together and took trips to Washington, D.C., and to New York where she met my parents.

We arrived late in the city, phoning my mother on arrival. She was her usual gracious self: *No, it was not convenient to come out to Queens so late at night.* (We stayed at the old Hotel Taft on 7th Avenue and 49th Street.)

Christine made friends with Betty Wheeler, the wife of an NCO, Henry Wheeler, who was not only working at Colonel Thomas's Training Headquarters, but practically running it. Betty had permanently rented a room in the home where Christine was staying. I too became acquainted with the Wheelers and they learned about me, my background, and my frustrations.

Toward the end of the two-month course we had a much talked about 48-hour exercise. It was reputed to be extremely strenuous. My reaction ultimately was that if others can do it, I can too. Once again the authorities at Ritchie proved themselves thoughtless and illogical, if not worse. It seemed folly to send men, by now mostly out of condition after sitting almost two months on their fannies without even engaging in daily calisthenics, out into the field for a continuous 48 hours. During this entire period, with barely any rest stops, we went traipsing day and night over mountainous countryside. A number of stations had been set up along the way in tents, where we stopped to solve various Intelligence tasks: map problems, questions on enemy organization, PW interrogation, and document translation. As soon as one exam had been taken, off we went to the next station. Especially dangerous was the descent down the side of a mountain in total darkness, without a trail and without a flashlight. The terrain was uneven and we clambered down through bushes and under overhanging tree branches, stumbling, sliding, often falling. Rumors had it that on each one of these exercises two or three people had had their heads and faces caught and their necks snapped by branches.

I came through it all right, taking no chances when struggling down the mountain in the black of night. At the end, after being up two days, we still had to walk back three miles to the camp. I had never been so worn out in my whole life. Within sight of Ritchie, some of us flopped down on the shoulder of the road to recover our strength, ignoring the pitifully unmilitary sight we offered. That evening, on pass and at my wife's place, I was barely able to lower myself into a tub and soak my worn-out body for an hour in warm water.

The final eight-day exercise was much less rigorous; in fact, it could not compare to the previous two-day one. It was not too well organized, much time was wasted, and under different circumstances, might have seemed more like a sylvan vacation with complaining elves, pixies, and male fairies clad in fatigues. We slept outdoors, two to a tent. The weather was so balmy, I tied my tent half to two trees to make a sleeping hammock. The exercise consisted of further Intelligence training — including interrogation techniques. I graduated on August 18, 1943, from this 9th Military Intelligence Training Course, having made no effort to place high in the class. Actually our graduation certificate, a simple letter, included no grade or rating. We had no idea about what would happen next, but expected assignment to teams and shipment overseas.

What we did not realize was that the entire concept of Intelligence teams, which were to remain assigned to MIS (Military Intelligence Service) while attached to armies, corps, divisions, and regiments, was still in its infancy and never had been implemented. No one in the U.S. Army knew about us, and the idea of MIS had to be sold to the various combat units. They had to be indoctrinated, briefed, and convinced about the services they might expect from us and how our teams could support their Intelligence collection efforts. Imagine the scenario: a senior officer, G-2 (Intelligence officer) of a corps or division, pretty set in his ways and not ready to take into his confidence a bunch of new recruits, some without Basic Training, others foreign — some from Germany — many with a thick foreign accent, merely because they spoke a foreign language most likely better than English. Their training at Ritchie, a place he never heard of, would hardly impress him. Can't you see such an officer welcoming with open arms a uniformed individual approaching his desk, leaning over and with both hands on it, smiling self-satisfied and with supreme confidence, saying with a thick accent, "I *sh*peak *z*even lang*uitges*, und *Tjer*-man da best." We joked about it later, but such incidents occurred.

Our time was taken up with final preparations for overseas duty. We fired weapons on the rifle range, crawled around on the ground under machine-gun fire, and received a driver's license. Each team was to have two jeeps at its disposal. I was glad I was an experienced driver and not a passenger at the mercy of a fumbling novice in a highly exposed vehicle. We practiced driving in convoys.

One Lieutenant on the Ritchie training staff had a small house built on the grounds. It was designed to teach us about booby traps and where the enemy would be apt to conceal them. The garden and courtyard of the house were used to teach us about land mines and other explosive surprises we might encounter in combat. Because of reports we had heard about warfare in Africa, booby traps and mines inspired in us the most fear. We suddenly realized that pursuing an enemy in retreat can be mighty dangerous if he had time to set such deterrents. No one knew at the time that operations in Europe would move with such lightning speed that the German troops would, fortunately for us, not have time to booby-trap abandoned buildings.

The tension at Ritchie was high and morale very low. Many of the soldiers, especially those speaking languages like Armenian or Greek, would probably not be used. Therefore, they grew increasingly anxious about their futures. The actions of the officers who ran Ritchie were completely unpredictable, if not scary. Some such fears were realized after I had left Ritchie, when most of the 14th class, unprepared and insufficiently trained, was sent out on a "cattle alert" to infantry units such as the 30th Infantry Division, many of them to be wounded or to die in combat.

I was very despondent. Christine would be leaving soon. I was headed overseas as a Private under the command of personnel I deemed myself superior to in education and knowledge, at least as far as language and familiarity with France and Germany were concerned. Rumors were also running wild. Most mysterious was a small building in which a Colonel, a Major, and a Tech-Sergeant had established their headquarters. Reputedly they ran a supersecret operation under very tight security.

In the meantime, Henry Wheeler from Training Headquarters and I had become acquainted. I had unburdened myself to him, complaining about my dim future in MIS. He had checked my school records and agreed that they were dismal. On their basis, I would not go far in assignments or promotions. He began to share my estimate of the situation. As things were going, my talents might not be utilized to the Army's best advantage. Soon thereafter, Henry told me the mysterious Colonel and Major ran some sort of a school and were looking for superior graduates from the Military Intelligence courses with an excellent knowledge of German. Fully aware of my background and trusting in what I had told him about my foreign language proficiency, he offered to call the Major, claim he was speaking for Colonel Thomas, and recommend that he take a look at me.

I went to see the Major in my snappiest and best military manner, standing at attention, saluting sharply, and reporting as ordered. The Major thrust a photostat of German writing in *Steilschrift*, the vertical angular writing in former years widely used in Germany, but by now replaced by rounded Latin letters. He ordered me to translate the document, which I easily did without hesitation. Satisfied with my performance, the Major asked me about my education. Then he dismissed me, saying I would hear from him later. This brief interview, for which I shall remain forever grateful to Henry Wheeler, was a turning point in my military career, if not my life.

The next thing I knew I was proudly enrolled with 20 officers and enlisted men in the second Order of Battle (OB) Course ever offered in the U.S. Army. OB was the brainchild of Mr. Tucker, a civilian analyst and editor of reports with the Army G-2 Intelligence in the Pentagon. He had written a little red book crammed full of information on the German and Italian military: all the German and Italian units by number and, if applicable, by name; commanding officers, when known; biographical sketches of high ranking officers; detailed organization of all units down to platoons; details on the Nazi *SS*; enemy weapons; specifications of tanks and armored vehicles — in short, everything that was known about the enemy. Our task was to memorize all this information cold. We also were offered valuable lectures on German military documents, personnel records, German strategy and tactics, Karl von Clausewitz and German war theory, and even geopolitics. This course was totally different from the IPW course I had taken in that it made us feel special, valuable, and about to play a significant role in the war. This time I made sure I graduated near, if not at, the top of the class.

Tucker (whom I was to meet again in 1956 in the Office of the Assistant Chief of Staff for Intelligence at the Pentagon) came from Washington to lecture to us, and we visited his office in the Pentagon one day during the course. The OB section consisted of Tucker and two enlisted men. Later, several graduates from the first OB class joined his staff. At that time I was envious of them, but I soon changed my mind. That was not where the action was to be!

Tucker was a hairsplitting, i-dotting, scholarly, if pedantic, sort of man, but his creation of the red *Order of Battle* book and its contribution to the war effort were absolutely invaluable. We have him to thank for our start in this area of Military Intelligence. Years later, when I worked with him during the Korean War, I felt truly sorry for him. Outside the soulless, sanitized, bureaucratic world of the Pentagon, he might have enriched our planet in more humane ways. He served us well in World War II by providing us with the springboard to start shaping our own roles in the campaigns to come.

I graduated from the second OB course on September 23, 1943. The projected teams were to comprise three individuals: an officer up to Captain and two enlisted men up to Master Sergeant. As future members of the first-ever OB teams in the U.S. Army, we were charged with a heavy responsibility and could now hope to play a crucial role in the war. We would always possess, at the disposal of Intelligence and Operations staffs, even Commanding Generals, the most up-to-date knowledge of the enemy forces opposing us. My self-esteem rose considerably. Would that my rank catch up with it! Rumor had it that to give us greater credibility and prestige with the unit staffs to which we might be attached, all enlisted personnel graduating from OB school would be promoted to Master Sergeant. It was too good to believe. Every day we clustered around the bulletin board awaiting orders and last-minute news.

In early October, most of the men who had graduated from either the Intelligence or the OB courses were, without any warning, given five days of leave to see their families before leaving the country. I flew to California on a DC-3 and spent the few days with my wife and her family. There was no time to see my parents in New York.

I had hoped to be promoted before leaving for California and have my wife sew on my Master Sergeant's stripes. Headquarters once again disappointed me and did not see fit to publish orders. But shortly after my return to Ritchie, on October 26, 1943, one year and two days after my enlistment, my hopes were fulfilled: my name, together with many others, was on promotion orders. (I had to look twice, but my eyes did not deceive me.) I was a Master Sergeant and there would be no more KP duty!

From then on everything happened in haste. All of us were assigned to teams. I was on OB team number I (out of VI teams). Hundreds of German-speaking men were assigned to IPW teams. French speakers for the most part were assigned to MI (Military Interpreter) teams. Armenian or Greek speakers as well as others not particularly proficient in any language made up PI (Photo Interpreter) teams. The latter had received added preparation in photo interpretation. We received additional, if superficial, training on the rifle range and on assembling and cleaning Colt .45-caliber pistols and carbines. After much deliberation about whether OB personnel should tote carbines or handguns, Headquarters, to my considerable relief, decided on pistols. Surprisingly, in view of Ritchie's previous multiple acts of stupidity, the right decision was made; aware that we would be dealing mostly with files and paper, they must have decided a pistol would be less cumbersome than a carbine.

The time for our departure drew near. Eighteen of us, 6 officers and 12 enlisted men, who formed OB teams I through VI, were bonded by our specialty and comparatively small number. The artillery Lieutenant in command of our team turned out to be somewhat unbalanced. He tried to act more like an infantry platoon leader and did not appear to grasp the role OB teams would play. He kept talking about acquiring a mortar as soon as we landed in enemy territory. I have no idea what he intended to do with an artillery piece! We ignored him as best we could and often teased him.

We were qualifying with the M-1 rifle on the firing range. While some were firing, others stood in a ditch near the targets. With a long pole equipped with a large white disk they indicated where we had hit the target. Our crazy Lieutenant was monitoring our performance, watching and correcting our every move, as though we were the greenest of recruits. Fed up with his superior attitude, without his catching on, we sent one man out of our group to the targets. Once he had reached them we started blissfully firing away with the confident assurance of sharpshooters. Our co-conspirator unwaveringly indicated bull's eye after bull's eye with his pole. The Lieutenant was puzzled by our seemingly unerring accuracy, torn between suspicion and admiring disbelief, but never caught on to the deception.

I was not only ready to go overseas, but even anxious to get on with it. My rank of Master Sergeant and my membership in an elite group of OB made my spirits high, enthusiasm strong, and self-esteem assured.

Our vaccinations were brought up-to-date and we underwent one more hasty physical. I alerted the dental officer to the deplorable state of my upper front teeth. There was no time for fancy orthodontics. Two nurses held me down by the shoulders because the Novocain did not completely desensitize the area close to all the facial nerves, where the dentist pulled four upper front teeth, energetically and mercilessly scraping the bone afterwards. "Have the medics aboard ship take the stitches out in three days!" was the only consoling farewell I received. How could I, like a Mortimer Snerd with a goofy toothless gap, face the enemy and inspire fear? I resolved on the spot to look grim and unsmiling, keeping my upper lip low, for the duration. Indeed, I had to wait until the end of the war and my return stateside to have the damage repaired.

We embarked at night, not knowing on what ship we were sailing, and left New York City on November 14, 1943. It was exciting: The dry run was over, the real thing about to begin.

May God hold us by the hand in winter, summer, and during all seasons of the year.
— Spanish Proverb

Chapter 12

OPERATION
NEPTUNE BIGOT — 1944

O NE OF THE MAIN concerns of any American soldier crossing the Atlantic by ship was of being torpedoed by German submarines. For us, those fears were quickly allayed shortly after we boarded what, to our surprised relief, was no slow leaky tub, but none other than the *Queen Mary*. The *Queen* had been converted from passenger to troopship and now accommodated 15,000 soldiers. It was no small relief to learn that the *Queen Mary* cruised at such high speeds that no German submarine could outmaneuver or overtake it. A state-of-the-art radar system provided additional protection. We were as safe as possible crossing the ocean on this ship. We would also reach our destination in much less time than we could ever expect to on any other vessel.

It was not exactly like sailing on a cruise. All the luxurious recreational areas, salons, dining halls, and ballrooms had vanished, miraculously metamorphosed into austere sleeping quarters for military personnel, with bunks stacked five high. There were, of course, many other troops besides the large contingent from Ritchie. Master Sergeants of the six OB teams remained together in the same cabin separately from our officers. The ship was run by a British Captain and crew under British rules, but American officers were in charge of our troops. Actually, there was not much for American officers to be in charge of as the British crew ran the ship. On a British ship, as on any other ship for that matter, the British Captain has the last word and his orders prevailed, superseding any existing American military protocol.

Some evil KP spirit must have had its predatory eye on me from the moment I enlisted in the Army and never ceased stalking me. To simplify the assignment of details without having to scrounge up live bodies for them, it had been decided to allow the luck of the draw to do the job. To each cabin corresponded certain duties, and its occupants were responsible for those tasks. The sign inside our cabin specifically stated that any personnel occupying the premises would be assigned to KP duty. In shocked disbelief we began scurrying about, attempting to tell officers or the British that in our grade we could not possibly pull KP duty. Our efforts failed. Consequently, the troops were treated to the sight of six Master Sergeants pulling KP at each meal. I am sure they thought a new world order had arisen.

Soon after our departure from New York, we had a general assembly outside on the main deck to inform us about safety procedures. A huge mass of soldiers, we were standing in tight formation waiting for the troop Commander to appear and harangue us. We waited a long time in the cold. An American field grade officer, craving our riveted attention, kept asking us to look as sharp as possible, because a "full Colonel" was going to address us. I asked loud and clear — but shielded by a thick wall of men around me — "Full of what?" It was impractical to administer mass punishment to thousands of men, and since it was not directed at the ship's Captain, *why would I be made to walk the plank?* The officer chose to ignore the remark.

The kitchen detail turned out to be a minor nuisance. We set the tables before each of the three daily meals, carried the food from the galley to the mess hall, and cleaned up after meals. The worst part consisted of the jeers our enlisted clientele, seeing six-stripers performing KP detail, heaped upon us. Actually, this duty turned out to be a blessing in that it enabled me to gather an important piece of Intelligence on the behind-the-scenes goings-on of the kitchen that otherwise might have escaped me.

One of the first times I entered the galley to pick up platters of food, I caught the British cook dipping his arm up to his elbow into a huge kettle of some soupy liquid. He brought his cupped hand full of the stuff to his lips, slurped some of it, tasting it thoughtfully, then spit the unconsumed portion back into the kettle. Waste not, want not! Having witnessed his sampling technique, I partook very sparingly from the chef's culinary creations, preferring for the short duration of the crossing to sustain myself with wrapped candy bars purchased from a small canteen on-board. It never occurred to me to disseminate this bit of privileged information to my comrades — although had I done so and thereby provoked an exodus of diners, my job might have been easier for scarcity of clients.

One morning, at breakfast, the jibes became too much for one of the servers. He reached down to the platter full of greasy bacon strips and *horresco referens* — I shudder to relate it — hurled a fistful of them at the man who had provoked him. Unfortunately, the latter was a German refugee of ultraorthodox Jewish faith. He grew livid, then enraged, when the bacon made contact with him. The ensuing free-for-all was an ugly spectacle to behold. Bacon strips were flying all over the mess hall. Never approving of wasting or mishandling food, even greasy bacon which I do not care to eat myself, I stayed on the sidelines. The melee finally subsided, and we cleaned up the mess before anyone in authority arrived to dispense punishment. I never expected to witness so violent a reaction to nonkosher missiles.

Weary of a diet of candy and a crossing that did not offer the amenities with which I had been spoiled on previous voyages, I was glad to reach Glasgow. The record time of 4 days and 16 hours in which the *Queen Mary* had completed the trip was the fastest to date. On November 21, 1943, after disembarking in Scotland, we officially arrived in England. There was a great deal of confusion as to who should go where. As OB teams, we had been made to understand that our arrival in London was urgently awaited. However, during the following weeks we continued to remain with all the other MIS teams, not immediately enjoying special treatment or individual travel orders. Our entire group proceeded to Litchfield Barracks near Manchester, an ancient Roman military encampment. The Commanding Officer, Colonel Kilian, we soon discovered, was marching to a different drummer and ran things very much his own way. He had, it appeared, set a goal to court-martial everyone in sight.

Regrettably, not thinking at the time of a future memoir, I never kept a journal of the daily happenings or the precise sequence of events during the war. Too much was going on, and at a time when not one of us knew what the future held, nothing mattered except that which had an immediate bearing on our welfare. Everything I relate comes not from later readings, but from purely personal observation. I rely on memory alone and on occasion, the chronology, if not the incidents themselves, are somewhat blurred and resist perfect recall.

Morale in Great Britain remained high, despite the bleak conditions, the tightly set jaws, and the drawn faces. Every day, the English people had put up with *Luftwaffe* air raids, blackouts, and food shortages. Later, in London, the insufferable German V-1 buzz bombs flew rattling overhead. Of note, this part of Europe has never been celebrated for its radiant sunshine. Except for the so-called British Riviera, near Paignton and Torquay — blessed by the warm drifts of the Gulf Stream — the English climate is damp, misty, and dreary. As I had learned in my literature classes at the *lycée*, European Romanticism, the entire Storm and Stress (*Sturm und Drang*) period in literature, from François Chateaubriand's *Memoirs from Beyond the Tomb* to Johann Wolfgang Von Goethe's *The Sorrows of Young Werther,* had been spawned by the cold barren mountains of Scotland, the dreary heaths of England, and the Ossianic legends clouded in mist, which flourished so well in such climes. I was on familiar ground, accustomed to these bleak surroundings from my years in Hamburg and my previous stays with the Chases. In a sense, I was returning to what had been my home for over half of my life.

Few of my companions felt the comforts of a homecoming, but at least they knew that they were more than welcome as allies and possible saviors of Europe. The British were mighty glad to see us, even if somewhat suspicious of how much we could deliver. British humor gently questioning the valor of the Yanks always prevailed. Our Good Conduct Medal for enlisted personnel (which, by the way, owing to some clerical error I was never awarded) was derided as the "Order of the Undetected Crime." Our Zippo lighters were referred to as individual flamethrowers issued to every Yank and reminiscent of the German *Flammenwerfer*. The Purple Heart, according to some unkind British, was won for sitting through a Rommel and African campaign documentary without fainting.

Litchfield Barracks was an old army post with gray stone buildings surrounded by an austere stone wall — like a fort. The *habitués* of this unattractive post soon informed us of the main do's and don'ts. Attending the daily retreat formation was an absolute must. Failure to do so meant a court-martial. Breaking into a chow line was also punishable by court-martial and three to six months of hard labor. To our knowledge, in the rest of the Army, court-martialed individuals lost certain privileges, such as the right to attend military formations like retreat. Not so in this camp. The Colonel may have thought some soldiers might choose court-martial over having to stand retreat. In any case, the prisoners stood retreat with, if at some distance from, the rest of us. There was a huge detachment of them, marching every late afternoon into the large yard where retreat was held. They wore fatigues and were under MP guard. I would not have been surprised to see them in leg irons. We wondered if, at the rate the Colonel was arresting, they would soon outnumber us.

The camp was a hotbed of confusion, and we feared we might find ourselves lost within its confines. Some Sergeant on the staff told us we could expect all kinds of details, but we made ourselves very scarce, only showing up for meals (making sure to stay docilely in line). One day, we were (at great risk to our unblemished military record) playing Ping-Pong during daytime hours in the Red Cross recreation building, when someone shouted, "The MPs are coming!" I ran for the restroom and crawled through an open window without being caught. It was a very narrow escape, and I never again took such a chance.

A week or so after our arrival, a large group of soldiers arrived after having spent a year or two in Iceland (or Greenland — I do not recall which). They seemed strangely morose, introverted — wild, hostile — very much psychologically affected by their long stay in the remote glacial expanses. Not being Cistercian monks or Tibetan lamas, they had not been equal to such a soul-testing experience. One night a strange noise, like that of splashing water, woke me up out of a deep sleep. I could not believe what I heard and saw. A soldier was lying prone on the very edge of the upper part of a double bunk, his body resting on its right side and turned toward the open space beside him. As though engaged in the most natural act while plunged in deep somnambulism, he was impassively urinating on the floor six feet below him. In the Arctic he may have been accustomed to see it freeze before it hit the ground. Until then the product of a fairly sheltered lifestyle, I was appalled, realizing to what behavioral deviations the stress of warlike conditions and strange surroundings can drive individuals who lack inner strength.

Very shortly after this incident, we were ordered to pack our bags and prepare for departure to the railroad station. Apparently, we were leaving Litchfield for London. Our expectations rose, but too soon. We spent several hours at the station waiting for something to happen. By nightfall, disappointed and frustrated, we were taken back to the camp. In the meantime another large group had arrived and now occupied our former barracks. We were told we needed to spend the night in tents. Three of us OB Sergeants immediately began making the tent assigned to us comfortable. It was the beginning of winter and cold and damp outside. Absorbed in our task (we had a good fire going in the stove that stood in the middle of the tent) we did not notice that all the other men had gone. An officer appeared and told us no one was allowed to sleep in tents because of the cold. Again I marveled at the changing nature of Army orders. The rest of the group had already been assigned to barracks. Pointing at the roaring fire, I assured the officer we would be most comfortable for the night. Pondering his decision for a while, he finally assented, insisting, however, that the next morning we find quarters inside one of the vacant buildings. We did enjoy a cozy warm night — one of the best ever in this camp.

The following morning we packed our gear and were assigned to another barracks. To our surprise, it was half occupied with men quietly asleep in their beds; by a miraculous stroke of luck we had been lodged with an AG postal unit that sorted mail around the clock. Continuously on the job in three eight-hour shifts, they were exempt from all details, inspections, or formations — even retreat. From then our main concern was to keep safely out of sight, but still remain in contact with the other members of the OB teams. We did not wish to be the forgotten MIS trio, sitting out the war in Litchfield, only to resurface after the armistice. Constant liaison with our outside comrades was imperative.

We could sleep as late as we wanted. No one came to inspect us. We were like honorary members of the postal unit. We lay low during daytime hours and alerted our OB buddies to our clandestine status. Fortunately, we did not have to meet this challenge for too long. Within a reasonably short time we joined the others and shipped out.

In London, we were assigned bunks in a large building that housed many other American military personnel. To the best of my knowledge, we were assigned to the Military Intelligence Service U.S. Forces European Theater (MISUSFET), our parent organization, and attached to no one in particular. MIS was possibly still in the U.S. and did not move to Paris until after D-Day. This administrative — in a sense orphaned — status, where we were for all practical purposes abandoned by, although always assigned to, MIS was to last for the duration of the war and often caused problems, especially when the time came for promotions. It was never remedied until 1951, when a new MISO (Military Intelligence Service Organization) Table of Organization and Equipment (TO&E) (30-600) was drawn up. As fate would have it, I cooperated on this project, being the only officer in the Pentagon at that time who had had experience with all of these teams.

Being quartered with other strange personnel from unrelated units caused some minor embarrassment. The Saturday after we moved into our building, we were deep in the "sleep of the just" when an officer burst into our room. He stared at us, unbelieving. We stared back at him, and as always, out of sheer habit, a little fearful in the presence of an irate officer. "Why aren't you ready for inspection?"

Fortunately, he was a reasonable man. I explained to him that we were independent teams of a classified nature, were merely lodged there, had nothing to do with the other units in the building, and would probably move out shortly to join regular units. He bought this explanation and withdrew graciously.

All OB personnel, officers and enlisted, were under the temporary supervision of British Intelligence. Christmas was drawing near, and the English were anxious to put us through another OB course before the holiday. In the usual — somewhat superior — manner often adopted by our Allies, we were informed that the Intelligence we were about to receive was the real thing, highly classified, and much more up-to-date than anything we had learned in the U.S. Much of it had been furnished by sources on the continent, like the *Maquis* — the French freedom fighters. We were to learn the current Order of Battle, including unit designations, strength, and location of all the German units now in France and expected to oppose us if and when we landed. It was very exciting as the immediacy of the invasion became almost certain. The information proved to be very accurate and there were almost no surprises later as far as the German Order of Battle in France was concerned.

The course lasted about a week, after which we were free, our attachment to operational units not finalized. In the meantime we could do as we wished, but were to remain in close contact with our officers, who would be the first to know of any orders affecting us. To facilitate matters, I was to meet one of the officers at the stroke of noon on certain days of the week in front of SHAEF (Supreme Headquarters Allied Expeditionary Forces). Later, as no orders were forthcoming, this was changed to one day a week. Each time I reported at the designated spot, I usually saw General Dwight D. Eisenhower, accompanied by a large retinue of officers, step out in front of the building on his way to lunch.

For reasons I have never understood, there had been a foul-up with my Master-Sergeant pay. I was receiving a $37.50 quarters allowance in addition to my pay. I had made a large allotment to my wife, since I did not expect to need much cash while overseas. However, when the time came to draw my first paycheck, the finance officer told me I would get nothing. All my pay had gone to Christine. My buddies thought the situation funny, but I did not share their amusement. It was not settled until after D-Day. Through letters, I advised my wife and parents of my financial straits. My father somehow arranged through friends in London to lend me money, for which Christine reimbursed him. These same friends also treated me to a nice dinner at *Le Coq d'Or — the* Golden Rooster — where, at a nearby table, I recognized Anthony Eden, Minister of Foreign Affairs.

While in England I visited Mrs. Bernard Chase. She still resided in Broxbourne Herts, north of London. It was not a cheerful reunion. Mr. Chase had died in Spain in an automobile accident. Her son, my friend John, had been killed while a squadron leader in the Royal Air Force. And Graham, the younger son, had also died. The daughter, I believe, was a nurse or in the Service.

I even saw the Steven Chase family in Harrow. Audrey had fallen in love with a German, as had the other Chase daughter, and was facing an insolvable dilemma. The war was devastating her country, killing her loved ones, and making a union with her fiancé unthinkable. I knew how she felt. I had been brought up in Germany, had been a happy boy there with many close friends. I did not like to see, because of the actions of a deluded dictator like Hitler, a country that had almost been, like my own, destroyed and now my enemy.

However, I had no problems discerning my loyalties. Audrey on the other hand grew bitter, torn apart by irreconcilable feelings. I took her out to dinner, but I sensed my company was no comfort to her. Besides, I did not wish to jeopardize my security clearance by getting involved in her affair with a German national. My apprehensions in this regard were not unjustified. After the war, Audrey asked me in a letter whether I could somehow help her contact this man. She stopped writing when I intimated that I did not care to become involved.

Three of the OB teams were attached to a higher headquarters, possibly the First Army Group. I confess that at first I was envious of what appeared to be a choice assignment. Now looking back at what was to be my role in the campaigns of France, Belgium, and Germany, I am grateful to whatever divine power guided the part I was destined to play in them. I learned from the experience that often the best plan is to have faith and trust in a higher power to make the right decisions for you. Despite one's skepticism, events bordering on the miraculous and inexplicable fortuitous coincidences — termed by Carl Jung synchronicities — make it at times difficult to experience them and not believe in a protective power.

I had a great deal of free time, but feeling very much a married man — in love with and totally faithful to my wife — I spent most of it alone. I went to a few movies, but found the run-of-the-mill slapstick British comedies not especially to my liking. Despite the air raids, the shortages, the wartime conditions, and the general fearful atmosphere, the well-known British ability of maintaining a stiff upper lip in the face of adversity was constantly evident. I, too, acted more like a tourist than a GI. I revisited the British museum and spent some time at the YMCA swimming pool. The food in the building where we were lodged was neither healthy nor attractive. There were no fresh vegetables or decent meat dishes. Powdered eggs for breakfast, starches, fried bologna, and salami did not offer an appropriate or appetizing diet. Also available to us were the Red Cross and British Service Clubs with inexpensive snacks such as meat pies, cakes, and doughnuts — not exactly ideal fare. I did not have the means or the desire to eat in expensive restaurants.

My companions often went to dance halls where for a nominal fee one could enjoy band music. A sufficient number of British women of all types and ages were present, so that one was practically guaranteed a partner. At first I refused to go, thinking it improper for a married man, but finally I went along and enjoyed a few dances. The ambiance at these socials was very proper and restrained, at least in my naive view. The young British women acted as though they were doing their patriotic duty by entertaining the Yanks before they went off to battle and maybe death. I always, if asked, immediately admitted to being married, staunchly clinging to the resolve of emulating the faithful knights of chivalry. I was as strait-laced as ever.

At one of these parties I met a young woman with whom I became better acquainted. I escorted her home and met her family. Still I continued to behave like the perfect gentleman. She talked in vague terms about having had a relationship with some man, but was imprecise. The nightly scene, when we walked the streets or took the tube, remained the same: planes flying overhead in the dark of the blackout, an occasional V-1, the thunder of explosions, and the constantly warning sirens wailing through the city. I was glad that I became impervious to all of it. I could see no reason why any bomb would choose to hit the spot where I happened to be.

Finally, this temporary respite in our military life came to an end. My OB team was earmarked for attachment to General Anthony MacAuliffe's 101st Airborne Division, while the other two were intended for V Corps and VII Corps, respectively.

The Lieutenant in charge of our team continued in his conversation, unbalanced, raving about the plans he had for using artillery after we landed on enemy territory. I thought it best to ignore him as much as possible, and he resented me that much more for it. Later I found out that, after being attached to the 101st Airborne, he had a nervous breakdown before D-Day. I was told he had gone on his knees before the G-2, begging to be excused from the landings. Instead of being court-martialed for cowardice, he had allegedly been assigned as an escort officer to SHAEF Headquarters, where if he kept his mouth shut he probably could not brag about his skill with mortars. The story proved my suspicions about his state of mind.

The CO of OB Team Number VI, which was intended for VII Corps, was Lieutenant Al Blazevicius, a Lithuanian-American from Connecticut. Serious, discreet, not very articulate, at times quite withdrawn, with no knowledge of foreign languages other than Lithuanian, he had been commissioned after attending infantry OCS. There was a certain cleverness about him and although no intellectual, he was sharp and perceptive. He was easy to work with, loyal to and supportive of the men under him, and utterly reliable. His outstanding quality was that he did not insist on hogging all the credit for himself. He was a team player and was content with being part of a winning team. Before our three OB teams left to join the units they were to support, he asked me if I would like to be on his Number VI Order of Battle Unit, assuming he could manage the transfer. He wanted me, as became evident during operations, not for my sunny disposition and irresistible charm (which were not patently evident) but for my perfect command of French and German and my recent knowledge of and familiarity with Europe, especially France, Belgium, and Germany. He also knew he could count on me to serve the team to the best of my ability.

Not dead-set on parachuting to my destination or reaching it by glider, I was delighted to join OB Team VI. He never told me what he did to accomplish the exchange until almost a year later. As a teetotaler, I was flattered to learn that to acquire me he had been willing to sacrifice a case of good liquor, which my former crazy CO was most eager to accept. The latter derived a double benefit from the trade: liquor to feed his delirious musings about setting up mortar positions and getting rid of a Sergeant he did not like. Lieutenant Blazevicius, on the other hand, may have saved my life with his willingness to sacrifice his liquid treasure. I heard that the Sergeant, who was originally on his team and for whom he traded me, came in on a glider around D-Day, became entangled in a tree top, and was picked off by a German bullet. Once again, I had been in the Lord's hands!

The day before we were to leave London, all three teams moved for a night to a British rooming house. With nothing to do, I decided to meet my dance partner one more time and say good-bye to her. We met and suddenly and irresistibly, I was seized with amorous thoughts. I asked her to come back with me to my room. Halfheartedly, yet in the beginning willingly, she agreed and we started walking to my new lodgings, though I was still not quite familiar with the location. Amidst a very thick fog I missed my place. By that time, both she and I had second thoughts about the proposed tryst and headed back to her home. We said good-bye and I restarted the search for my lodgings. The fog was now so thick and the night so black that I could not see my hand before my eyes. I was groping my way along a wall, when I heard some steps. The passerby, better acquainted with the locale, directed me to the nearest tube station. I found my rooming house and spent my last night in London alone in my bed.

OB Team Number VI arrived at VII Corps Headquarters in February of 1944. The headquarters was located at Breamore, Hants, not far from the historic city of Salisbury. The VII Corps, originally activated in 1940 at Fort McClellan, Alabama, had preceded us to England by about a month. The Corps personnel had served together in different areas of the U.S. and on various maneuvers and formed a tightly knit group. Most of the men had developed a strong kinship for their unit. MIS teams could not yet aspire to such feelings and to our new fellow soldiers we were initially outsiders. However, the G-2 section received us, if not with open arms, at least with an open mind — willing to give us an unprejudiced opportunity to show them how we could support them in the forthcoming operations. For all practical purposes, on a working level if not on a social and intimately personal one, we were to become an accepted, integral part of the Corps.

The enlisted personnel were not housed in barracks, but in small individual cabins scattered throughout the English countryside. I shared a cottage with Brewer, an Austrian Jew, who made a good roommate and pleasant companion. Our manner and tastes were similar, and we made a very congenial twosome both at work and at play. We worked in the G-2 section, gathering OB data from reports sent by higher and adjacent headquarters, to bit-by-bit set up complete files on the German units we might some day face. Our tools were filing cards and the red *Order of Battle* book to which we made many corrections. Eventually we discarded the book as out-of-date and superseded it with our files. The latter were kept in a small folding field desk, a box-like filing cabinet with a front panel that could come down or be removed. It served us well throughout the war.

Brewer and I did most of the work, but the Lieutenant coordinated with the rest of the G-2 staff. The acting G-2 Commander was a Lieutenant Colonel, a wonderful person to work with. We were all hoping he would be put in charge when operations started in earnest. A little later, we were joined by Lieutenant Effrussi, a well-educated and polite individual, originally Swiss, who spoke German and French well. He had not been assigned to an OB team after graduating from the course, but remained a kind of supernumerary. Eventually, he acted as an OB aide and interpreter to Major General Collins, Commander of VII Corps, and we saw little of him. He seemed very appreciative of my European background, my fluency in French and German, and treated me more like an equal than an NCO.

In the beginning, it was my impression that the G-2 section was concerned with our security clearances. Some members of the team were foreigners or very recently naturalized U.S. citizens. I was the only one born in the U.S. Security was an important and touchy subject.

Brewer and I were free in the evening, had our meals together, took walks, and talked. Several times we took the bus to Salisbury to tour the old city and cathedral. On weekends, we often journeyed to Bournemouth, a lovely seaside resort, which I knew from my summer in nearby Chichester with the Chases. Bournemouth was known for the restored HMS *Victory*, Admiral Nelson's flagship in the war against Napoleon. We slept at the Red Cross for a nominal sum, went to the Sunday afternoon concerts to satisfy the music lover in Brewer, and walked around town. We kept to ourselves.

No one had any idea when or whether an invasion of France would take place. We kept a complete Order of Battle of German units, read classified reports, and kept ourselves otherwise busy. Toward the end of March 1944, the VII Corps held Exercise Beaver, but we played no role in it.

I was still having trouble with my pay. I saw a Second Lieutenant in the AG section. He claimed the foul-up was due to some statement I had made waiving my quarters allowance. This was ridiculous. Why would I waive $37.50? In an interview with the officer, I offered to make a sworn statement that I had never waived anything. He looked me straight in the eye and said, "You've been in the Army long enough, Sergeant, to know an enlisted man's word is not worth shit!"

I never forgot those words and, once again, the frustration of not being an officer welled up in me stronger than ever. I learned the address of the OSS in London and asked for a few days to see if I could obtain a commission from them. I told them about my qualifications and offered to volunteer for work behind enemy lines in exchange for a commission. The interviewer said OSS would be glad to have me, but direct commissions were no longer available. I gave up all hope of ever becoming a commissioned officer in the U.S. Army.

Until then our desk work was completed under comfortable conditions, no different from the clerical work we might have done as civilians in a cushy office at home. General Collins, who had had extensive battle experience in Guadalcanal, was concerned that we might not function as smoothly once we were on the battlefield. In the Service 18 months, I had, with rare exceptions (such as the Ritchie 48-hour exercise), never been exposed to extensive rigorous training and had been spared all field maneuvers. Many soldiers in the VII Corps had been on maneuvers while in the U.S., but the General thought it might be good for the sedentary headquarters staff to have some more field exposure before engaging in real warfare: he thought we should get off our butts before D-Day!

Thus, it was decided that all of us working in the headquarters staff sections would work for a few days outside. It is a sobering lesson to shuffle papers in the wind and the rain. A site was selected in the countryside. We moved all our gear into tents and were ordered to start digging foxholes. Very reluctantly, I picked up a spade and began shoveling dirt, not looking forward to spending the night outside in the cold, damp weather under a pup tent. Once again some guardian angel, as averse as I to the discomforts of field conditions, came miraculously to the rescue. I suppose, like all good guardian angels, he realized we were in it together. Where I went, he went, inside or outside! It started raining and judging from its somber looks, the sky did not allow for false hopes about a weather change. The Colonels and field grade officers, exposed like us to the inclemency of English weather patterns, quite logically concluded this dry run might get us soaked. The Chief of Staff made a quick decision testifying to his prudently practical leadership. To our well-dissimulated joy, the exercise was scrapped; we would be trusted to meet the challenges of the field valiantly and adequately, when called upon to do so, without any further preparation.

MIS, as always, vacillating about the final makeup of its teams in regard to rank, decided that OB teams could not afford two Master Sergeants. All other teams had only one. Consequently, one of the two enlisted slots was lowered to Staff Sergeant. Since Lieutenant Blazevicius did not wish to lose me, he allowed a very unhappy and bitter Brewer to be transferred out of our team. The replacement was Fred Singer, a good-humored Austrian Jew, recent immigrant to the U.S., who, of course, spoke perfect German, although of the delightful Austrian Johann Strauss variety, and had a strong accent in English. Regrettably but understandably, the VII Corps G-2, not targeting specifically Fred, but on general principles, did not wish to grant him full access to all the top-secret material. I felt sorry for Fred, understanding his wounded self-esteem and disappointment at such discrimination. I knew full well how I would have felt in his place. Regardless, Fred and I got along famously and we valued each other's abilities. I might add here that Fred's reliability proved to be of sterling quality. I could not have hoped for a better coworker.

The next crucial event was Exercise Tiger, which took place from April 26th to 29th, in an area known as Slapton Sands, near Paignton and Torquay. The true purpose of the exercise was kept as secret as possible, but any time three divisions — the 4th Infantry and the 82nd and 101st Airborne Divisions — are observed disembarking at the same time on the same beach, even a layman would recognize the dress rehearsal. Anybody can guess to what degree all of us were now gripped with the feverish anticipation of D-Day. We had more and more reason to be convinced it would occur, *but when and where?*

Never having focused before and at length on this aspect of the unit command structure, I personally began to deeply sense the fundamental distinction between the two staff functions, G-2 Intelligence and G-3 Operations, as they fused and culminated in the mind of the unit Commander, in this case Major General J. Lawton Collins. The G-2, of which I was a part, was the General's eyes and his ears with regard to the enemy's Order of Battle. We had to provide for him a mental picture, ultimately his knowledge, of the total enemy situation. We were not concerned with operations. The G-3 monitored the capabilities of our troops and advised the General on what was feasible in the way of operations. However, Collins had to combine both of these inputs and act accordingly with wisdom and efficiency. My role as an OB Sergeant was to produce as much pertinent and timely information as I could muster.

Suddenly, I found myself on my own. Effrussi took ill, and Lieutenant Blazevicius asked for some leave and then became ill himself. Both officers were away from headquarters. Thus, the entire responsibility for the OB participation in Exercise Tiger fell on my shoulders. But there was little to worry about, since I was well capable of doing the work myself and would have probably ended up doing so anyway. My role was naturally very limited and specific. I had to invent fictitious identities of imaginary enemy soldiers, with name, serial number, unit identification, and other details, and condense them into brief scripts. The latter were to be distributed to individual soldiers of the "invading" forces, who would after being "captured" by "enemy" troops, use them to reply to the questions put to them by PW interrogators. We could by this means monitor the flow, timeliness, and accuracy of PW interrogation Intelligence as it was channeled rearward. Singer helped me with the scripts, but did not accompany me to the exercise.

On the 23rd of April, I left for Torquay. Everything was hush-hush, security was airtight, everybody was told not to talk about anything military. I constantly wondered and feared whether other soldiers, possessing classified information, could be trusted to keep their mouths shut. I am certain it was a primary concern for higher headquarters. I was given lodging in an English building in Torquay together with other enlisted personnel, whose affiliation or purpose I did not know.

An officer, noting my rank of Master Sergeant, immediately made me acting First Sergeant of the building. I fervently hoped I could improvise adequately if ever called upon to actually perform the role — fortunately, the circumstance never arose. I took a walk around this quaint tourist town, looked at the shops, walked down to the beach, and found an isolated spot and took a short dip, my last one for a long time to come. The water was cold, with little trace of the alleged warming influence of the Gulf Stream. The civilian population of Torquay, as always friendly, had evidently not the slightest idea as to what all the American soldiers were doing in the area. My presence must have been known to someone at headquarters, for I was picked up on the 27th of April, the eve of the exercise, and taken to an empty house inland. I was told to spend the night there. As I usually sleep on my stomach, I had no problem adjusting to the conditions, found the right posture, adapted my hips to the hard floor, and rested reasonably well.

I have but a hazy recollection of what happened during the exercise. The next morning I thoroughly briefed a group of soldiers, who would play the role of PWs, about their scripts. I assured them I would keep track of their progress through the exercise. On April 28th and 29th, I was aware of a great deal of air activity and knew the three divisions were landing on the beaches, but I observed nothing directly. I remember asking a Lieutenant Colonel from VII why we were using the 4th Infantry Division, fresh out of Fort Dix, New Jersey, to spearhead this invasion and perhaps the real one later on. He replied quite chillingly, "Precisely because they are inexperienced. They'll storm inland, not knowing any better. The men of the 1st and 9th Infantry Divisions are seasoned troops. They've been in Africa and Sicily, they'll dig in and won't advance as readily and recklessly." For a while I pondered the logic and cruel rationale of his answer. Such detachment from the human consequences involved in military decisions does not come easily to all of us. I heard after D-Day that Major General R. O. Barton, Commanding General of the 4th Infantry, was heavily affected by the enormous losses inflicted on his men.

It turned out to be a very long day, like the one which, a month or so later, was to become known in history as "the longest day." There was not much for me to do. Eventually, I reached the beach where the PWs were to be eventually taken. I wandered around the headquarters of Colonel Eugene Caffey's 1st Engineer Shore Brigade, observing the beach cluttered with men and equipment. This brigade, also known as the 1st Engineer Special Brigade, just returned from Italy, was in control of the beach, and was responsible for making sure the landings took place as planned.

My prisoners arrived and I interviewed them. They were a sullen, complaining lot — tired, hungry, cold, and anxious to rejoin their units. I detected no enthusiasm among them about the part they had played in the exercise. I continued waiting on the cold beach, not really knowing what to do. I talked to some men and they said that, according to rumors, a few German E-boats — small, fast torpedo boats — had penetrated our formations at sea and managed to sink some of our ships. It sounded ominous, but I dismissed the news as something beyond my power and, indeed, alarming if true. Strange, how in battle, news that does not immediately affect one is swiftly put out of mind. I am sorry to say that, although generally most sympathetic to other people's misfortunes during the war, I quickly learned to adopt the selfish reaction: "Better you than me!" I and many others never knew until 45 years later, from reading about it, that 749 of our men died in the E-boat attack, were buried in a mass grave, and the whole affair kept secret for security reasons. That night, I never gave the rumor another thought.

My "prisoners" continued to complain bitterly. Finally, with the courage of one who does not plead for himself but for others, I asked to speak to Colonel Caffey. I was, of course, rebuffed. I had no idea at this time that Colonel Caffey had many more worries on his mind besides my prisoners. He must have known of the disaster, the loss of men, and the possibility of his being blamed for the loss. (He was at first held responsible, and

General Omar Bradley, unfairly and not fully informed of all the details behind the tragedy, is said to have thought of either relieving him or at least not using him and his Brigade on D-Day.)

Some time during the day I had also focused on the geographical location of Exercise Tiger, and I wondered where such a scenario could be duplicated in France. The only location that came to my mind was the Cherbourg or Cotentin Peninsula. I was almost hoping to be wrong in my guess, figuring that if I could think of it, so could the *Generalstab — the* German General staff.

The men never ceased complaining. I again asked to see Colonel Caffey and in the end, an aide, smiling good-naturedly at my persistence, took me to the Colonel. I emphasized that I was not asking for myself, but for the men in my care. He listened to me patiently and promised me prompt action if at all possible. Soon, indeed, a truck arrived on the scene and loaded my now more joyful prisoners for return to their units. Quite satisfied with the role I had played in helping them get off the beach, I waved them proudly good-bye. I felt I had done my best for the men under my care. It was the first time such an opportunity had presented itself since I had been promoted to Master Sergeant. With no other task ahead, I searched for a likely place to spend the night, then settled for a deep natural hollow in the sand where I managed to catch a few winks before dawn.

After Exercise Tiger I was ordered to join my officers in Falmouth, to the west of Paignton, and closer to Lands End, where I had spent the fabulous summer of 1932 with the Chases. On arrival, I was told I would be housed by the Naval units under the command of Admiral Don P. Moon. I was assigned a bunk in a Quonset hut, where I met a very disgruntled Fred Singer. Because of security clearance concerns, Fred was not permitted access to the huts where the VII Corps staff was now working. He felt like a pariah. I was issued a special pass and for the first time entered the highly classified area, where operation NEPTUNE BIGOT, as I came to know it, was being planned. The general public knows it as OVER-LORD.

Lieutenants Blazevicius and Effrussi greeted me most cordially and quite ceremoniously, then led me to a map covered with a cloth. They pulled back the cloth, informing me that this was where we would land on D-Day. I immediately recognized the Cherbourg Peninsula. *So I had guessed right after all!* All of a sudden I was in the know. It was right there on the map in front of my eyes. VII Corps was scheduled to land on Utah Beach supported by the 82nd and 101st Airborne Divisions, as well as the 4th, 9th, 79th, and 90th Infantry Divisions. I was pretty excited.

We were all fairly certain that D-Day would soon take place, probably in a month or so. Of course, no one knew exactly when. More than ever before, the secret of the exact location lay constantly and heavily on our minds as we went about our daily business. Especially in the evening, when, free on pass among English civilians, I had this strange feeling of pride and responsibility to be one of the privileged few to know. The outside world was still impatiently and skeptically wondering if there would ever be a D-Day. Inside the restricted area, the two Lieutenants and I continued updating our situation map and now extensive OB files on the basis of the highly classified reports that kept pouring in. The majority of German divisions on the Cherbourg Peninsula were on R and R according to our Intelligence, beaten down, almost decimated by, and now recuperating from the disastrous campaigns in Russia.

Every single NEPTUNE BIGOT document had to be strictly accounted for. This delicate task was now incumbent upon one person — the young, tousled, now very nervous AG Second Lieutenant, who had told me, in less socially acceptable terms, my word was worthless. We saw him now all day long, a sorrowful expression on his face, running around the sections, distributing, collecting, desperately trying to keep track of every scrap of paper inscribed NEPTUNE BIGOT. His nightmare ended some time after D-Day, when a truck from the Corps rear echelon loaded with this supersecret material sank and was lost forever on disembarking. From then on, every missing NEPTUNE BIGOT paper was declared to have been on that truck, contributing greatly to a much less harassed Lieutenant's peace of mind.

Outside the classified area, my lifestyle had considerably improved. The Navy carried its own food and was well fed. No substitutes for the U.S. fleet! For the first time since my arrival in England I again tasted fresh food: real eggs, steak twice a week, vegetables, pie à la mode. Why could I not have joined the Navy? Only twice a week did we have to stare at beans for breakfast and we were always free to skip them. The barracks was clean, the showers heavenly, the ambiance terrific, the Navy personnel friendly, including the Petty Officer who awakened us every morning with a resounding, "Rise and shine! Let go of your cocks and grab your socks!" While I was working in the classified area, Fred Singer was still twiddling his thumbs, free as a bird, but not for long.

Our team still was without the jeep we were entitled to. One morning I received orders and a requisition slip to pick up a new one in Bristol. I arrived by railroad and stood in front of the station, wondering where the motor pool might be. Someone told me and simultaneously called out to a man on a motorcycle. The man motioned for me to hop on the back seat and hold on tight. Off we went through the English countryside to a giant American depot and motor pool. I signed for the jeep and decided to set a record driving back to Falmouth. My officers were delighted to see me back so soon.

The nasty, dirty task of waterproofing our jeep went to poor Fred Singer. He did a good job, under the supervision of our motor pool mechanics, waterproofing the bottom of the jeep and extending the exhaust pipe way up to the sky. Every late afternoon for a week, I saw him in his fatigues, sweaty, filthy from the waterproofing compound, not exactly the picture of a debonair Intelligence specialist. It was a greasy job, and it took him days to complete it. As it turned out, he did a good job, as we found out on D-Day.

In the very beginning of June, the fateful day arrived. We were told we would be leaving Falmouth the next morning in a convoy to somewhere in the east of England. We were encouraged to go out on pass that same evening to prevent civilians from suspecting anything. I went to a dance, organized by the British for American servicemen, as usual hoping no one would let out the word of our early departure. I watched the dancers and finally, rather shyly, asked a young British woman, with a large blotchy red birthmark across her face, for a dance. I felt sorry for her as no one was dancing with her. She was a nice, quiet girl and she asked me to accompany her home, introduced me to her family, and we chatted. She gave me her name and address, expressing the wish to see me again. I had to lie and promised I would call on her. I wrote her from France later, explaining we had left the next day. She replied, hinting in her letter that, had she known about my leaving, she would have made sure we had more privacy in her home. I could only guess as to what she meant, but it sounded belatedly intriguing and seductive.

We traveled in convoy to, I believe, Southampton. I was not really paying much attention, merely driving behind the vehicles in front of me, with Singer as my passenger. The two Lieutenants were traveling separately with the G-2 section staff. My jeep was loaded on an LST (Landing Ship, Tank) and, as instructed, I made certain to note, in order to ensure future smooth disembarkation, the exact location and numerical designation of the deck and the spot where the jeep was stored. Then Fred and I boarded the ship with hundreds of other GIs, reasonably sure D-Day was about to dawn with us very much a part of it.

Pray to God and flail away with your mallet.
— Spanish Proverb

Chapter 13

D-Day and the
Invasion of Normandy

T DAWN ON JUNE 6, 1944, our ship was lying at anchor with a great many other vessels on both sides, all parallel to each other with bows facing Utah Beach. It was for me like being on an excursion to a quite familiar place (although I had never been in that particular spot before). I felt as though I was returning to one of my previous homes. There was nothing to worry about, the more so as there was no German air activity whatsoever. What a relief! We had dozed off during the night wherever we could make ourselves comfortable. The ship was packed with troops, milling about on deck, looking at the shore, wondering, *When do we disembark? What happens next?*

I roamed around on deck and, opening a door at random, noticed a shower. Who knew how long it would be before I could indulge in showering again. I did not realize that once on land, after things got settled, we would have a mobile shower arrangement at Corps Headquarters, with a water tank, heater, and a pipe equipped with shower heads, and would be expected to stay clean and shave every day. Whenever possible, such discipline and cleanliness must be enforced, even under combat conditions, to avoid a breakdown of morale, the complete disintegration of civilized habits, and of course, subjecting your buddies to olfactory stress beyond that of battle.

The shower had been taken just in time. Shortly afterward a member of the crew locked the door to the shower, as well as all others leading to and from the deck, I suppose to keep track of all on board. It was unusually peaceful for such a crucial, long-awaited day. Under these circumstances I do not understand why anyone would be afraid. I seek reassurance, if necessary at times like these, by telling myself, "You've got lots of company!" I noticed a soldier opening a large case of rations, picking out some of the cigarettes, and heaving the rest of it, food and all, overboard — a shocking reminder of the wealth of supplies we could boast of and waste. If the Germans could have seen him chuck his food, I thought to myself, they would probably surrender, convinced at least of our material superiority. As we soon found out, the Germans were suffering shortages of everything: food, gasoline, and in some cases, morale.

Suddenly, the quiet was disrupted by two lone German planes flying north fairly low toward us. All ships were facing west. The planes dropped a bomb or two that missed the ship immediately to the south of us. They kept flying over our ship, as we all watched with keen interest, some anxiety, and disbelief to see them alone. Another bomb dropped. It missed our ship and the one immediately to the north. The next time the planes scored. The bomb landed on the second ship to the north of us, and the hit vessel started burning and sinking. That was as close as the action got to me all day. I really felt pretty lucky. The details of rescue operations, if there were any, were not visible, since there was another ship blocking my view.

We were all wearing impregnated fatigues and carrying gas masks. It was, in my opinion, a highly unnecessary measure, as I repeatedly told my officers during the next few weeks. The Germans would not dare use gas against us because they did not enjoy air superiority. It took the higher command a long time to see things logically and excuse us from carrying the cumbersome masks.

Finally, the crew started unloading equipment and personnel on a continuing basis. After a few hours it was our turn. Our jeep was hoisted from the ship's hold and gingerly deposited by the crane unto a small landing craft. The trick was to get smoothly off the landing craft into the surf, gun the engine so as — God forbid — not to stall in the water. I hit the gas pedal, the motor roared, but nothing happened. "Shit!" Then I remembered the handbrake and off we went into three feet of water. We didn't even get very wet. It had all been so simple. It proves there is no point in worrying ahead of time.

Once on land, it was almost like disembarking off any car ferry. MPs were directing traffic. Hastily put-up traffic signs indicated the direction to follow to various units. The general mood was exhilarating. Of course, we were not landing at H-hour, facing resistance and death. I followed the signs for VII Corps Headquarters. The tents were already up and both Lieutenants were waiting for us at the G-2 tent where field desks were set up and maps installed. (They had landed earlier with the G-2 staff.)

We were all hoping that the Lieutenant Colonel and acting G-2 would take charge of the unit. However, during the very last days of planning in Falmouth, a new G-2 for VII Corps had arrived from Washington, D.C. He was a Colonel King, a West Pointer, and we were all disappointed. Colonel King was certainly not the kind of officer we expected. Although a full eagle or "bird" Colonel, he was somewhat casual, suave, detached, not the decisive and imposing personality expected in this position. Colonel King in some ways did not seem to take charge. He was very easygoing, more like a debonair gentleman one might meet at a cocktail party. It was almost as if he had said, like some remote observer, "Don't mind me! Do your thing! I'll just watch." Yet behind this was a certain stubbornness, a spoiled-child streak, as though he was accustomed to having his way.

Early in the operation, we were all concentrating on prioritizing, trying to get a handle on the job, and developing a *modus operandi* for the future. We were located in the middle of the Normandy hedgerow country with some forested areas here and there, a terrain easy for the enemy to defend, difficult and costly for us to take. Ste. Mère Eglise was not too far away, and about 30 miles separated us from Cherbourg, our target. We needed to capture the major port so that our ships could land there, instead of on beaches, to adequately supply our troops during the rest of the war. Our airborne troops, as well as the 4th and 9th Infantry Divisions, had landed before us. The plan was to cut through and isolate the Cotentin Peninsula, making escape from Cherbourg impossible for the Germans, then advance north and liberate the port.

A large number of Germans had already been captured, and we had a mass of soiled enemy documents to study. I scanned, as fast as possible, the various pay books (*Soldbücher*), personnel files, maps, whatever was being carted back to the G-2 section, in the hope of finding valuable information that might save lives. It was like sifting through trash, but it was no time to be finicky. A few times I was lucky and discovered maps and sketches of minefields drawn up by German engineers. I hastily translated any vital language on such documents so that our operations personnel could understand them. In a few cases, maps of minefields were discovered in time to save lives and facilitate our advance. I had a strange feeling rummaging through some personal items, such as the pay books — with pictures of wives and children, torn, dirty — some stained with blood. The soldiers they had belonged to — many now prisoners or dead — were like us, away from their families and had the same emotions, fears, and joys. But they were on the opposite side and not always by choice. I found wallets, paper money, coins, an enormous number of photographs and correspondences, as well as military records and documents, company rosters, and such.

Over time, we developed procedures that were to prove valid and productive for the rest of the war and which eventually became exasperatingly monotonous and trying. Naturally, such procedures had to be adapted to whatever field conditions prevailed, reaching their optimum stage when the headquarters was not constantly on the move, but could function in one location quietly for more than a day.

We received G-2 reports from units above, below, and adjacent to us, primarily from Twelfth Army Group, First Army, adjacent corps such as V, VIII, and XIX Corps, and all the divisions under us. I had about as good a picture of operations as one can have, much better than the poor doughboy in the front lines.

We constantly received PW interrogation reports from lower units. These were raw, unedited, and unevaluated, as gleaned from captured enemy soldiers. Knowing the German Order of Battle by heart, we were in a better position to evaluate the raw data, incorporating what was reliable and deemed by us consistent with our OB files, and rejecting the rest. It was like fitting missing pieces of a puzzle into the entire picture when one has a general idea of the latter.

We worked closely with the G-2 staff, making sure that all our information was coordinated each night with the G-2 report, estimates of the situation, and other such documents. Lieutenant Blazevicius left much of that work to us. He was very good at drawing maps and overlays. He spent hours fiddling with a large situation map, painstakingly transferring all the Intelligence Fred and I collected onto it, so that there was a fairly complete graphic picture of the enemy facing us. General Collins, most probably more a man of action than of contemplation, then sent for the map and could at a glance, without reading the detailed reports, acquire a good idea of the enemy situation. In this manner our team truly functioned as one, and everyone on it contributed to the production of good, German Order-of-Battle Intelligence. As time progressed and the Corps advanced more slowly, Lieutenant Blazevicius spent hours on that map, tracing, retracing, erasing, making the subtlest of changes on the overlay, as though he was copying a Rembrandt. I still see him now, grease marker in one hand, a rag in the other, in front of the map, taking a step back to look at his masterpiece, approaching it again to change something, his tongue protruding between his teeth, lost to the world around him, enthralled. Maybe he never looked at another map after it was all over!

Discipline, order, and personal hygiene were never relaxed. Naturally we were not in the front trenches, but reasonably close to the front and constantly exposed to enemy artillery fire or sporadic strafing by German planes. On rare occasions, in Northern France and Belgium, we were moving so fast that Corps Headquarters was set up for a day or two ahead of the divisions under our command. We, of course, had a rear echelon comprising all support sections of VII Corps, such as Adjutant General, Quartermaster, Medical team, and others. They followed far behind us. The order came out to shave every day, which we did by pouring water into our helmets and shaving in the open air. Most of the time, if around headquarters, we wore only the helmet liners. The helmet itself, if turned around, made a wonderful stool.

The first night, some of us wanted to sleep inside the G-2 tents, but an order was issued forbidding it, a security measure in case we were bombed or strafed by *Luftwaffe* planes. We were told to dig foxholes. Now physical exertion, in my book, was a no-no. I looked for a nice ditch near a hedgerow and spent the night in the hollow, a very natural and painless way to bypass the unthinkable exertion of digging a hole on your own time. At night, lying in my ditch, I often had a recurring, very disturbing thought, especially when I heard enemy planes flying over us with their rat-tat-tat machine-gun fire. I visualized the bullets drawing a dotted line across my body. I thought it was a funny, if morbid, idea. Once the Germans strafed our position and most of our motor pool. The next morning, I inspected the damage. Sure enough, our trailer had a few holes, as well as my barracks bag. I took out my olive drab dress shirts; both of them had bullet holes right in the middle of the front. Invisible mending was not immediately available!

As an enlisted man I was not issued a sleeping bag, merely a blanket. After a few days in France, I took a walk in the forest and looked for one of the 82nd or 101st Airborne gliders that had come in before D-Day and crashed into tree tops. Each one was equipped with an inflatable boat in case of engine failure over water. I soon found one, hauled out the rubber boat, and cut a large square piece from it. It was not a neat job, but served my purpose. I then tied the rubber material together with string to form a bag. Inside of it I spread my blanket. Every night, I crawled inside the blanket, which in turn was inside the rubber shell. The contraption kept me dry and warm in the ditches of Normandy. The Lord helps those who help themselves.

For someone who had never been a Boy Scout, I made up for it — adjusting to life *alfresco*. The engineers dug latrines, not sufficiently inviting to encourage lingering any longer than necessary. We were issued pills as anti-pollutants for the drinking water. (Having grown up in Europe, I did not harbor the innate American fear of drinking water abroad.) We were to be on K-rations for not more than 30 days. However, so many prisoners had a higher meal priority than we had that we ended up on a diet of the unpopular boxes for about 90 days. I suppose SHAEF in London, while its officers dined in good restaurants, endeavored to act the gracious host and give our guests the best. *Está en su casa* — my home is your home, as they say in Spain. We had to be content with the cans of concentrated ham and eggs, pork, and other types of pasty — not tasty — lunch meat, a bar of chocolate hard enough to break one's teeth, crackers, a tiny pack of cigarettes (I gave mine away), and powdered lemonade, the memory of which I have unsuccessfully tried to ban forever from my mind. Eating this stuff for days on end, three packs a day, was like scouring out one's intestines with a strong detergent. It made worrying about being irregular in bathroom habits totally unnecessary.

Colonel King must also have felt relaxed, perhaps even bored, after a few days. He did not appear to be too concerned with the details of daily G-2 routine. He surprised us all by announcing he was going to forage around on the front lines with four other officers, hoping to run across wartime souvenirs such as German Lugers and parade daggers. Actually, hearing this, I thought he was out of his mind. We tried to dissuade him, but he persisted. One cannot tell a Colonel what not to do. He organized a little hunting party, took off with his brother-in-law, a Lieutenant Colonel in the VII Corps MP detachment, and three other officers. We did not hear from him for six or seven hours and feared the worst. The tension grew by the hour. After all, it was not just King, but four other officers he had talked into this tomfoolery. At dawn we received the bad news. The five officers had blundered straight into machine-gun fire from German positions set up behind hedges. Colonel King had been killed and was later buried in the cemetery at Ste. Mère Eglise. The other four were more or less seriously wounded. VII Corps was minus a G-2, a victim of his own reckless stupidity.

Years later, in 1955, having been recalled during the Korean conflict, I was assigned to a special two-man detachment of the Assistant Chief of Staff for Intelligence in Washington. Lieutenant Colonel Reitz and I represented the interests of the Department of the Army in CIA (Central Intelligence Agency) defector interrogations. Operating in and near Frankfurt, I was further attached to the Military Intelligence Group, also known as Camp King. On arrival in the area, I followed Army protocol and went to introduce myself to the CO of the Camp and pay my compliments. I was waiting outside the Colonel's office and spotted a portrait with a familiar-looking face. I walked up to it and read the inscription. I do not recall the exact words, but it was in memory of Colonel King and his "heroic" death in Normandy. I was stunned. I had always known about Camp King, visited it before, but never associated its name with our short-timer G-2.

Within a day of Colonel King's death, we had a new G-2. Colonel Leslie D. Carter, a Virginia Military Institute graduate, was a model officer and gentleman. A former Cavalry officer, short, and tough, he immediately established himself as a leader. He was a hard worker, always at his desk, expecting the best from himself and those under him. He was fair, sharp, loyal to those he commanded — feared in a sense — but human underneath it all. One might on rare occasions see a twinkle in his eye, but overall he was a no-nonsense individual. I gave him the utmost respect to the end of the five campaigns and never served a better officer. After his arrival, the entire G-2 staff worked as a team. I really believe we produced good Intelligence, which helped General Collins and Operations in their tasks.

At this time, our troops were advancing slowly but steadily. Tired of a diet consisting exclusively of colon-cleansing K-rations, I ventured away from headquarters in the jeep on one or two occasions, looking for something to eat. Normandy is apple country as well as a region of cautious peasants known for thinking like lawyers and never giving a straight answer. Ask a Norman how the apple harvest turned out and he will reply, *"Pour une année où y'a des pommes, y'a pas d'pommes. Pour une année où y'a pas d'pommes, y'a des pommes"* — "For a year when the apple harvest is good, there are no apples. For a year when it's bad, there are apples." The perfect reply in a court of law! Lieutenant Blazevicius, hoping I could find him some of the renowned Norman firewater, asked me to look for the very potent, almost 100 proof *calvados*, a clear cognac made by distilling cider. While I was at it, I looked for other goodies: plain cider or anything else edible, in that precise order of priority. I was the right man for the job, but my priorities were the reverse of his. Food was first on my list.

I had no trouble locating some monasteries, where I was able to trade cigarettes for French Port-Salut cheese, fresh bread, cider, and *calvados* — all produced by the monks. I disliked the bitter Norman cider and instead, for myself, took nonfermented apple juice. The monks were delighted to trade. In a way, like all Norman farmers, they were worried about their ability to sell their products. The Germans had always bought their entire harvest. Now the war was interfering with the Norman economy. More than anything else, they wanted to be sure our invasion would not prove an obstacle to their prosperous trading. Ridding them of the Nazis was commendable, but it must not be done at their expense.

A few weeks later, SHAEF, in a completely misguided attempt to do the right thing, committed a grave error. Eisenhower's Headquarters issued an order forbidding, under penalty of court-martial, all purchases by our troops of Norman food products. We were not to deprive them of their food. All the farmers I talked to were in alarm over this — in their opinion — stupid measure. They all wanted to sell whatever they had and reap the benefit of their harvest. They faced a trying quandary. Which was better: liberation from the hated Germans or being deprived of making a living? However, had anyone posed the question, the Normans would never have given a straight reply.

As we neared Cherbourg, around June 24th, I was asked to draft surrender terms for the German garrison in both German and French. I carefully composed the two documents. I was then ordered to broadcast them in both languages at 20-minute intervals from a radio truck. I was the only one at VII Corps able to speak both German and French with a native accent. That night, together with Signal Corps personnel, I advanced in the dark to the front lines and broadcast the surrender conditions all night long. The Germans never replied, still it was an exciting effort which, had it been successful, would have made me very proud. Even trying for a surrender was a thrill. The next two or three days our troops continued their assault on Cherbourg. The last resistance was eliminated, a mere three weeks after we had landed on Utah Beach. My officers decided I should drive into Cherbourg, while the fighting was still in progress, and look for German documents.

My motto was usually not to volunteer for a mission, but if ordered to do something to go ahead without hesitation. My mission was to enter, if possible, the Fort du Roule, a fortification protecting the city and its harbor, and look around for anything of interest to us. Upon my arrival in the immediate outskirts of the city, I found sporadic fighting still taking place. I drove around and asked for directions. I came upon a German antiaircraft position, which had been silenced by our artillery and presented an unusual, gruesome sight. The entire German crew was dead, but looked very much alive, each body as though preserved in motion. The blast that killed them must have done so instantaneously; every German was in a different position — crouching, squatting, kneeling near the weapon, like figures in a wax museum. It was my first confrontation with sudden death and strangely enough I was not very much affected by it. It looked rather like a staged mime presentation.

As I drove on, a German in uniform, evidently fearful for his life, begged me to take him prisoner. He was running around confused, looking for someone to talk to, afraid of being shot, and most anxious to surrender. Our men had not noticed him in the confusion. Seeing he was unarmed, I ordered him to the back seat of the jeep and took him to a PW collecting point. Credit for the capture went to OB team number VI.

I finally found the hilltop Fort du Roule and entered it from below. It was like arriving into a huge cave-like warehouse dug into the hill from the bottom. There was no trace of any documents, but a large quantity of canned goods was found. I saw many cans of Portuguese sardines preserved in olive oil. My heart jumped — they are one of my favorite *hors d'oeuvres*. A second glance, unfortunately, convinced me that every single can was bulging, the contents inedible. The constant artillery blasts must have caused the damage. I was bitterly disappointed, fondling the bulging cans in my hands, hoping to find some intact. There was none. However, I discovered a multitude of canned German *Schwarzbrot*, the tasty German black rye bread, which I loaded on my jeep and with which our team supplemented its meals for weeks. Then I headed back to Corps. On the return trip, some stray bullets punctured both my rear tires, but not me. The motor pool took care of the repairs.

All German resistance in the Cherbourg Peninsula was over by July 1, 1944, and VII Corps with its various divisions (4th, 9th, 83rd, 30th, 1st Infantry and 2nd and 3rd Armored) prepared for the drive south. We initiated OPERATION COBRA to break out of the peninsula and start the advance to the east and across France. The Germans resisted fiercely in the Coutances and St. Lô areas. In the meantime, I received some good news! First of all, my payroll mess was finally straightened out. I received a large sum of money and only remember sending a money order for all of it to my wife. I really had no use for any of it in combat; besides, every once in a while, we found some bank notes with the German documents and personal papers that reached us (although more and more of it was being intercepted by teams attached to lower units).

The other good news item came as a complete surprise. The Army discovered in those early days of combat that many officers had been put in charge of Intelligence teams mainly because they were commissioned officers, not because they were particularly suited for the task. They did not always possess the ideal qualifications and did not provide the right leadership for the specialized work we were doing. Generally, the Army wants its officers to be jacks-of-all-trades. However, there are times when one individual, either because of inclination, inborn talent, or even training, will prove inadequate for a particular job. He might be terrific at storming pillboxes or driving an armored car, but be very poor at interpreting aerial photographs or translating enemy documents. There is nothing for him to be ashamed of; it is merely good policy not to force a square peg into a round hole.

Having become aware of this during the planning of the invasion and initial operations, SHAEF Headquarters issued a directive requesting qualified senior officers to recommend soldiers for battlefield commissions. NCOs who had distinguished themselves in specialized Intelligence work would become Second Lieutenants. Our Lieutenant Blazevicius and Lieutenant Effrussi, with the approval of Colonel Carter, urged me to fill out the necessary papers. Colonel Carter was willing to recommend me. I was, of course, elated. Later, during a lull in battle when we were near Avranches, the two Lieutenants with Singer took a sightseeing trip to Mont St. Michel, the delightful unique monastery-fortress off the Normandy shore. I stayed at headquarters in case the General needed something and filled out a long application with data mainly required for a security clearance. The Army loves paperwork, and I had to try and remember my many addresses for the past ten years, as well as all my educational and job background data: no small task!

On July 25th, two days before my birthday, the IX Tactical Air Command (we referred to it as the 9th Air Force) flew 9,000 sorties during a very short time. It was a scenario, the impression of which I shall never forget. Three-thousand aircraft took part in this saturation bombing, about 1,800 heavy bombers, 400 medium bombers, and the rest fighter planes. The targeted area was only five miles wide and two miles deep, south of the St. Lô-Périers highway. It was close to our lines and purported to hit German positions, facilitating an eventual St. Lô breakthrough. We were all told to leave the huts and farm buildings where we had set up shop and to stay outside close to the ground. A tremendous deafening roar filled the air as this sky armada delivered its load very close to us. The earth trembled with the shock. The noise was unbelievably earsplitting. It went on and on for two hours or more, sortie after sortie, explosion after explosion.

I thought it would never end as I tried to shut out the noise by holding my hands to my ears. We were convinced the German positions in front of us had been pulverized. Apparently it did not turn that way. Some of our troops, being too close to the target area, were hit by mistake. It was also rumored that the Germans got wind of the intended raid ahead of time and in an incredibly daring move, squeezed right up close to our front line, coming out of it allegedly unscathed, but no doubt groggy. The result was that we bombed much empty terrain. In the end, the drive succeeded. We fought ourselves out of the dangerous hedgerow country and in one mighty push advanced more than 30 miles, enabling the VIII Corps to advance west into Brittany and Patton's Third Army to enter the fray. It was a good way to celebrate my birthday. We were free of the Cotentin Peninsula and ready to drive east across France.

VII Corps Headquarters set up shop in abandoned farm buildings and houses instead of tents. It saved time and effort and offered more protection in inclement weather. Fred and I usually found ourselves a comfortable and sheltered place to spend the night, like a barn or house. I recall the first time we literally hit the soft hay in a barn after working, as usual, until the early morning hours.

The nights were the busiest part of the day. The reports had to go out and we often worked through the night. I have forgotten much of the details of what occurred as we raced across France. A few incidents worth relating stand out nevertheless.

One morning, Lieutenant Effrussi, who was now spending all of his time accompanying Major General Collins as interpreter, asked me to drive with him on a special mission. The OSS had apparently established contact with members of the French *Maquis* who might provide us with worthwhile Intelligence data.

During battles, a great number of cattle were being killed. The farmers could not always immediately remove the animals, which lay in the fields rotting and exuding the unmistakable sweet odor peculiar to dead carcasses. I am not always too good at remembering landmarks. Since I was driving, I wanted to make sure I would find my way back to VII Corps at night on strange country roads. (It would not be wise to miss a turn and end up in enemy territory.) Therefore, every time there was a change of direction, I made a mental note of it, and if there were some sweet-smelling dead cattle near a particular curve or fork in the road, I took extra notice of that too. It would be for me one more reference point to look for, that is smell for, in the dark. Actually, in this particular case, the odor proved very helpful when we came back in the darkest of nights. It alerted me to the final crucial intersection and the road back to our unit.

I had no idea what to expect, wondering what my first encounter with the famous OSS cloak-and-dagger agents would be like. Quite a surprise was in store for us. Lieutenant Effrussi and I found the village far to the rear of our troops where we were to meet the OSS representatives. (The cloak-and-dagger boys were indeed operating behind the lines, but not those of the enemy.) They had a real eye for real estate. They had taken over a magnificent property with a gorgeous garden; it was like an elegant villa. The Lieutenant and I had been in the field for about two months and did not exactly look like fashion plates. We wore our crumpled impregnated fatigues, combat boots, and helmets. The men that received us with evident distaste for and visible annoyance at our unannounced casual appearance blended admirably with their lovely surroundings. I could not believe my eyes and felt like a hobo crashing a party.

The OSS people all wore officers' insignia. From head to toe, they were immaculate in their perfectly pressed uniforms: green blouses, pinks, clean starched shirts, ties, and meticulously shined shoes. How did they get to there from England in this crisply unblemished state? They must have been delicately deposited by magic carpet and in cellophane wrappers. The setting was also charming and pastoral. A large table had been set outdoors, with tablecloth, china, and silverware. There was wine on the table. Servants were busily running back and forth from the main house, obviously preparing to serve an elaborate lunch. Our arrival was evidently ill-timed.

I deferred to Lieutenant Effrussi for the social introductions and niceties. He explained our mission and the fact that it had been cleared between Major General Collins and the OSS. That did not make much of an impression. The officers, each one with a drink in his hand, had been engaged in gay banter as we arrived, and told us with inconceivable arrogance, contempt, and lack of graciousness to wait somewhere in the garden until their Epicurean repast was terminated. No one even threw us a bone. As a Sergeant, I could understand being left out. However, I could not imagine the affront to the Lieutenant, a representative of the Corps Commander. He, although as always polite and outwardly calm, must have been seething with rage. We both withdrew out of sight, nibbled at our K-rations, and drank from our canteens.

The lunch lasted a very long time. Finally, an OSS officer told us we could speak with the two Free French, both young men who had come through the German lines. He warned us we would not obtain too much information. Our presence was definitely not welcome. Lieutenant Effrussi thought I should handle the interrogation, while he would observe, since they might even take me for French and be less reluctant to talk. I briefly introduced myself, as I still often do in France, with a white lie, claiming to be French and living in the USA. I immediately noticed that they were

somewhat embarrassed about not providing information. Finally, in openly frank language, I blurted out something like, "What is the problem?
Why don't you talk? We're on the same side, fighting the Germans!"
Again embarrassed hesitation. I pressed on. Then it all came out: "We
were told not to give you any information."

We were nonplussed; the Lieutenant outraged. "General Collins will
hear about this!"

Many years later, from 1956-1958, while serving as a Soviet case officer in the CIA, I constantly ran into this kind of secretiveness among
allies. We had an inter-agency defector interrogation project run by the
CIA with Navy, Army, Air Force, and State Department participation. We
all were supposed to share the information provided by defectors, but my
implied orders always were to see to it that CIA received the lion's share
of everything — Intelligence and credit — if necessary at the exclusion of
the other agencies.

We terminated our interview, which did not yield too many valuable
Order of Battle data. I tried not to judge the OSS by this unfortunate incident, assuming that under other circumstances they may have rendered
valuable service to our country. Lieutenant Effrussi reported the story to
the General, and the latter made certain that the OSS *prima donnas* would
henceforth no longer operate in our Corps sector. I still have before my
eyes a vivid image of the scene: the exquisite luncheon for the impec-
cably dressed, with Effrussi and me slinking off in the bushes to eat
K-rations — straight from *"Les Misérables."*

It is a fact that in a war, while many fight and die unselfishly, others go
through it unscathed or even profit from it — exploiting it like some game.
I certainly do not belong to the second category. I am grateful to my guardian angels for protecting me and taking few breaks while on the job. I can
truthfully say that I did my utmost to serve my country in whatever capacity it thought I could do some good, given my training and qualifications.
I never shirked any assignment. I tried to live up to the expectations of my
superiors and was ready to assume any risk. Still I did not volunteer for
reckless missions. For instance, I had fully expected to serve in the 101st
Airborne, but of course, did not turn down the opportunity to go to VII
Corps. I merely assumed it was meant to be. I did not take advantage of

wartime situations to commit acts that would have been reprehensible, if not criminal, in civilian life. Not everyone was that scrupulous.

The VII Corps, besides our OB team, also had IPW (Interrogation of Prisoner of War), PI (Photo Interpretors), and MII (Military Intelligence Interpreter) teams. The first two were busy interrogating PWs at Corps level and studying aerial photographs in the G-2 section, respectively. The French Military Intelligence Interpreter team had essentially nothing to do and made certain never to deviate from this *dolce far niente* — sweet idleness. As a matter of fact, after the war a *Story of VII Corps — Mission Accomplished* was sent to all of us who had been part of this tour, arranged for by the Army with the cooperation of Adolf Hitler, through Normandy, Northern France, Ardennes, Rhineland, and Central Europe. It was a nice gesture on the part of a grateful General Collins, who became a Lieutenant General, and reminded me of those souvenir brochures travel agencies send their clients after a package tour. Amongst other data it listed all units ever attached to VII Corps. The 419th French MII team was mistakenly included with the German Interrogation teams, rightly demonstrating how fuzzily its heroic and valuable contribution was remembered.

The members of this team, of whom I only recall three, were a picaresque lot. The CO had worked in some capacity or other at Hector's cafeteria on New York's Times Square and found his niche in the Army. He knew French, being of French or Canadian origin (he was cagey about giving out information), had been commissioned in the Infantry, and really looked the part: neat, snappy, with a trim warrior's mustache. Beyond that his main skill was forever to avoid the G-2 section as though it were a minefield and to successfully dodge work at all times. I had known one of the Sergeants under him as a student in the French Department of New York University. He was Polish and went by the nickname of "Lunch Meat" because he was constantly snacking. The other Sergeant, Jorge, was of Hispanic descent, a somber individual of volatile moods. I stayed clear of them, which was easy, since they were conspicuous by their absence. If there was any need whatsoever for French, I was always called in to do the honors.

When the MIS planned the various MI teams, it thought that besides the need for Order of Battle, PW Interrogation, and Photo Interpretation, French interpreters would be required for liaison between American troops and the French population. The occasion for such use never arose, at least not in VII Corps. Perhaps, knowing that once we entered Germany, they would automatically be out of work (unless they planned to tutor the German population in French), our French MI team may have thought it wise not to get too busy on French territory so that the transition to legitimate idleness in Germany would not prove too traumatic and disruptive to their lifestyle. In any event, while we all worked hard at Corps Headquarters, the French team, ably led by the spick-and-span Lieutenant, was roaming the countryside in search of worthwhile, personally satisfying collection efforts — making use of their knowledge of French.

Once they went too far in their acquisitive zeal. The team "liberated" a magnificent German Maybach limousine and then used it as a primary means of transportation in lieu of their less impressive jeep. Had they used it off-duty, they might have gotten away with this conspicuous show of new wealth. However, General Collins caught a glimpse of this splendid example of German automotive craftsmanship, as the French team proudly, if unwisely, drove it around the Corps Headquarters area. Men in authority usually do not like to be outdone by those below them. Besides General Collins was not in the mood for a classic car show. He called in the red-faced Lieutenant. Outwardly snappy as ever, the latter was at a loss for a satisfactory explanation. He never thought of claiming that all along he intended it as a gift to Collins.

Interestingly enough, after I received my battlefield commission, I became supernumerary on the VI OB team. There was no slot for a Second Lieutenant in Order of Battle. First Army was about to reassign me to an IPW team at regimental level. An irate Colonel Carter called First Army, bellowing into the phone in his very persuasive manner, "I don't commission my Sergeants to lose them! Work out something!" I was assigned to the 419 MII team, which had a vacant slot for a second officer, but never ceased working in OB for Carter. After the automobile incident, the MII team made itself even scarcer than before, proving at least its members had the stealth to remain permanently underground. They could at least boast of one working member — me — on detached assignment with the OB unit.

My commission did not go through for months, a delay I found difficult to live with. I must have been hard on Lieutenant Blazevicius and Sergeant Singer with my impatience and disappointment. Much later, through an officer of an IPW team assigned to us long after D-Day — Second Lieutenant Helmut Strauss, I learned the real cause of the delay.

When Ritchie had heard that SHAEF wanted field recommendations for promoting noncoms to Lieutenant, Ritchie as usual did the inconceivable. A group of over a hundred new recruits were lined up, mostly Privates, some without basic training, proficient in German, and given direct commissions. This was not exactly the method for remedying the shortage of good Intelligence officers that SHAEF had had in mind.

Second Lieutenant Strauss had been one of them. This put a screeching stop to our battlefield appointments, as SHAEF feared a glut of new Intelligence officers. Eventually the consequences of this irrational act by Ritchie were ironed out, and I belatedly received my commission on November 22, 1944.

Despite Eisenhower's edict against buying food or drink from the local population, my two officers urged me to go foraging again. Bowing to their wishes, albeit reluctantly, I found a farm which was doing a great business despite the prohibition and bought *calvados* and cheese. I was not alone. Four officers, one a major, from other units were doing the same. No sooner had we terminated our shopping than we were surrounded and trapped by MPs, who cordially invited us to follow them. I was scared stiff. They led us to some tent where, they said, we would all undergo a summary court-martial. In the Army, rank always comes before beauty. The Major disappeared first in the tent. In an act of sheer desperation I turned to the MP Sergeant, telling him I had been ordered by my CO to buy food and that a court-martial would sink all my chances for my pending battlefield commission. Perhaps my stripes stirred a vague instinct of tribal cohesion and compassion in his soul. He looked around quickly, then whispered to me, "Go! Get lost!" I never obeyed an order faster or more gratefully. My officers were duly informed by me that henceforth I was out of the shopping service business.

The German troops were fleeing east across France with us close behind. Many of us were convinced that had SHAEF been willing to give the available gasoline to General Patton instead of the 9th Air Force, his Third Army could have cut off the retreating Germans and forced a surrender, perhaps ending the war much sooner. I think the Germans, when driven into a pocket, would have found a logical justification for surrendering.

During that period, a friend of mine from Ritchie, OB Sergeant Bailey, came to visit us from his division headquarters. He told me that during the Germans' hasty flight he had become disoriented and separated from his unit. In the distance in front of him he glimpsed some fleeing trucks. Convinced they belonged to his outfit, he raced after them in his jeep. As he drew near, the soldiers standing in the rear of the last truck began frantically waving him back. Bailey looked more closely. They were Germans fleeing before him. He jammed on the brakes, made a U turn, and took off in the opposite direction.

The Germans abandoned Paris and did not attempt to defend it. For diplomatic reasons and to please De Gaulle, SHAEF ordered American generals to allow the French to enter the "City of Light" first. The honor went to French General Leclerc and his 1st Armored Division. Leclerc marched triumphantly into Paris to the jubilant cheers of the population. At that time our VII Corps was at Chartres. Somehow, Lieutenant Blazevicius obtained permission to take a day off and drive into Paris. He asked me if I would drive him there in our jeep. *Would I ever!* I had never allowed myself to hope for or count on such a wonderful surprise. VII Corps was supposed to bypass Paris in its advance east. Blazevicius knew he could rely on me to know my way around the city.

When we reached Panam, Lutèce, whatever you wish to call the most beautiful city in the world, I naively thought the Lieutenant wished to do some sightseeing. He quickly disabused me. The only thought in his mind was entertainment and companionship. He had been deprived of it too long. I had to find some, and, his well-being in mind, I wanted to find him the best. Driving along familiar streets and squares, I was amazed at how normal everything seemed. No one could have guessed that the city had been so recently freed from years of Nazi occupation. I stopped the jeep, asked some policemen, and they directed me to the Boulevard des Italiens, near the Madeleine Church. They guaranteed me the impeccable quality of the establishments there, adding that only the highest German officers had been among the clientele. I dropped him off and arranged to pick him up in the late afternoon or early evening, as he bade me not to hurry.

I immediately went to a pay phone and through directory assistance, obtained Lucien Bailly's telephone number. Everything seemed to be functioning like in peacetime. Within the hour, I was sitting in Lucien's apartment surrounded by his relatives and friends and besieged with excited questions. I vaguely remember some agitated neighbor appearing with a rifle and screaming something about barricades, no doubt inspired by his readings on the French Revolution of 1789. I told him to calm down and not shoot himself by mistake. The Germans loved Paris and did not want to leave it damaged (hoping perhaps some day to come back). It was a wonderful day. Imagine returning to your boyhood city right after its liberation! It felt strange having to tell them there still was a war to be fought. This merely was a very, very short break. We fitted into the jeep as many people as we could and drove around Paris in a festive mood. Then all of a sudden, it was time to think of saying good-bye.

I drove back to where I had left the Lieutenant and rang the bell of the truly palatial house: marble columns and staircase, beautiful rugs and furniture, gorgeous women. In the center of this tableau of luxury, a sheepishly grinning Lieutenant Blazevicius was surrounded by a group of women. No wonder the Germans loved Paris. The women greeted me invitingly, but I told them it was time for us to go. I did not wish to risk any disease the German High Command left behind in lieu of booby traps. I introduced the Lieutenant to my friends, who had waited outside guarding the jeep. They said they would find their way home, since all means of transportation were, amazingly enough, working. (Only in peacetime do Parisian workers strike and stop functioning.)

When we reached Chartres it was late and we were hungry. I showed the Lieutenant the magnificent cathedral, my favorite in France, and saw a restaurant sign. I knocked at the door, the boss opened it, and I asked him if we could have some simple meal, like an omelet. I also requested permission to drive the jeep into his courtyard and hide it from the MPs. I did not want the threat of a court-martial. We had a delicious omelet with French bread, the best meal we had enjoyed since leaving England. This episode brought us closer together. We were grateful for this short break in what might be a very long challenge to our endurance.

I am a man;
nothing that relates to man
do I deem alien to me.
— Terence, 195-159 B.C.

Chapter 14

The Drive into Germany

HAVE BUT A HAZY recollection of all the detailed happenings in our lightning-fast advance east through Northern France toward Belgium. The minutiae of each day's work schedule, the hundreds of data we gleaned on German unit strength, weaponry, morale, location, are forgotten. No salient incidents occurred, no lasting impressions were made, merely the never-ending deadly drudgery of keeping up-to-date our files on the German forces opposing us and consigning the ever-changing order of battle data to daily G-2 reports and map overlays. A healthy memory, in my view, has a way of refreshing itself by ridding itself of trivia every so often. The novelty and excitement of combat also had worn off — not that, working at Corps level, I did not count my blessings!

My risk was limited to occasional *Luftwaffe* raids and German artillery shells. My job was to fight a paper war. Of course, there was always the possibility of cutting oneself on a sharp paper edge or running a splinter under the fingernail while handling enemy documents. Don't laugh! An undoubtedly true rumor was circulating that some Ritchie *wunderkind* had done that very thing, reported to First Aid, had the splinter removed, bled a little, and received a Purple Heart for a wound caused by enemy action. In a war of this magnitude, actions are often taken and decisions made *nach Schema F* — according to a flat rule, without discrimination or evaluation of the exact circumstances.

In the heat of combat, anyone requesting and receiving First Aid as a result of enemy action was often automatically listed as qualifying for the medal, no matter how insignificant the wound. I guess some of the men graduating from Ritchie were still prone to do the unexpected and draw unwelcome attention to themselves, like accepting an award on such a flimsy pretext. Then again I can understand why he didn't turn it down.

Strange things happen with medals. The G-2 section acquired a Lieutenant Colonel — a West Pointer. He was the only person I ever knew capable of sitting upright in his chair, sound asleep, holding up the *Stars and Stripes* as though immersed in its lecture without dropping the paper. He was awarded the Bronze Star Medal for a period during which he had received emergency leave to be present at his daughter's brain operation in Washington. The mistake was discovered and the order rescinded. Then again, many heroes deserved decorations they were never awarded.

After nine months in battle, I started feeling differently about my safety at Corps level. I was burnt out, weary of the routine and of working day and night with the same people, craving change — any change at any cost, even at the risk of forsaking the relatively safe haven of my present duties and confronting immediate danger at division or regimental level. I even asked Colonel Carter whether he would be willing to release me for assignment to an IPW team operating at regimental level. It was late at night (or rather early in the morning). We had worked for hours on the nightly reports. Colonel Carter was at his desk, as always, the very picture of iron discipline. I, now a Second Lieutenant, stood at attention in front of him and amazed at my own nerve for daring to ask such a question. He looked up at me in his quiet way, his face grave, his gray-blue-eyed gaze

unflinchingly commanding respect and obedience, his voice a tad grav-
elly. "Don't you think I'd like to be where there is more action? You and
I have a job to do and we'll stay here as long as it takes!" I felt ashamed
for having put the question to him in the first place.

Our quick advance made it impossible for the retreating Germans to
booby-trap any buildings or lay many fresh minefields. This freed us of
one big worry so that we could devote all our energy to scanning, all day
long, the Intelligence reports that came to G-2, extracting and evaluating
any Order of Battle information they contained. However, the OB team
did not issue its own independent reports. Whatever we contributed found
its way into the G-2 summaries, estimates of the situation, or other documents. In that sense, as mentioned earlier, we were an integral part of the
G-2 section, yet still maintained our separate OB identity. It is strange that,
even when working as closely together as we did with VII Corps personnel, under circumstances where teamwork is essential, there was that tangible distinction between those who had always been assigned to Corps
and those who were only attached to it. This distinction was not noticeable
in our relationship with Colonel Carter who considered us an integral part
of his team. However, it was rather evident in that Singer and I did not
form strong ties or hobnob with the G-2 enlisted personnel. There must
remain in man some vestige of tribal instinct, whereby newcomers to the
flock may remain strangers forever.

Fred and I worked closely together without any friction whatsoever and
with confidence in each other's work. We were both married and shared
together the pain of missing our wives. Fred had a fleshy physique, was
jovial like many Austrians — except, of course, Hitler — and liked to
nibble on sweets when goodies were available. He and I kept up our spirits with jokes, often in German, since he found it easier to crack jokes in
his native Austrian. It is amusing to think of two American soldiers jok-
ing in colloquial German while fighting a war against a German-speaking
nation. When Lieutenant Blazevicius discovered a German encyclopedia
of erotica, which became the most popular and circulated book in the G-2
section, occasionally my linguistic talents were called upon to explain a
few items that seemed unclear. However, most of the time, not being
inclined to engage in scholarly analyses, the officers, who avidly borrowed the book, contented themselves with the bare illustrations.

As far as our everyday life was concerned, C rations had replaced
K-rations, and the three meals a day were not exactly an elaborate

dress-up affair. We ate from mess kits, drank from tin cups, dipping the eating utensils into hot water to clean and rinse them before and after each meal. Our uninspired cooks took no pains to work miracles with the meals. After the end of the war, we had German cooks who took pride in their job, adding a little here, a little there, and creating culinary wonders with C-rations. (I believe one can tell a caring cook by the way he slings the food down on your plate.) The ambiance was not conducive to socializing, and we did not tarry around the open-air mess after eating. A nonsmoker, I gave all my cigarettes away. I did not drink any liquor either and have no idea whether others did. The quartermaster laundry was operating, and we could get our clothes washed fairly regularly. Showers, too, were available most of the time, if not hot, at least warm or lukewarm.

Mail, in the form of V-mail, was pretty regular. I do not remember how it was processed, but it was, I believe, microfilmed and then printed out in a small format. The V-mail letters we received were about four by five inches. Sometimes we received packages with cake or cookies, which we usually shared, unless the contents were personal.

One problem with correspondence, which contributed to my wanting to be an officer, was the fact that all enlisted personnel had to have a commissioned officer censor their mail and certify it free of military information. I believe some of the officers, like Lieutenants Blazevicius and Effrussi, acted decently and sympathetically by scanning our mail rather superficially, trusting in our common sense not to reveal anything vital.

On September 2, 1944, we entered Belgium and fought for a while in the Mons, Charleroi, and Namur area. We crossed the Meuse River, a significant step in our advance toward Germany. The Germans were resisting fiercely to prevent our setting foot on their sacred soil, the *Vaterland.* However, on September 12, the 1st Infantry and 3rd Armored, who quite consistently were among the units under VII Corps command, fought their way into Germany. By September 15, we had penetrated the Siegfried Line, nearing Aachen, the ancient capital of Charlemagne and the Holy Roman Empire. Key strategic points in this region were the Roer River Dams. As long as they were in German hands, we faced the threat of the Germans demolishing the main dam and flooding the Roer Valley. This would block our crossing the river or isolate any of our troops that might be on the other side when the dam was blown. On October 21st, after heavy street fighting, Aachen capitulated to VII Corps, the first major German city to fall to the Allied attack. I was not present in Aachen, but heard that a few regrettably ugly incidents took place. A GI firing point-blank at a young girl's head? Who knows? I did not witness it.

When we were west of and close to Liège, the Walloon, French-speaking city of Belgium, General Collins — tired of racing after his divisions and moving his headquarters almost daily — decided to risk advancing the VII Corps forward echelon a good distance east, past Verviers and Eupen, south of Aachen and ahead of division headquarters. The perfect place was found in Kornelimünster, an abandoned monastery with many rooms, corridors, courtyards, and a basement and attic. It was to be our headquarters for two months and gave us an opportunity to really settle in. Our rear echelon was going to be just outside and east of Liège. Courier jeeps would run back and forth from Kornelimünster to Liège through Verviers. The day designated for the move was announced without much warning, and I was told to drive Lieutenant Blazevicius and all our office equipment to Kornelimünster. Every Belgian town we crossed was in a festive mood. It was like being in a 4th of July parade at home.

Liège had been liberated along with many other small villages. The Germans were retreating and Aachen was about to fall. As we drove through populated areas the people kept cheering, brandishing flags, and waving at us. I had not often witnessed such exuberant enthusiasm of entire communities. Pretty women were at the windows smiling and beckoning to us. In some instances their meaning was brazenly clear. I am always amazed at public displays of uncontrolled joyful behavior. It has never been in my nature to let myself completely go on such civic occasions.

We drove through Liège, an important coal and metallurgical center, on the northern edge of the Ardennes. Our precision bombing had not been very accurate. Our bombers must have dropped their load in a hell of a hurry, without getting too close to the antiaircraft fire. I could not blame them. Why take a chance? The bridges over the Meuse River were intact, as was the railroad station, and everything else that mattered. However, the main church had been hit as well as the cemetery, making a mockery of the RIP grave markers.

When driving through the city, more than once we glimpsed an angry screaming crowd of people chasing some poor woman, shouting threats and obscenities, and throwing stones at her. It was a revolting sight. I remembered as a child how sick I felt reading in the Bible about women being stoned by a mob. I still seethe watching films dealing with a lynching mob in the American deep South. The woman's head had been shaven clean, crude swastikas deeply carved into her bloody scalp. I shuddered.

The crowd was screaming insults of "Nazi sympathizer" and "whore" at the poor dazed creature, who staggered along, unable to find protection from her unrelenting pursuers. I felt immense compassion for that woman. This whole scene might have been triggered by one false accusation. But what can anyone do with a determined mob under such circumstances? I remembered the cruelly true Spanish proverb *más vale salto de matas que ruegos de hombres buenos* — it is better to hide behind bushes than rely on the pleas of good people.

This incident poses the interesting question whether bystanders should intervene. Doing so can make things a lot worse for the victim, as Cervantes illustrates in *Don Quixote*. The knight orders a man not to beat his young servant, but as he leaves the scene, the thrashing resumes worse than ever. I could not have shot every one of her pursuers. Fortunately, I personally witnessed few of these spectacles, but there must have been many.

It was rather late when we reached Kornelimünster. I was looking forward to the return trip, happy to be driving back alone and without an immediate deadline. It was almost like taking an evening drive for fun back home. I watched all those cheering people, and I marveled at the magnitude of their childish exuberance. Were they really that happy at getting rid of the Germans, or was it just an excuse for having a party and letting off steam? I was not, at that time, fully aware of any distinctive traits peculiar to the people living in that part of Belgium. They are more like the French, not at all like the other more stolid Flemish types. In Europe, there are great differences in the character of people according to regions. The Parisian is quite different from the citizen of Marseille in speech and behavior, and the austere Calvinists from Geneva have absolutely nothing in common with the fun-loving cheerful citizens of nearby Lausanne.

I was crossing Liège at a very slow pace, stopping continuously so as not to hit any of the many pedestrians running in the streets, when a pretty, highly animated, dark-haired girl took advantage of my low speed, ran toward my jeep, grabbed the windshield and back of the passenger seat, and managed to jump on the vehicle. Mindful as I was then of regulations and military discipline, I was not too happy at her action. Then I said to myself, "Oh! What's the difference, if it is just for a few yards?" I was certain she would jump off quickly.

But as we reached the end of Liège, I began to worry about her. It was going to be a long walk back, and I was not running a taxi service. Finally, feeling not at all comfortable with the situation, having no idea what, if anything, was on her mind (although she looked like a decent girl, not a tramp), I stopped the jeep. As politely and nicely as possible and to her immense surprise, I asked her in perfect French how she planned to return home. She was flabbergasted, but perhaps sensing the bond of language between us, stubbornly refused to get out of the jeep and said she would manage. I believe she asked me if I was American, and I told her, "Of course!"

The situation was becoming very difficult, as I had to drive on. Strange as it seems, in view of what happened afterward, I have either forgotten or purposely erased from my memory her name, like a dream we cannot recall unless we write it down after awakening. Let us call her Georgette. She kept on telling me that, no matter where I left her, she would find her way back. Now, strait-laced and faithful to my wife as I was, I had no designs whatsoever on this girl. I just wanted to get rid of her, wishing I had been more firm and ordered her unceremoniously off the jeep right from the beginning.

It was getting quite dark, and I told her I could not possibly take her back to Corps Headquarters and hide her there. We stopped at a farmhouse. I was tired. Everyone reaches a breaking point; I guess a lifetime of sticking to principles, setting duty above everything else, doing what Pierre Corneille's heroes do in plays, and minding the warnings of my mother, suddenly crumbled. I found out what the Bible meant by The Fall. I just let go and went along with everything, swept downward by a current I could not resist.

We very simply and naturally made love. I was letting go of months of tension and pent-up anxiety, thinking of absolutely nothing, neither my wife, or the Army, or my pending commission. Naive as it may sound to some, for me this was a very significant step.

The next morning, I told Georgette that I would manage to pick her up on my way back and return her to Liège. It would have been much easier to behave like a cad, and leave her to fend for herself. She appeared to have no regrets.

I returned to the area where parts of VII Corps Headquarters were still encamped, picked up Fred, explained to him vaguely that I had been delayed on the way, had spent the night somewhere, and began the drive back to Kornelimünster. Georgette was waiting. Fred was puzzled beyond words. I found it easier not to explain anything. He could not possibly understand, since I was at a loss to account to myself for what had happened. It was out of character.

I felt drained, guilty, unclean — trying to wipe the entire incident from my memory. I reached for other worries to fill my mind. It was the end of September or very early October, and I was still impatiently waiting for my battlefield commission. What on earth was holding it up? Almost every day I had an inner tantrum, unable to control my impatience, wondering if there had been a snag, and I would not receive it. The interlude with Georgette made me think of my wife all the more. It had been a pure sexual release. Still there was something more and if there was not, I had to invent it for my own satisfaction. This girl had given herself to an unknown American driven by some strange emotion brought about by the joy at the end of Nazi dominance. . . . Sometimes it is easier not to sort it out.

The days dragged on and on. We had set up our OB office in a corridor adjacent to the G-2 section, with windows facing west onto a large courtyard. We were still being shelled by German artillery fire and the General, thinking of himself as less expendable than we were, had had an underground bunker built in the center of the courtyard for his personal safety. We all slept on the floor of the attic and took our chances. A few times the building was hit by German shells, once severely, but most of us survived without injuries, although the entire wall next to Fred and me came crashing down in pieces while we were working there. Another time, as I was walking to the showers in the company of some others, an artillery shell hit nearby. I was not hurt, but some people in the courtyard were injured by debris and shrapnel.

VII Corps troops — the 1st, 4th, 9th, 104th Infantry Divisions and the 3rd Armored — fought hard in the Eschweiler, Roer Dam, and Hurtgen Forest areas. Eschweiler was finally taken. The 4th Infantry lost many men in the Hurtgen Forest. It was unwise on the part of Collins to have them fight there, since the Germans, some even near invalids mobilized by Hitler as a last resort into the *Volksgrenadierdivisionen* (German divisions hastily activated from haphazardly recruited, often unfit, citizens), stood behind trees and thus protected, easily picked off our soldiers as they advanced through the forest. One of these German soldiers was reported to have a wooden leg. We heard that Eisenhower was critical of our General for committing our infantry in the Hurtgen Forest and incurring so many fatalities. Later in the war, Eisenhower acted more cautiously about giving Collins *carte blanche* to commit troops without carefully weighing the consequences.

To the east, the XXI Corps was being activated. Some of their staff officers spent a few days with us observing our staff at work. Among them, Lieutenant Colonel Wilbur Wilson, XXI Corps G-2, spent considerable time becoming acquainted with our OB section. On one occasion, a group of the highest-ranking Generals, including Eisenhower, Bradley, and Hodges, met at our headquarters.

While we were immobilized in the monastery, I could not help wondering whether it would be possible to see Georgette again. Now, we always worked late into the night and were reasonably free in the morning. I started scheming about some way to go to Liège. I found out that we could, with luck, hitch a ride on the courier jeeps running back and forth between us and the rear echelon of VII Corps. I asked Lieutenant Blazevicius for some time off. He granted it and I managed to reach Verviers and Liège. Hitchhiking by military personnel was not unheard of at that time. In Verviers, if one happened to be there at the right time, one might see the German V-2s sputtering by high in the sky, making a noise like a Model T Ford or a very loud motorcycle, on their way to London. They were a weird sight, and I saw them several times. In spite of their speed, they seemed to be moving in slow motion.

The first time I went to Liège to see Georgette, I walked from the VII Corps rear echelon over the Meuse bridge into the city. I was in uniform, of course, and having asked for directions, found Georgette's apartment and family. They were middle-class people, excited about visiting with a French-speaking American. Georgette was glad to see me, but hardly ready to resume where we left off. She did not want her family to know about our very brief tryst and acted accordingly. The recklessness of Liberation Day was gone. In the meantime, always candid, I had told her I was married, which may have contributed to her diminished ardor. I no longer represented a free ticket to America. Here began a series of very trying and risky episodes, which at times made me wonder about myself. I committed several acts of pure folly, taking incredible chances. I returned to Liège three or four times.

The second time, I found out that Liège was patrolled by our MPs and off-limits to all American personnel who had no official business there. I managed to reach Georgette's home without running into any problems. I explained the situation to her family, and they came up with the idea that I should dress up in a civilian suit belonging to her late uncle. The suit was a little short, but the fit was passable. I must have been out of my mind, since were I caught in civilian attire, I would be considered a deserter and face court-martial. In any event, with everything to lose, I took the risk, motivated by a crazy impulse to see if I could get away with it, confident in my foolproof knowledge of French and in a way, ready to test my skill at being incognito by impersonating a Belgian national.

I soon found out that my previous abstinence from complicated relationships with strange women had had its advantages: peace of mind. With Georgette problems began to crop up. She claimed to be pregnant, which might or might not have been true, insisting she needed cigarettes for which she could obtain money for an abortion. Anyway, I gave her the cigarettes, and began to seriously regret my involvement; but I had been brought up with a sense of responsibility for my actions. Maybe I was challenged by the adventurous appeal of the situation. I did not just disappear, but continued my visits and once spent the night in their attic, where they had a small bedroom. I asked Georgette to sneak up there at night, but she refused. I forget what excuse I gave Lieutenant Blazevicius for being delayed overnight. He was understanding and did not press me for an explanation.

I regret to admit that I was pursuing Georgette for another tryst. I was going to a lot of trouble to see the sights in a city off-limits to American personnel. I believe I felt I deserved just compensation for the incredible hardships to which I was subjecting myself. However, Georgette became uncooperative. She reluctantly agreed once more and took me to some very nice place, which as much as I could tell, was run by some lady for just such meetings. It was outright luxurious. I began to wonder how Georgette was so knowledgeable about such things and became slightly suspicious of her vast connections with that layer of society. It was high time to break up the relationship. Our meetings were no fun and stressful for me. I decided they had to stop before a disaster occurred. Fortunately, events took care of the situation.

On November 21, 1944, Lieutenant Blazevicius, with a big grin on his face, told me that my commission had finally come through. I was to take a jeep to VII Corps rear to be sworn in as a Second Lieutenant. I was beside myself with joy, having finally reached my goal. I was the first American officer in our family. It really meant a great deal to me. Blazevicius gave me one of his infantry insignia and gold bar. On November 22, I appeared before the AG Lieutenant (who had once told me my word was not worth "shit" and who had regained his peace of mind and equanimity by claiming that any missing secret document had gone down to the bottom of the Atlantic). Cautious as ever, he first swore me in as a commissioned officer, exactly one year and one day after we had reached England. Then, and only then, did he hand me my discharge as a Master Sergeant. I am surprised he did not put me in irons during the ceremony.

As I left the AG's office, my gold bar and crossed rifles pinned to my shirt collar, and walked along the street, two Privates walked by and saluted at the very same time. I returned the salute, then quickly remembered the age-old custom. I ran after them and called to them to stop. They turned around, looking really worried. I took two $1 bills of scrip money out of my pocket and gave one to each, explaining they were the first to salute me after I received my commission. Both looked much relieved. For just an instant I thought of walking into town and telling Georgette about my promotion. Then I thought better of it and caught a jeep back to Kornelimünster, a commissioned officer in the U.S. Army. I never visited Liège again.

The enlisted men in the G-2 section, who had known me for a long time, continued calling me by my first name and I did not mind at all. However, one evening, Colonel Carter summoned me to his desk. Never looking up at me, the Colonel in a very low, almost inaudible, voice said, "Lieutenant, if I ever hear an enlisted man calling you again by your first name, I'll rip those bars right off your collar!" His meaning was quite clear. "Yes, Sir!" I passed the word around the G-2 section, begging everyone not to get me in trouble with the "old man."

As a commissioned officer I was entitled to a sleeping bag, which made my nights more comfortable. During this period I was told one evening that some officer from the U.S. was looking for former Ritchie graduates now in VII Corps. He turned out to be the officer in charge of teaching us about mines and booby traps at Camp Ritchie. We met and he informed me he had been sent on TDY (temporary duty) for the sole purpose of acquainting himself with real minefields. Goethe in *Faust* wisely observes:

> All theory, dear friend, is a mere lifeless gray,
> life's golden tree alone sparkles in green array.

We decided to meet at chow the next evening to talk and bring each other up-to-date. I looked for him in vain. He had stepped on a real mine and killed himself. Goethe was right.

During the early days of December 1944, Fred and I in the OB section, as well as enlisted G-2 map Sergeant Harper, had gathered from many IPW reports that there were ten Panzer divisions — a very unusual concentration — in the enemy sector across the Rhine River. We naturally reported this to First Army, who disregarded the warning. We thought they should have taken it seriously and at least looked into it more closely, possibly having the 9th Air Force bomb the area. On December 17, our concern proved to have been justified. German Field Marshal Karl von Rundstedt had launched the Ardennes counteroffensive, a desperate, ultimately futile effort to throw the Allies back into the Atlantic. It was a bit late in the war to achieve such a lofty goal.

During that time, a German Colonel had ended up in the VII Corps PW cage. Carter thought I should interrogate him. I was told to pin on a borrowed Lieutenant Colonel's silver oak leaf for prestige. The German soon realized I knew a great deal about the German situation, but protected by the Geneva Convention, did not give much more than his name, rank, and serial number. It was not in my power to force more Intelligence out of him. I only knew he was lying about his unit and why he had ended up in this sector of the front.

Von Rundstedt's armor had broken through 35 miles into Belgium and

Luxembourg. VII Corps had been picked by First Army to counterattack the penetration. If we at Corps had been bored for the past two months, the lull in excitement was over. The situation was very confused, but we moved as quickly as possible back into Belgium and the Ardennes. I recall very little of what happened next. I only know I was very fortunate to be at Corps and not in the trenches. The weather was very cold, the snow deep. Hardship for me, if any, was limited to working long hours, being cold, trudging back through deep snow each dawn to catch a little sleep in a deserted house we had taken over. I remember some dog barking ominously at me one lonely frozen night, and I got my Colt .45 out of its holster just in case.

For the next month we were in the region of Marche, Houffalize, and Bastogne. I received a Bronze Star Medal for whatever I did in Intelligence work, but it was not much compared to what others suffered and accomplished. Perhaps I was awarded the medal for spending Christmas and New Year's in combat. At the time I knew exactly what had happened, but I have forgotten all but the most general facts. A famous Viennese Colonel and spymaster, Otto Skorzeny, working for SS Intelligence, had devised a plan of dressing German soldiers in GI uniforms. They tried to cut through our supply lines, which ran through Liège, but failed to even reach it, as most of the German vehicles ran out of gas. It had been a truly bold, but desperate, plan.

British Field Marshal Bernard L. Montgomery was appointed Supreme Commander of the Allied Forces engaged in this battle. He showed up many nights in our G-2 section, unmistakable, just like his photographs: hawk-faced, swagger stick tightly held under his arm. He was interested in our Order of Battle data and instructed us, henceforth, to include in our nightly report of enemy units in contact every single German unit identified, no matter how flimsy the basis for identification. Previously, we would only list units of which several members had been identified and which we could be reasonably sure of being present on the basis of carefully evaluated IPW reports and multiple substantiated sightings. However, Field Marshal Montgomery wanted every straggler listed, even if we were convinced the man's unit was somewhere else, perhaps in Russia, and he had somehow ended up in Belgium, possibly conscripted into a new unit in a kind of emergency while on furlough back home. We thought such reporting highly misleading, but we were not about to argue with a British Field Marshal. So our lists of units in contact grew longer every night, occupied pages instead of short paragraphs, and were, in our modest opinion, pretty meaningless. On the overlay maps we continued listing only significant, evaluated, corroborated identifications of enemy units.

The Germans had committed at least three Panzer Corps, four elite SS Panzer Divisions, and four regular Panzer Divisions. By the end of January, we had definitely defeated the German Ardennes counteroffensive and won the Battle of the Bulge. We were completely out of contact with the enemy and out of earshot of the guns. We had destroyed an enormous amount of German equipment, including 850 railroad cars. VII Corps assembled in the vicinity of Ochain, Belgium, for 12 days to rest its personnel and to service and repair its vehicles and equipment after the grueling winter battle. Just prior to that, Colonel Carter had sent me on an overnight trip, merely for a change of pace, to Luxembourg — the capital of the principality of the same name.

I was to represent the Corps at a demonstration of a new piece of equipment Army Ordnance had just perfected, the Infrared Spectroscope. The latter, much like a telescopic sight, could be mounted on a carbine or rifle and allowed one to see targets in the blackest of nights. I was part of a small group of officers sent from various units, who listened to a lecture on the new scope. At night we all went out in the snow to test it, firing at targets. The device really made the targets visible enough, in a reddish, fuzzy way, to be fired at and hit. Upon my return to Corps, I wrote a brief report on the trip and the demonstration. What I remember most vividly of that meeting is the gaunt, weary, distracted look on the faces of those in our group who had led platoons and fought in the front lines during the Bulge. Some looked as though they had been staring death in the eyes for eternity. Once again, I had a great deal to be grateful for. We were all exhausted and worn, but some of those officers had seen really cruel action, constantly aware that they would be in the front lines until wounded or killed.

During the rest and recovery period at Ochain some of us were offered three-day passes. In my case, by granting this brief change of scenery, Colonel Carter also wished to give me an opportunity to buy an officer's uniform and accessories at the well-stocked Paris PX. Until now I had been wearing my enlisted man's uniform. I traveled with two other officers who were counting on my help to get around in Paris. We were assigned rooms in a large hotel somewhere near the Paris Opera. The rooms were dark, unheated, and hot water was available only at limited, usually unpredictable times. I ended up taking the line of least resistance, which meant cold showers.

The first evening in Paris, I was at a loss as to what to do, not even thinking about the possibility of contacting friends like Lucien Bailly or Jacqueline. In retrospect, I am really sorry I did not. I thought, wrongly, that her family, being Jewish, might not have fared too well during the German occupation. Later, I found out they had not suffered; somehow, Jacqueline's father had been able to procure all the food they needed on a regular basis from the provinces. I never found out in detail how he accomplished this. When we talked about it in July 1945, he airily dismissed my sympathy about his war-related sacrifices.

My two companions wanted action and asked me to take them where they might find it. We went on a long walk north to the Clichy and Pigalle district, the ideal place to meet ladies of the night. I was not keen on the idea, since I never drank and had firmly resolved not to become again involved after the now much-regretted Georgette episode. I took my friends to a few dreary bars, not places I frequent on my own, and singularly lacking in customers, especially female.

The entire situation was awkward for all of us. My two companions could not speak French and the average client in a Parisian bar is not apt to be fluent in English, particularly in that section of Paris. In Clichy or Pigalle one is more apt to hear the quite distinctive "slaughterhouse drawl" of the macho guys of La Villette. I am never at ease in bars. It was a bizarre scenario: three American Servicemen on leave after three campaigns and seven months in the field, two of them raring for action in a city known for its *risqué* entertainment, facile women, and unlimited access to hedonistic pursuits; the third, although not an award-winning guide to Parisian nightlife or red light districts, able and willing to dedicate his consummate knowledge of French and the city to the attainment of their goal. Yet the operation had hopelessly bogged down in the depressing ambiance of an unattractive half-deserted neighborhood bar, and my two companions were gradually losing their interest.

With me it was different. I was simply enjoying using French and showing off my ability to be perfectly at home in a foreign setting, thanks to skills I had spent years fine tuning. For the sake of the other two, I was hoping that some attractive women might show up. One lively, pretty young woman finally did. The way she handled herself, greeting everyone there and being greeted in return, she was obviously an *habitué* of this and other similar establishments. She was exuberantly in control. Naive as I was with women, always seeing the best in everyone, it hadn't dawned on me that she might be a prostitute, even though I knew this was a high-density section of Paris for that social class. She immediately noticed our presence and realizing I spoke French, focused on me rather than on my friends, to whom I would have preferred she direct her attention. Much later, she claimed to be a dancer, which I accepted at face value, failing to interpret it as a euphemistic job description.

We talked, and as never fails to happen, my being an American in uniform, speaking and acting like a Frenchman, made for an easy rapport between us. I tried to draw her attention to my two companions, but failed. Ultimately, not taking part in the conversation and not knowing what was going on, they felt left out and became discouraged. Despite my pleas and promise to keep trying, they went back to the hotel under the pretext of being tired. I should have gone with them, but was enjoying bantering in French with the clients in the bar and showing off.

I ended up making a big mistake. I allowed myself to be shamefully persuaded to spend two nights with the girl. The war had taken its toll on my character.

She had a small apartment in the neighborhood and very casually had me spend the night with her. She never asked for money, but later on hinted at a gift of cigarettes. She appeared to be amused by the entire affair. She was outgoing and seemed to be enjoying herself with me. She said she made a living as a dancer in bars. Everyone knew her by name; she was definitely not a streetwalker. Although a bit worried, I was giving her the benefit of the doubt. Actually, I was attempting to alleviate worry and convince myself I had not committed a stupid mistake.

I spent the next day making purchases at the PX tailor shop of uniforms and insignia. I enjoyed a long walk around Paris, amazed at the large number of lucky GIs stationed there while the war was in full swing. I did not feel too good about myself and was almost glad to return to VII Corps. A week or so later, I developed a gonorrheal infection better known as " the clap" and received penicillin shots from First Aid. In the eyes of the Army, any venereal disease was a sin and a possible court-martial offense. First

Aid reported the incident to Colonel Carter, who one evening called me into his office.

He addressed me in a very serious, fatherly tone, pointing out that he was informed of everything that happened to those under his command. He lectured me on family values, one's responsibility to one's family, and the dangers of extramarital sex. I listened gravely and really felt penitent, very much relieved when he told me he would not take any further action in the matter. But to tell the whole truth, this was not the end of it. Four years later, when taking a routine physical in the Army Reserve, my blood test for syphilis came up positive. I was in panic. Everything had cleared up nicely and I had experienced no further symptoms. I rushed to a specialist in internal medicine. He was not as surprised as I was. A massive dose of penicillin, he explained, can obscure for years blood tests for syphilis. I had to tell my wife and take a very long series of shots. I was ultimately completely cured, as was confirmed by two very painful spinal probes taken three years apart.

On February 5, VII Corps moved back to its previous position on German soil, but remained inactive. The XVIII Airborne Corps on our right attacked to seize the Roer River Dams and to force the enemy's hand with respect to this continued threat of water engulfing our troops. Previous efforts made to capture the dams had been unsuccessful. Aerial bombardment of the largest dam by the RAF had not affected the huge earth and concrete structure. The dam had to be captured or be blown up. Slowly but surely the Americans closed in. On February 11, the Germans destroyed the outlet gates on the largest dam, releasing the water, but not fast enough to precipitate the devastating flood that had been feared. The Roer River rose significantly and for several days blocked our advance. However, the threat had been removed. We would be able to proceed toward Cologne as soon as the water had receded.

VII Corps troops were being regrouped during this period. Our 3rd Armored Division and 4th Cavalry Group moved back into Germany from Belgium. By February 23, VII Corps had attacked across the Roer River. We took and cleared Düren. German prisoners were taken by the thousands. On March 4, elements of the 3rd Armored reached the fabled Rhine River, fighting its way into Cologne with the 104th Infantry. Our advance was spectacular. Cologne, now largely reduced to rubble by Allied bombardments, once the Queen City of the Rhine, the third largest city in Germany after Berlin and Hamburg, became the largest city in Germany to fall to the attack of British and American forces in the war. Berlin was later captured by the Soviets, and Hamburg was declared an open city in the face of the British advance.

I spent some time in Cologne near the magnificent *Dom* — cathedral. I had visited it in 1922 when first arriving in Germany. My father had met some business clients there. I conferred with German authorities, who asked me to convey to VII Corps Command the imperative need of cordoning off the cathedral, as any vehicular traffic and resulting vibrations might cause the highly unstable structure to teeter and crumble. We, of course, respected their wishes and took the necessary measures.

We took the university city of Bonn, Ludwig van Beethoven's birthplace. Last time I had been there, the British occupation forces from World War I were still there. By now, VII Corps Headquarters was ruthlessly occupying German homes and buildings for its headquarters. Not partial to occupying strange bedrooms with personal belongings, I recall tossing the bedding out of a window so that I could place my sleeping bag directly on the bedstead. Suddenly, we received the electrifying news: on March 7th, elements of the 9th Armored Division, part of III Corps, had seized intact a crossing over the Rhine, the Ludendorff railway bridge at Remagen, a few miles south of VII Corps sector.

An honorable death is better than a base life.
Tacitus, A.D. 55-117

Chapter 15

From the "Rose Pocket" to "The Music Plays Softly"

ONCE THE REMAGEN crossing had been secured, VII Corps engineers established three additional pontoon treadway bridges. The first one was built on March 17 and was 1,176 feet long. Despite fierce German resistance, our advance was impressively fast. Operations occupied center stage; Intelligence merely offered the best possible timely support. Our momentum was so formidable that information, although always essential, may have only offered our Generals the comfort of knowing that nothing could stop us. Still, we never ceased our OB work and it was no doubt helpful that we identified eight enemy divisions, most of them of low quality. A thousand PWs a day were being taken. On March 28th, we started swinging our attack around from a northern to a northeasterly direction. At one time we advanced 90 kilometers in three days. Our armor, particularly the 3rd Armored Division, thus enabled us to take, by surprise and undamaged, Marburg, a famous university town with a population of 25,000. Marburg's 13th-century cathedral and university, founded in 1527, escaped all destruction.

Usually all the loot, if any, goes to the forward elements of any army. However, VII Corps Headquarters reached Marburg so rapidly that even some of us were able to find souvenirs. While looking around for documents in the Marburg City Hall and adjacent buildings, I found four parade daggers, one for each German branch of Service: Army, Navy, Air Force, and SS. I kept them, of course, but after the war, not being a collector, I gave them as a present to Henry Wheeler, the Camp Ritchie Training Section Sergeant who had indirectly enabled me to go to Order of Battle School. He had, with one single phone call, opened a door for me, which in turn gave me the opportunity to gain both satisfaction and recognition in our European operations by putting my qualifications to good use. Wheeler had finally been sent overseas, after Ritchie went out of business, and I saw him again near Frankfurt after V-E Day and before returning home.

American armor continued its lightning advance, taking several thousand prisoners, and reaching an area just south of Paderborn. The German troops defending their precious Ruhr Valley were cut off by VII Corps units, which encircled them from the west, south, and east along a 200-mile front. Our successes were spectacular, and the end of the war could already be glimpsed. Another ominous development for the Nazi cause was when the Ninth Army managed to cross the Rhine north of the Ruhr and drive eastward. The looming linkup of the First and Ninth Armies represented a crushing blow to the enemy. Then we were dealt a tragic loss.

On March 31st, the United States Army lost one of its great battle leaders, who had been with us since the Normandy breakthrough. Major General Maurice Rose, commanding the 3rd Armored Division, was killed in action near Paderborn. Under his leadership the division had earned its nickname of the "Spearhead Division." The great work and the brilliant success of this elite unit reflected the ability and spirit of General Rose. Because of the importance of the attack in which he was leading his division when he lost his life, and to honor his personal courage in battle,

VII Corps and First Army adopted the name of the "Rose Pocket" for the operation that isolated the Ruhr. To my knowledge, General Rose was the highest ranking officer to die in the operations in which I was involved.

Intelligence was received of a pending attack from the rapidly closing Ruhr trap by a tank-and-infantry drive east in the vicinity of Winterburg, but the 104th Timber Wolf Infantry Division — with characteristic speed — deployed to the northwest to counter the threat. The division reached the enemy's line of departure before the Germans could initiate the attack and for the next four days beat back all attempts to penetrate the VII Corps ring in that area. Elements of the 3rd Armored Spearhead Division made a firm junction with elements of the 2nd Armored and 83rd Infantry Divisions (XIX Corps) at Lippstadt on April 1st and closed the Ruhr trap.

The "Rose Pocket" isolated about 5,000 square miles of enemy territory, including parts of the most highly developed industrial region in Europe, and 350,000 enemy soldiers. The troops inside the pocket were completely cut off from supplies and reinforcements. It was one of the greatest operations of its kind in history, equaled perhaps only by the brutal warfare on the Russian front. Anyone viewing pictures taken at that time of the German prisoners flowing into our PW enclosures can hardly believe the endless masses of Germans, including men and women, surrendering, huddling together, their faces tired, worn, without any bravado or enthusiasm for the Reich's cause. They were a beaten lot.

While other American units worked at shrinking the pocket, the 3rd Armored Division, now commanded by Brigadier General Doyle O. Hickey, launched a new drive to the east. The new objective was to cross the Weser River south of the Harz Mountains. Some elements of VII Corps had to remain engaged in securing our sector of the Rose Pocket until completely relieved therefrom. Other troops drove eastward and on April 8th crossed the Weser River, another major step forward.

At the rate we were going and to put it plainly, it looked very much as though the *Wehrmacht* was soon going to be *kaput*! The number of prisoners taken had overtaxed our PW facilities. At that time we ran into a shockingly ugly sight, one that perhaps received less publicity than Dachau: the infamous German slave labor and concentration camp at Nordhausen. We found thousands of slave laborers of Russian, Polish,

French, and other nationalities. I was destined to have a long hard look at this abomination, since besides my Order of Battle duties, I was asked to investigate the role the citizens of Nordhausen played in this grisly scenario.

Many of the men and women kept there were used as slave labor to operate the huge V-bomb factory built deep into the hillside a short distance out of town. The inhumane living conditions of these people were appalling and gave me cold chills as, disbelieving, I walked through the sleeping quarters and barracks. I saw live skeletons just lying there, next to corpses that far outnumbered the living. I personally saw hundreds of these wretched human beings, weighing perhaps 70 to 90 pounds, in filthy bunks, cots, and on the floor in the corners of rooms. I had read about such atrocities, but nothing prepares one for the real thing. There were hundreds of bodies, some lying in the fields, or stacked at the crematory, waiting to be burned. It was a truly revolting spectacle. I asked to be shown around and, grim-faced, escorted by frightened, apprehensive Germans, inspected everything including the underground V-bomb factory and incinerators.

The German guards were quite obsequious, acting more like tourist guides, thoroughly familiar with the history of the sight, but spieling off their well-rehearsed lines to visitors with superb detachment and from an absolutely neutral position in regard to the subject at hand. Of course! What did this have to do with them or their lives? I reported what I had observed to Carter and my colleagues in the G-2 section.

My next order came indirectly through the G-2 section from a very incensed Corps Commander. I was told to speak to the mayor and some of the prominent citizens of Nordhausen to determine how much they knew about the atrocities that had been committed in their town. I could have given them their answer to that question without talking to anyone. Only the most sophisticated means of torture developed over centuries by mankind and now expertly applied to the upstanding burghers of Nordhausen might have produced an answer closer to the truth. However, I was not given *carte blanche* to experiment with tools I have only seen described and depicted in medieval books on the subject of productive interrogation. I was limited to speaking to many people and asking a multitude of questions and was not at all surprised when no one admitted to anything more than having heard very vague rumors about what had been going on. What else would they admit?

Fifty years later, we are accustomed to being routinely stonewalled by anyone ranging from the highest political figures to the lowest criminal. In Nordhausen someone might have confessed, but no one did. It was much like asking students in a class who among them was guilty of shooting spitballs while the teacher was out of the room. No one ever knows anything. My next task at the time was to have the mayor order every prominent male citizen in town to take part in digging mass graves in a hillside overlooking the city, and to carry all the bodies to this makeshift cemetery and bury them. There was at least some small satisfaction in watching these allegedly blameless citizens, shovel in hand, dig a big hole and bury the corpses, thus becoming more intimately acquainted with the local horrors, which seemed to have previously escaped their attention. A few voiced the complaint that they had played no active part in those inhumane acts. I told them with little sympathy that this was ultimately a very small price to pay for being even passive participants in the Nazi Regime and to keep on working. However, in my heart I knew that the average citizen cannot do much about the acts of his government, regardless of how he feels about them.

Despite German resistance in the Harz Mountains, we moved eastward toward the Saale River, taking between 2,000 to 4,000 or more PWs each day. After Nordhausen, VII Corps established headquarters in Eisleben, which I thought rather significant, since it is Martin Luther's birthplace. While there, I received another special task that I was rather proud and pleased to carry out. It was nothing of great import, and although I am no autograph hound or chaser of celebrities, it is always a thrill to meet someone who figures prominently in history books. Lieutenant Effrussi, who seemed to be the spokesman on such occasions for General Collins and who most probably recommended me for the job, asked me to dress up in my Class A uniform, take my jeep, and pay a call on no lesser personage than Princess Hermine of Reuss, widow of the late German Kaiser William II of Hohenzollern. Hermine had been the Kaiser's second wife and had married him, not to become empress, but rather out of love — to share with him his exile.

Apparently, Princess Hermine lived in her own world of memories, blissfully unaware of the wartime situation and without any idea of how far American troops had penetrated into Germany. My mission was to pacify and reassure her that soon the war would be over and she could proceed with her plans to visit Baden-Baden in the Black Forest. She was accustomed to adhere to a tight yearly social calendar and no world war was going to interfere with it. I was flattered at Effrussi's confidence in me to attend to this mission with as much courtesy, diplomacy, and finesse as was required on such an occasion. I do not remember the name of Hermine's estate, but vaguely recall it was near and to the south of Eisleben. Once there, I stated the purpose of my visit to what I took to be a majordomo. I was promptly introduced into a large study filled with antique furniture and a beautiful large desk. I immediately recognized a photograph of the late Kaiser, as always posed in a manner that would conceal the infirmity he bore from birth, a paralyzed useless left arm, usually masked by the folds of a coat. I was a world away from everything I had experienced since D-Day.

When Princess Hermine appeared, I introduced myself as the representative of the American Army and General Collins, explaining in the most reassuring words that we would very much appreciate her patience and forbearing with respect to her travel plans to the thermal hot springs and baths. Choosing my words very carefully and avoiding as much as possible any reference to the crushing defeats inflicted on the German *Wehrmacht*, I assured her of my conviction that quite soon she could make plans to travel unimpeded. I thought that this would sound a great deal better than, "Look, Lady: Don't you know there is a war on? This is no time to think of trips or thermal baths! Germany is in enough hot water already!" She listened somewhat distracted, obviously unaware of the momentous changes that had been occurring in her country. She was of another world quite remote from Hitler and Nazi Germany. I thought her a gracious old lady. True to myself I resisted any temptation to ask for her autograph and left, happy to have met the widow of Kaiser Wilhelm II, the last emperor of Germany, of whom my Fräulein had told me so much.

The 104th Timber Wolf Infantry Division resumed its drive eastward toward Halle, another famous university city, as well as an important metallurgical and chemical industrial center. (These names were as familiar to me as New York or Chicago to the average American.) On April 15th, the Mulde River was designated as the restraining line for our advance, and the Spearhead Division withdrew the bridgehead it had seized over that river. The advance of Marshal Koniev's Soviet Forces east of the Elbe was driving steadily westward, and to prevent any accidental clash of American and Soviet troops, a sort of no-man's land was established between the Elbe and the Mulde Rivers. Halle resisted in a house-to-house battle that lasted for five days after it had been encircled. Germans were flooding our PW camps to the tune of 5,000 to 10,000 daily. Our dive-bombers destroyed German vehicles as enemy troops were compressed into a smaller and smaller area. On April 20th, all resistance ceased in the VII Corps area with the capture of 18,000 prisoners, and on April 23rd, our last combat mission in Europe was accomplished. For us it was over!

Initially, VII Corps was to remain near and to the west of Halle. The work of the OB section was done, but we still included in the nightly report an endless, useless enumeration, not of enemy units, but rather of identifications of stragglers or individuals that had become separated from their units and had no tactical significance whatsoever. Occasionally I wandered over to the VII Corps PW cage and straggler collecting point. We were beginning to capture a great many women and kept them separate from the men. (Even in PW cages decorum should be upheld.)

One day the MPs, who at this stage of the war could even find in their heart a touch of sympathy for some prisoners, drew my attention to an elderly German Brigadier General. He was very polite, submissive, and no longer conscious of his rank. The MP wondered whether we should treat this officer more gently and keep him out of the dense bustling crowd of other prisoners. We had too many PWs to worry about separating commissioned officers from enlisted personnel. I felt sorry for the General and had the MPs transfer him to the women's cage. It was the least I could do for a General, especially one of advanced age. At that stage of his career he deserved to be in female company — before it was too late.

The General was quite grateful and I engaged him in a conversation. He was the first German PW in the grade of General I had ever met. A soft-spoken gentleman, he told me he knew Field Marshal Hermann Goering, chief of the German *Luftwaffe,* since the old days when they had served together. He had also met Hitler and could only reiterate something I was fully aware of, namely that Hitler was a dynamic speaker and could keep his huge audiences enthralled. He seemed to realize the terrible mistakes Hitler had made and was now tired and detached from it all. I did not, under the circumstances, probe too deeply into his past. He did not appear to be a confirmed Nazi, merely an old air force officer who, tempted by his rank and seniority, had taken the easy route and remained in the air force too long. I asked the MPs to treat him kindly and with respect.

The Corps was dreaming up new uses for me and my knowledge of German, since our OB work was no longer needed. My next assignment was in the laundry and dry-cleaning business in which I had no expertise except as a customer of such establishments in private life. Now that we were going to remain in one place, the VII Corps Quartermaster decided to make good laundry and cleaning facilities available to the troops. My job was to recruit every laundry and dry cleaner in Halle to work for us. In the company of a Quartermaster Corps officer knowledgeable on the subject, I interviewed all these people, acting mostly as an interpreter until I had caught on to all the different terms and understood what we needed and what the Germans could provide. I learned a great deal about commercial laundering, as all the Germans I dealt with were most helpful, which under the circumstances was to be expected. Being on the winning side always provides a favorable introduction to one's former opponents and insures cooperation on their part.

I also spent some time in an underground mine in Halle, where the Germans had hidden many library books and documents. However, I did not discover anything of great military interest. Just about this time, President Harry Truman, Prime Minister Winston Churchill, and Premier Josef Stalin met in Yalta. As a result of the strategic decisions agreed on at the lofty level of this conference regarding the occupation of a defeated Reich, the VII Corps operational responsibility was to move to nearby Leipzig in Saxony to facilitate negotiations with the Soviets.

The initial contact between American and Soviet troops was made by Major General Emil F. Reinhardt's 69th Infantry Division on April 25th. The contact point was just south of the VII Corps zone, and on the following day patrols of the 9th and 104th Divisions met elements of Marshal Ivan Koniev's First Ukrainian Army along the Elbe. At this time, the respective zones of V and VII Corps were altered and operational emphasis was now placed on the organization of the Corps zone for military occupation and government, centered about the Corps Headquarters located in Leipzig.

On May 6th, the First Army — its mission accomplished — prepared to become nonoperational, and VII Corps was placed under the control of the Ninth U.S. Army. The war in Europe ended officially on May 9th,

1945, eleven months and three days after D-Day. We could be grateful to the Lord for granting us the blessing to reach our goal in this relatively short period.

On June 1st, my long-anticipated promotion to First Lieutenant, held up for weeks (I am convinced, by a jealous Chief Warrant Officer of the G-2 section) finally came through.

At midnight, June 11, 1945 (D+370), VII Corps Headquarters became nonoperational, relieved of its command by XXI Corps, and two days later began its redeployment to the United States. Lieutenant General Collins was most anxious to be given a new assignment to the Pacific, no doubt to gain another star to full General. After all, career officers have to make hay while the sun shines, thriving more on warfare than peace. (As Talleyrand, French Minister of Foreign Affairs at the 1815 Congress of Vienna, said, "You can do everything with bayonets, except sit on them!") Collins and the entire VII Corps cadre left for the USA and a new assignment in the Pacific.

"Lightning Joe" eventually became a four-star General and Chief of Staff of the U.S. Army, but V-J Day and the end of the war with Japan frustrated his earlier hopes to return to active combat in the Pacific Theater of Operations and earn his fourth star there.

Before VII Corps left, I had one more run-in with our "sleep-reading" Lieutenant Colonel, now in charge of a G-2 section with no real useful purpose. Since the war was over and there was no longer any need for German Order of Battle data in the nightly routine G-2 report, I asked him for permission to cease publishing the endless list of German unit identifications.

I was sure the *Wehrmacht* had its own list of all its members, so why duplicate it nightly here in Leipzig, except to use up the surplus paper left over from the war? My silver bars were no match for the Lieutenant Colonel's silver oak leaves. He grew very angry and told me in no uncertain terms, "Just do your job, Lieutenant!" Field Marshal Montgomery's wishes prevailed to the bitter end! The Lieutenant Colonel left a day or two later. So did my old buddies, now Captain Al Blazevicius and Fred Singer, who was promoted to either Tech or Master Sergeant. They both had enough points, earned through years of service, time overseas, campaign ribbons, and such, to be sent home. I did, too, but I was not technically on an OB team and could still be useful because of my knowledge of German. In any event, I stayed.

Leipzig, where I was now stationed, had been heavily damaged by our bombing raids. As always, the section of town most severely hit was its cultural center: opera, municipal theater, museum, all dedicated to the peaceful pursuit of the arts and humanities. Hotels were also badly damaged with only a large one left intact. It became the BOQ (Bachelor Officers Quarters) and Officer's mess. I shared one of its rooms with Lieutenant Helmut Strauss, who had received a direct commission from Ritchie without the benefit of 90 days of grueling OCS training. While this still rankled me, we became good friends. After all, what should he have done — refuse a direct commission, when offered, out of sheer integrity? I wouldn't have either!

All the MIS teams were assigned on paper to a distant MIS Headquarters (by now possibly debauched after being sequestered for the entire duration of the war in such a hardship post as Paris). We never heard from or knew anything about them, having long concluded that we were forgotten — or at best represented nothing more than a number on a list. We were not even very much aware of being under XXI Corps — or cared — as long as we were housed, fed, and paid.

Many of the team members, unlike Helmut and me, who had opted for the impersonal hotel surroundings, preferred to live in German private homes requisitioned by the Corps. Officers and enlisted men usually were housed together. Some of the MIS teams (with the only exception of the French one) had worked continuously very hard for 11 months. The PI team, for instance, had slaved day and night over thousands of aerial photographs. Excusably or not, after this long period of straining under a tight rein, sudden freedom can have strange effects on one's behavior.

The Army had imposed very strict rules regarding fraternization with the Germans in occupied zones, including a nightly curfew for German civilians at either nine or ten o'clock. Violations of any kind could lead to a court-martial. Black market activities, such as selling or trading food, cigarettes, and clothing to Germans, was *Streng Verboten* — strictly forbidden! I never attempted to research all the shenanigans that took place during this short period I remained in Germany and during the remainder of the occupation of Germany by our troops. I shall only relate incidents I observed, but readers may extrapolate on their own to realize that the potential for abuse by our troops was unlimited. Before I recount some of my observations and own acts, I must point out that some of us, particularly those fluent in German, were still given work to perform. I do not even remember who gave us the assignment, but after VII Corps had departed, the IPW team personnel and I, handpicked out of my French team (the other members of which had no applicable skills) commuted daily to a giant German PW enclosure holding 200,000 or more prisoners.

This camp was a good hour's jeep ride west of Leipzig. Our job was to screen the prisoners, to find out who among them were mere soldiers ready to go home, and who were confirmed Nazis or SS personnel that should be retained. Helmut and I adopted a quick screening method that allowed us to process a great number of Germans every day, allotting about five to ten minutes to each one of them. Our method may not have been foolproof, but, I am convinced, was effective enough to catch the bad guys and allow the good guys to go home. We asked each German for his papers, usually the *Soldbuch*, which indicated the units he had belonged to, when he entered the Service, and whether he was a member of the party or had belonged to any Nazi youth organizations. If he had no early Party affiliations, we passed him. If we noticed a suspicious entry or observed nervousness on the part of the prisoner — shifting eyes, hesitation in speech, inconsistencies in his paybook — we grilled him further. These people were afraid of us. A great deal was at stake, and Helmut and I acted our part well. I yelled at them like a German officer would, a grim look on my face, and stood for no nonsense.

I remember catching one man in a lie. I ordered him to stand at attention until I ordered him at ease. The next man I caught lying I placed in front of the other at attention, noses almost touching. I had them stand in this position, face to face, eye to eye, for quite a while. Even I thought at the time that it was childish of me to abuse my power over these two men. Then again they had brazenly lied to me and insulted my intelligence — let them understand what it is like to forego one's dignity, a feeling the Nazis inflicted on many of their victims. Then we interrogated both of them again and found them to have been good loyal Nazis. It was a game for me, but for those people it meant the difference between going home to their dear ones or suffering continued uncertainty in a camp.

We had picked a few PWs to serve as orderlies. They were more than happy to please in exchange for a few privileges like food or cigarettes and to escape being thrown in with the dense mass of captured men. It is not much fun to serve the Reich for years, see your country defeated, then be herded into enclosures with thousands of others, wondering when you will see home again, and worry meanwhile how you will survive, after your uncertain return, in a country partially in rubble. We had these orderlies build a steam bath. We discovered near our interrogation tent a small stone structure and had our "slaves" seal it, build a makeshift fireplace out of rocks and bricks, and light a big wood fire, which in turn heated some large rocks. Then Helmut, others, and I indulged in a wet sauna, pouring water over the hot rocks, generating lots of steam, and hosing ourselves off with cold water after enjoying the heat. This may not have equaled the luxurious excesses of Nazi bigwigs in occupied Paris, but it felt pretty good in the June heat.

Once in a while I strolled to the straggler collecting point in Leipzig, where every day a stream of refugees of all kinds ended up. I spoke to some of them. I recall one senior German staff officer telling me, "You Americans have made a big mistake! You should join forces with us and fight the Russians." I could not really disagree with his proposal, sensing the truth of what he said. In theory he was right. (At that time I did not know the Soviets well at all, unaware that ten years later I would serve as a Soviet Intelligence specialist in the Army and the Central Intelligence Agency.) I explained to him that America does not have a long-range foreign policy and handles such matters on an *ad hoc* basis. Americans had not as yet developed a taste for long wars as a way of life and would rather put this one behind them. He just shook his head prophetically.

I discovered that one of the Corps MP officers was carrying out a program of personal vendetta against Hitler Germany. Every evening he came to the collecting point, picked a German at random, and gave him a good shellacking. From my point of view this is not the best way to get your daily exercise, but wars drive people to do strange things! Suddenly Nordhausen seemed just a tiny bit more comprehensible. Was it all a matter of degree?

Every American Serviceman was interested in acquiring some of the products for which Germany was famous, most of all cameras such as the Leica, one of the best and fastest in the world. On the other hand, one could acquire such items only illegally — looting, fraternizing, black market bartering. For years to come, the black market in Germany and other European countries became a way of life, and no German was ever seen without the telltale briefcase containing anything from money to cartons of cigarettes, smoked fish, or a large salami — often neatly stashed side by side. I enjoyed slightly more freedom to talk to Germans, as I could always claim to be looking for valuable information for either CIC (Counter Intelligence Corps) or the burgeoning Military Government. Near our hotel was a camera shop, still in operation, but without any visible merchandise. I entered the store several times and asked the owner about the availability of cameras. He claimed to have no Leicas, but said he could get me a Robot, a fast-shooting sports camera capable of taking 50 pictures in a very short time.

While I was mulling over the possibility of acquiring such a camera without being caught and court-martialed, one of the MP Lieutenants — having heard of my ability to communicate with Germans — asked me if I could help him get Leicas. I immediately realized the splendid opportunity offered me by our evidently corruptible enforcers of the law. If I could operate under the cloak of their fairly certain immunity, I might be safe. Perhaps I could profit from being the intermediary in this moderately heinous deed.

I had long conferences with the camera-shop owner and finally put together a deal agreeable to all. He would procure two or three Leicas in exchange for a large quantity of rations and cigarettes. He was not shy with a long list of food hard to obtain for Germans. I was not offering my negotiating services altruistically for the pure joy of helping my comrades in arms as well as throwing a few crumbs to the German underdogs. Unbeknown to the MP Lieutenant, the German would slip me a Robot for my selfless efforts, having no doubt figured the cost thereof in the quantity of goods he had requested. The MPs did not care, since for them everything was on the U.S. Army.

I arranged a time for delivery and with utter fascination, watched the masters at work. The MP Lieutenant with his enlisted henchmen committed the perfect crime. He procured a truck, loaded it up behind the kitchen with cases of rations, drove it to the alley behind the camera shop. Serving as *consigliere* in this operation, I was not required to participate physically, merely giving the others the benefit of my *savoir-faire*. The MPs took off with their Leicas and I picked up my Robot the next day. As I had never been issued a footlocker like other commissioned officers, I had one made out of wood by a German carpenter, in exchange for cigarettes, and locked my newly acquired toy inside of it. My European schooling was finally paying off.

Compared to what others did, this camera episode would not even have counted as a misdemeanor in today's penal code. Our famous French team, to which fortunately I belonged only on paper, operated at a much more sophisticated level. Its three members were occupying a large residence all by themselves. They roamed around the countryside and managed to pick up some small cattle with their jeep. Just how they did it, I shall never know. Then they found a butcher to slaughter the animals in their basement and dispose of the meat on the black market. I often wondered what the German owners of their house, once they moved back in, thought of all that blood in the basement. I only know and saw with my own eyes the valuable loot they acquired with the meat. They collected a large quantity of all kinds of valuables: jewelry, small antiques, silverware, and such.

Another incident of minor interest, the details of which we never learned, occurred with the Photo Interpreter Team. I had known some of them as far back as Ritchie, but avoided having dealings with them. They were not a congenial group and evidently did not get along together too well. The story passed along was that the enlisted men sat together in a room of the house the team occupied in Leipzig, cleaning their carbines, preparing themselves for shipment back to the U.S. One of them was an Armenian, from Los Angeles, who had always bragged to me in Ritchie about his wealthy family and the terrific family rug business he expected to return to after the war. Was it an accident? Was it a long-time grudge nurtured during a year of working together day and night in their own tight office? We shall never know! Suddenly, a weapon discharged and very seriously wounded the Armenian. And we never learned whether he recovered.

One evening, Helmut and I were taking a walk after dinner near the hotel when we spotted, and were spotted by, two young German women. One was dark, average-looking; the other had blue eyes and was blonde, svelte, and pretty. We knew what the risk was, but the women, especially the dark one, acted as though they were curious about us. They did not encourage us, but neither did they discourage, when we followed them to their apartment building. The blonde ignored us, but the dark one kept on looking back at us, giggling, talking to her friend, seemingly interested in becoming acquainted. At the door of their building, the dark one looked back once more. We took a chance, following them inside and then to their upstairs apartment. The dark one let us in, the blonde remained sullen and neutral.

To their surprise, the women quickly found out that Helmut and I spoke perfect German. We offered them cigarettes and sat with them making idle conversation. I focused all my attention on the blonde. She had class, a certain presence — the Marlene Dietrich type I thought. She seemed torn between the curiosity of knowing more about two German-speaking American officers and a certain understandable hostility toward soldiers of an army who had just defeated her country. Furthermore, she surmised from his looks, as she later told me, that Helmut might be Jewish. He, relegated to the less attractive woman, did not care to stay much longer and finally left.

While the blonde never encouraged me, she nevertheless never asked me to leave. We seemed frozen in a kind of strange cat and mouse play, a verbal exchange, where no one really knew where the other one stands. Both women had been a long time without their husbands and presumed them dead. And I seemed to be living outside my self, not even acknowledging at that moment that my marriage existed.

It was quite late and because of the curfew for Germans, the blonde could no longer return to her own home. She apparently was accustomed to staying overnight at her friend's apartment and went straight to a bedroom. I followed her. It was the strangest situation. She did not object to my being there, but simply got undressed down to her slip, and lay down on a bed. I also undressed and lay beside her. She just lay there, and I did not wish to force myself upon her. I wanted her to like me. Finally, I fell asleep.

In the morning, the blonde left. I went back to my hotel, baffled and frustrated, my desire to know this woman still very strong, inflamed by the ardor inherent in the chase. The next evening I found the apartment and had a long talk with the dark-haired woman. She was sympathetic and promised to intercede on my behalf. My persistence was rewarded. I obtained "Marlene's" address. We clicked, became lovers, swept along in a strong natural wave of mutual passion, as I would like to believe, and which grew as we learned about each other.

We simply lived for the moment. She knew I was married. Her husband might resurface. We were brought together and would be separated by a mad, purposeless war. Don't think flowers cannot bloom in rubble! Our meetings ironically almost had a tinge of domestic bliss. It was deeply sincere on my part. Was it make-believe on hers? I went to her place after work always attempting to bring her items I could easily procure, mostly cigarettes. Of course, she kept asking me for things. And why not? The Germans were going to pay a big price for losing the war. She prepared modest, but nice meals, set the table carefully near the window of her apartment. I spent the nights there. I had never experienced married life before, since I had never been with my wife in a domestic setting, only random nights with her — and very few at that. My Marlene was a loving person, and sang to me at times. I shall always remember her singing, "The Music Plays Quite Softly a Song About Love," as haunting as the famous "Lili Marlene."

The only dark cloud always hovering over this scene was the knowledge that I was breaking the rules and could be court-martialed if caught.

She told me about the occupants of her apartment building, especially one old man universally disliked by all the neighbors. He had made their lives miserable during the war, ramming Nazism down their throats. He had joined the Party from the very beginning. Hitler had even awarded him the German Cross in Gold, the highest decoration for Party members. Our CIC personnel, by nature a very cliquish bunch who, convinced they alone had a high enough security clearance for whatever they were doing, never thought of calling on our expertise and were spending their time with limited linguistic resources ferreting Nazis and possible spies. I kindled their interest in this old man and with their tacit approval, grilled him one afternoon, first by myself, then in the company of a CIC agent. I was after the Cross in Gold, which I was certain he had secreted away. It would make a terrific souvenir! I tried everything: threats, promises, rewards if he came clean. He refused to budge, claiming it was lost, although he was scared to death. He finally gave me the cloth insignia which replaces the original decoration for normal wear and is sewn on a uniform or suit. Then I let the CIC have him. They drew a blank also. He was a very stubborn old man, one of Hitler's finest.

My friend usually asked me for trivial items I found easily procurable. However, one day she came up with a major request. She wanted a lady's bicycle. Hers had somehow been lost in the war. It just so happened that near the hotel and the Corps Headquarters, Germans had to dismount from their bicycles before proceeding. If they failed to do so, the MPs relentlessly confiscated the bicycles for good. There were warning signs to that effect, but many Germans either ignored them or failed to notice them. Every evening the MPs had a large stock of forfeited bikes. My friend had observed this practice and now insisted I obtain for her a nice lady's bike with a light. I finally told an MP about it, who without asking me any further questions, proceeded to get me what I wanted. By this time it was for them a daily routine.

It did not take long for the right rider with the sought-after bike to come along, fail to dismount, and lose her precious possession. After the bike was added to the mountain of others, the woman hovered anxiously for a long time nearby, crying, imploring the MP for mercy and begging for her bike back. I really felt bad; what I had done went against everything I had thought I believed in. She had forfeited her bike by not dismounting, but I felt guilty for picking her out of the crowd. All I had to do was to remain passive, not intercede on her behalf with the MP. As yet she did not associate me with the confiscated machine. However, after seeing me talk to the MP, she sensed my presence was specifically linked to her bike. In a sense my conscience told me I had sealed this poor woman's fate. To my immense relief, the tearful woman finally gave up. I rode the bike to my girlfriend's building and carried it up to her fifth-floor apartment. She was very grateful and I tried hard to forget the whole incident.

Although I took every precaution to keep my presence in my friend's apartment secret, I was certain some neighbors knew. Living under Nazi or Communist regimes makes people alert to and suspicious of everybody and everything. I had made an enemy of the old Nazi Party member in the building and had no illusions about other tenants. One night, after 10 p.m., we noticed a multitude of MPs swarming all over the neighborhood, in front and around our building. With my bad conscience, knowing full well my precarious position if discovered in Marlene's apartment, I was terrorized. I was convinced the old man had given me away and that the MPs were looking for none other than me. There was no escape. All I could think of was being arrested, court-martialed, sent to prison, my future ruined. It was too late for regrets. I worked myself up into a real lather. These were among the worst two to three hours of agonizing suspense I had ever spent. My friend was, of course, also very upset. We stood at the window, behind the curtains, watching for hours. No one can imagine my intense relief, when at last the MPs disappeared as quietly and swiftly as they had come. I discreetly found out the next morning it had been a routine curfew check and had nothing to do with me.

In those days I had no knowledge of Russian and was in no way involved in the negotiations between Americans and Soviets. The latter showed up at intervals at our mess, and I saw their coats and Service caps with the hammer and sickle insignia hanging outside in the lobby. One day, I could not resist and took one of these cap insignia (I was picking up some very bad habits). We were leaving and handing over Leipzig to the Soviets on July 3, 1945. The Germans did not know, but feared such a move on our part. I told my friend, and she was panic-stricken. The Germans dreaded the Russians beyond all imagination, their fear magnified by rumors of rape, violence, and inhumane acts.

I could do nothing for her. I brought her whatever cigarettes and food I could manage, but in the end we had to say good-bye. For me, the parting had always been a lurking inevitable conclusion of our wartime affair. For her, it was one more in an endless chain of heartbreaks and hardships. I drove away from Leipzig with a very heavy heart, hoping she would manage to cope as she had done all along, not jealous at all of any Soviet officer who might treat her with care and decency — even love. Since I was a member of the French MII team, I had to travel with them; in some ways it made it easier, because we had absolutely nothing to say to one another. I could remain steeped in my thoughts.

Leisure begets vices.
— Latin Proverb

Chapter 16

Time to Go Home!

I WAS IN LIMBO WITH regard to work and fixed duties. I had no specific assignments, being merely the second officer on the 419 French MII team. Not in charge of it, certainly I was not needed by its members to participate in their nefarious dealings. I was just with them for the ride and did not even know our destination. I finally found out we were going with XXI Corps from Leipzig to Schwäbisch-Gmünd, situated an hour's drive east of Stuttgart. Schwäbisch-Gmünd, literally "Swabian Fall or Flow," is a small town, at that time also known as the Silver City of Germany, because of its large number of expert silversmiths. The Swabians speak German with a strong regional accent, which sounds quaint and amusing to anyone raised in northern Germany as I was. Upon our arrival, I was told by the CO of our team, who had been promoted to Captain purely on the basis of being around, that I could obtain a week of leave to go to Paris. Two members of the French team were going, and I was welcome to ride with them if I wished. I accepted, of course. It might be my last chance in a long while to see Paris again.

I traveled with the two enlisted men, Jorge and Lunch Meat. The latter was, as ever, munching away on some tidbits, no doubt storing up for the time he would have to pay for his own snacks. Although a commissioned officer, I never tried to pull rank on these two dark characters, always afraid lest I precipitate a regrettable confrontation. I was very leery of them. I was on the team for TO & E purposes only, but had never been involved in their work (which, I believe, had never been a clearly defined observable reality).

Jorge had lived in France and had a girlfriend residing in a small town east of Paris. We dropped him off. Lunch Meat took the wheel and the two of us continued toward the City of Light (and Pleasure). On the way both men had discussed all the loot they had collected from their clandestine operations — jewelry and silver — and joyfully anticipated its disposal. Jorge had taken his share. Lunch Meat had his in a large box, which he kept on the back seat of the jeep. It contained a great deal of valuables. I had only glimpsed its contents, but they looked like something out of *Treasure Island*. We had been driving with the top of the jeep down behind the back seat, and I had warned Lunch Meat to tie down his box before it slid off the back of the jeep, as we drove over very bumpy roads. He, gruff and morose as always, would not hear of it.

With the top down, traveling in the wind, there was a great deal of noise. We would not have heard anything fall off the jeep. Every once in a while I looked back to see if our luggage was still there. I noticed the box was gone. I called out to Lunch Meat to stop and told him about the missing box, reminding him of my previous warning. He was shattered, disconsolate, a tragic figure overwhelmed by grief. This very moment he would have been a movie producer's dream for the role of Job. Still, he alone was to blame.

By now, it was pointless to turn around and look for the lost box. Some poor French peasant was certain to have stumbled across it on the road, picked it up, opened it, found the treasure inside, and henceforth believed in Guardian Angels, Providence, God, Fairies, and all the company of Heaven. Outwardly, I shared Lunch Meat's grief, consoling him as best I could. Inwardly, thinking of his team's escapades and outrageous excesses, I could only visualize the lucky finder of the treasure and know the Lord works in mysterious ways. The loss considerably dampened Lunch Meat's spirits and he even let me drive, a good move on his part I thought, considering his present distraught condition. Besides, I always love to drive. His trip to Paris was wrecked, and all the surprises he had in store for his friends there had vanished in the dust of the road.

Upon arriving in Paris, we parked the jeep in an Army lot guarded by MPs, made an appointment to meet and check with each other in a few days, and went our separate ways. I decided to look for a hotel in the Clichy and Pigalle section and found a reasonable room. I noticed prices were sky high, much above what I wanted to pay. I decided I would have to conduct a little business on the side, since I did not think it fair to my marital finances to spend my hard-earned funds on myself. I had managed to obtain a second Robot and carried it around for a few days, asking in stores and bars if anyone was interested in purchasing it. I eventually found a buyer, the owner of a bar. He wanted to try out the camera before consummating the deal.

I was feeling pretty tough at the time and told him I was not the least bit worried. Should I not get my camera back, I hinted with a grim smile and in my most polite French, I might just be tempted to drive by in my jeep in the darkest of nights and rearrange his front window with a brick (at a cost higher than that of the camera). The man took pictures with the Robot, was satisfied with the results, and paid the price agreed upon. The front window retained its pristine condition, and my short vacation in Paris was paid for.

I decided to look up Jacqueline and her family. Much to my surprise, they were living in their old apartment and had weathered the German occupation without too many hardships. I did not pry, but his being Jewish had had no apparent ill effects. His wife was her usual gracious self, and Jacqueline, my first real date in St. Germain in 1935, had not changed. We agreed to meet for dinner before I left for Germany.

The old man, always interested in profitable deals wondered whether, with my perfect knowledge of German and my being stationed in Germany, I could not manage the acquisition of valuable merchandise at bargain prices. The German people were hard up after losing the war and he hoped to capitalize on their shortages. If required, he even offered to keep the goods for me in Paris until they could be disposed of advantageously later on when it appeared safe to do so. We all stood to come out ahead. I politely declined, pretexting that merely because there were money-making opportunities, I did not plan to initiate a career in crime. I distinctly remember telling him I would never exploit the misfortunes the Germans had brought on themselves.

During my stay in Paris, I went to a few bars, and just by inquiring, I located my previous date who had given me more than I bargained for during my earlier trip to Paris. She was still dancing in bars and acted very surprised when I told her about the medical souvenir she had bestowed upon me. She claimed complete innocence, but I really did not feel up to debating her and left, despite her expressed interest in being with me again. Had there been in French an adequate equivalent of "I would not touch you with a ten-foot pole," this would have been the right time to use it.

There was not too much I could do in Paris, since everything was very expensive. I took walks, went to the PX, and enjoyed what I thought to be my last free time before going home and starting work on my Ph.D. I met with Lunch Meat in the guarded Army parking lot and we checked on the jeep. To our consternation, someone had stolen our spare wheel and tire. Evidently, crime was flourishing inside the enclosure while the MPs were focusing all their attention on keeping it out. We decided to steal one back just before leaving the parking lot. It was either that, or pay for the items out of our own pocket. Any upright Jesuit would have granted us dispensation for this retaliation. I have often wondered who finally ended up without a spare in this game of musical chairs, or spares.

My date with Jacqueline turned out to be somewhat of a surprise. We went for dinner to a nice local restaurant of her choice. (One could eat well in Paris, if willing to pay the steep prices.) Ten years had passed since we had last seen each other. She was still quite attractive, with her animated manner and flashing dark eyes, and fun to be with. I was now 28 years old, an officer; she in her middle 30s and unmarried. She did not mention her love life. We reminisced about St. Germain and she told me that the son of the hotel owner, with whom we had double-dated in 1935, had gotten the other girl pregnant and caused a major scandal in the two families.

We were eating our dinner, talking, laughing and — what an unforgettably strange moment — suddenly looked at each other at the very same instant, in wordless mutual agreement. It was time to leave. I paid the bill, and we walked to my hotel. The concierge silently gave me my key, and we went up to the room. Later, while still lying together, Jacqueline found this an opportune moment to hint at a love affair she had had during the war with an older man and to compare the experience favorably with the one we just had. Who needs a critique at a time like that? I saw Jacqueline very briefly one more time. We corresponded for a few years, until time spun its inevitable cobwebs.

I was certain, upon my return to XXI Corps, that with my points for service overseas — the arrowhead for landing on D-Day, and five campaign ribbons — I would be sent home immediately. However, I had another surprise coming. The G-2 of XXI Corps, Lieutenant Colonel Wilbur Wilson, said that he had been much impressed with the work of the OB section and with my qualifications. He told me he knew I was scheduled to go home, but asked me to stay with him until the Corps was deactivated. His request caught me unprepared.

I told him I was married, my wife was expecting me, and I had plans to start on my Ph.D. Wilson replied that he would love to have me stay and had some good use for my services. Besides, he said, the delay would not be long — three to four months at the most. If I waived my right to return, the Adjutant General could easily arrange for me to remain with the Corps. I would be assigned as CO of the 166 IPW Team, which was now attached to XXI Corps. Wilson wanted an immediate answer. I thought about it and, on the spur of the moment, decided that after a year of combat duty, I could use some more relaxed work and the pay that went with it; at home, I would be an unemployed graduate student. I agreed to stay. On August 14, I was assigned as CO of IPW Team 166. The enlisted personnel on the team essentially had nothing to do, and I told them I would not breathe down their necks as long as they stayed out of trouble. The Colonel and I remained good friends for years.

The XXI Corps had a very active Officers Club, membership in which was mandatory. Every evening it was filled with officers, American female personnel from the Medical Corps and other Service organizations, local women working for us in one capacity or another, and even German female guests. Fraternization was less and less frowned upon — in fact, was tolerated. Drinking was heavy, but I still never indulged. There was also music and dancing. Everybody was relaxing after the war. Instead of accepting housing in one of the fancy single homes the Army had requisitioned from the Germans, I had opted for a plain modest room without private bath in the only hotel on the town's main square, the *Marktplatz*, immediately next to the Officers Club. I liked simple quarters and preferred to be centrally located. The homes were far away on the other side of the river.

The first job Wilson gave me was to give private lessons in German conversation three times a week to the top brass — all Colonels, heading the various sections: Corps Engineers, Medical, Adjutant General, Operations, and such. It was a small group and I enjoyed basking in this exalted company. The task was simple enough, required no preparation on my part, and in this setting all the Bird Colonels were a gracious flock.

The second job was even better. I was going to be the liaison officer between XXI Corps and the French First Army of General Leclerc in Baden-Baden, my main mission being to buy liquor and wine from them for the club. Who in all of Swabia, nay Germany, could be more ideally suited for this job? As a product of the French educational system I could deal with the French. As a teetotaler, I would not sample the merchandise. Hitherto, no one had been able to pry any liquor loose from our French allies.

The Corps placed a Maybach luxury limousine and a driver at my disposal for this, my first trip to Baden-Baden. The car was the wartime idea of a stretch limousine and obtained a minimal amount of miles per gallon (but the Army did not charge us for gas). I arrived in Baden-Baden, after a three-hour trip via the only viable through-street in Stuttgart, severely damaged by our bombing raids, and was stunned by the resplendent beauty of this luxury spa. I had forgotten the wonderful parks and gardens I had last seen in 1922 as a kid arriving in Germany from America. (I had also watched then in childish wonder my first storks flying over nearby Karlsruhe.) The French received me well, like one of their own.

I have a foolproof introduction to the French — better than a password, a fraternity handshake, or a Masonic sign — insuring instant rapport:

"*Ah! Vous parlez français?*" — "You speak French?"

"*Oui, naturellement! J'ai fait Carnot.*" — "Yes, of course. I studied at the *Lycée Carnot.*"

"You'll join us for lunch, *naturellement?*"

"Vous êtes trop aimable." — "You are too kind!"

There followed a two-hour lunch and nostalgic conversation about Paris. (It was so hard to be in exile, away from Paris, suffering the hardships of a world-renowned spa!) We chatted about life in Paris — education, the war, everything we had in common.

My father had taught me never to bring up business before lunch when dealing with Frenchmen. So I just enjoyed their hospitality. After lunch, (it was almost three in the afternoon by that time), I casually mentioned that I had a long road ahead and would soon be leaving. "Incidentally," I added, "was there any way we could buy some wine and liquor for our club?" It worked like a charm! They loaded my limousine with bottles, I paid them, and we all looked forward to our next meeting, absolutely essential to Allied understanding and friendship. Of course, any time they wished to visit us in Schwäbisch-Gmünd, I would personally make them feel welcome. They never took me up on my invitation. Elegant Baden-Baden was far too great a place to leave — even for a day — to visit the humdrum burg that XXI Corps was occupying. Leave it to the French to pick the choicest spots!

I drove back to Baden-Baden several times, always with the same success: a car full of liquor. Once, we had to accept a load of unpacked bottles which the driver and I arranged loosely on top of the back seat of the car. But somewhere between Stuttgart and Schwäbisch-Gmünd, there was an MP checkpoint. All military vehicles had to stop for verification. I was driving, and just before reaching the checkpoint I hit a bad bump in the road. Many of the bottles broke, creating not only a mess of broken glass on the seat and floor of the car, but also perfumed the entire interior with an overpowering fragrance that would have done Falstaff's Boar's Head Tavern proud. I opened the window just a crack and the MP waved us on. *That was close!*

While on the subject of liquor, I shall relate an adventure that occurred before the Corps was deactivated. The club was rolling in money. As the time approached for deactivating the Corps, the club officer, a pleasant, jovial *bon vivant* — ideal for the job — wondered what he should do with the surplus of cash. His first thought was to distribute it among all the members. The military authorities, when consulted, ruled his plan out as unfeasible. Money could not be returned to the members under any circumstance; illogically enough, liquor could. Our club officer left for Paris (where else?) to purchase a large quantity of the best France had to offer.

I did not hear of all this until Colonel Wilson called me to his office and in his usual poker-faced way simply asked, "Lieutenant, how would you like to go to Paris?"

Catch 22 had not yet been written, but I immediately knew there was a snag of some kind. "What's the story, Sir?"

"The story is that you cannot stay, you have to turn around and come back right away!"

I laughingly told him I could not go under these conditions. No one can go to Paris and turn around right away. It would be like Ulysses resisting the songs of the sirens without tying himself to the mast of his ship. Then I asked for more details.

Apparently, our club officer had called from Paris asking for me. He had been able to obtain all the necessary permits to buy the liquor — cases of it — had the permits to pick it up in his pocket, but did not have the faintest idea of how to go about getting it. The cases had to be collected from all around Paris. He did not know a word of French, was totally unacquainted with the city, and did not have a truck. Besides, he most probably could think of better things to do in Paris than "*cherchez*" — find — the liquor, much preferring to "*cherchez la femme.*" Time and speed were of the essence. This was a challenge my normal desire for showing off could not resist. I told the Colonel I was ready to leave.

With a "deuce-and-a-half" ton truck, and an enlisted driver, I left at noon the same day, doing all the driving. I was afraid that, should I make the enlisted man take the wheel for unreasonable amounts of time and there was an accident, I would be responsible. We drove to the Rhine and found the bridge I was planning to take blocked. We had to go miles out of our way to the north and cross on a temporary pontoon bridge. Without stopping, I drove through the night, spurred on by a flow of adrenaline, and arrived at the *Place de l'Opéra* around seven in the morning. I had been up for 24 hours. The club officer met me as agreed, gave me a map of Paris, the addresses of the warehouses, and the official documents serving as payment in lieu of cash. I told the enlisted man to take the day off, but warned him to meet me without fail at the same place at five o'clock in the afternoon. Then I started looking for the warehouses around Paris.

I found them without difficulty. I had no problem completing the transactions with the warehouse workers. The papers were all in order and the French were happy to deal with, for all intents and purposes, one of their own. (My friends, often critical of the French attitude toward Americans, always tell me, "You cannot judge. You speak their language." However, I do not believe that language alone is the key. The crucial point for Americans to mind is as follows: do not expect from the French more than they expect from themselves!) We filled the truck to absolute capacity and everyone warned me that the vehicle, loaded as it was with valuable liquor, was worth a fortune on the black market. Under no circumstances should I leave it unattended.

By five o'clock I was back at the *Place de l'Opéra* and, of course, as I feared, my driver was nowhere in sight. I immediately went to an MP, told him about the circumstances, and to my utter surprised admiration, he and his colleagues had my driver back in 30 minutes, a little the worse for wear and not quite sober. They were really on top of the situation, perhaps because they patronized the same establishments where they found my driver. I explained to him we could not leave the truck unattended and must immediately return to home base. On the way out of Paris I took a little detour, north to the Gare St. Lazare, along the street to my father's old office building that overlooks the bridge, *Pont de l'Europe*, built by my classmate's father, to Jacqueline's parents' apartment.

They were eating dinner and extended an immediate invitation. I explained to them the situation, told them I had an enlisted man guarding the truck downstairs, and had to leave right away. They gave us a snack of cold chicken, which I gratefully accepted. We ate in the truck, and I started driving again through the evening and the night. At about two or three in the morning, I could no longer keep my eyes open. I pulled over to the side of the road and slept an hour on top of the cases of liquor. My driver was sleeping all the way in the passenger seat. We stopped at an American military base for breakfast, reaching the *Marktplatz* and the Officers Club about two in the afternoon. I had been up, except for the short nap, over 50 hours. I vaguely remember taking a dip in a swimming pool and sleeping until the next morning.

I was the hero of the day, which immensely flattered my ego. Everyone heard about the guy who drove nonstop to Paris and back, sleepless on the job for two days. The club had converted all its cash to liquor, which would be distributed free to all the members, insuring a zero inventory when the Corps disbanded. The club officer, on his return from Paris, corroborated that without me it could not have been done and offered me a dozen bottles of expensive liquor as a reward. First I refused, then I accepted with the intention of giving it away.

As I think back to the end of the war in Europe, that period of celebration, of relaxing after months of tension, uncertainty, grief, and hardship for so many, it all seems like a phantasmagoria, a strange shadow pantomime, wherein the actors are faceless blurred figures. However, the events do not vanish that easily from my memory — would that they did! Unfortunately, they stand out clearly against a live, better-forgotten background. I now wish I had not been so naive, so heedless, had not opened that door to the forbidden chamber. The metaphor of irremediably tasting the apple takes on a poignant meaning!

It seemed that this was a time when ancient taboos, the normal rules of conduct, the *do's* and *don'ts* programmed into us since birth, by parents and mentors, were engulfed and lost in the maelstrom of the war and its immediate aftermath. Always sober and lucid, I do not have the excuse of a mind befogged by spirits. I knew right from wrong, but I allowed myself to drift along. I had no business in the milieu I had been frequenting and should have stayed away.

With regard to the Germans, the reasons for their moral erosion are more evident and excusable. Americans have never known what it is like to have the enemy invade their territory. Many Germans were deeply damaged both in body and spirit by a disastrous war of their own doing. Their judgment of right and wrong was severely shaken. Strange, when you think about it, how the most massive, vastly destructive, and bloody upheavals in human history are rarely, if ever, brought about by a Socrates, a Plato, or an Einstein, but rather by ordinary men from among the people like Luther, Mohammed, the Mahdi, Hitler, and Stalin. Ordinary men can move masses in unexpected ways.

I had a great deal of free time during which I enjoyed becoming acquainted with Schwäbisch-Gmünd and its people. It was too early after the end of the war to find anything worthwhile available in stores, and I had no interest whatsoever in scavenging or bartering for valuables. I had a silversmith make a modest ring for my wife. It was of rather fine workmanship, with the coat of arms of Schwäbisch-Gmünd surrounded by minuscule silver balls. He was a proud man and only asked a fair price, not any handouts, though was not adverse to a gift of cigarettes. The surrounding country was rather spectacular, and I enjoyed some nice walks.

One day I had the pleasant surprise of having an old friend from Camp Ritchie show up. Hugh W. Nibley had been a member of the first six OB teams and a fellow student in my class. We had remained together across the ocean, at Litchfield Barracks, in London, until our teams had been assigned to various units. A very scholarly and dedicated Mormon, he already had his Ph.D. in classics or in religion and was never seen without a book in his hands. Waiting in line for chow, on the road, during breaks, no matter what the occasion, he was always oblivious to the world around him, absorbed in his reading.

At that time he was studying Arabic. Both of us, with similar academic backgrounds, hit if off rather well, although Hugh, under all circumstances, did his own thing and always remained an intensely private, self-sufficient person. I believe our good rapport was based on the interest we shared in research, foreign cultures, and languages. He found me somehow at XXI Corps, and I took him all over the countryside to some nearby ruins and photographed them for him. He acted very grateful, paid me for the film and developing, and I regret to this day being stingy enough to have taken his money. He had no interest in the military, performed his duties well, awaiting the day he could return to his beloved teaching and research. He was a good man!

In the late '80s I saw his name mentioned in *Newsweek* in regard to some religious subject at Brigham Young University. I wrote to him and stopped by to see him on my way through Salt Lake City and Provo, Utah. He had not changed a bit, either physically or intellectually. Still deep into Mid-Eastern studies and the Mormon religion, author of scholarly books, totally focused on his work. He was one of the pillars of Brigham Young University and a revered teacher. My wife and I had driven miles out of our way to visit him, though he could allot only so much time to our visit and then, with the same relentless focus I had know him to devote to Arabic, went on to the next item on his crowded agenda.

But to return to the subject of mores within the military at this time, there was a great deal of "shacking up" going on between military personnel and the natives. German women had access to the clubs and it was not difficult to form liaisons. As the military government was beginning to set up shop, there were also many Germans or other displaced nationals from other countries, Czechoslovakia for instance, beginning to work for the Army. I became acquainted with some of them and discovered indirectly, a certain underground network in this small town. Many of the women knew and eventually introduced me to a strange person occupying a small apartment opposite my hotel on the *Marktplatz*.

I have no idea what shady business she was really involved in or how she made her living, but she seemed to know everything that was going on at all times. If I wanted to know where someone or something was to be found, she would invariably be able to tell me. Like a kind of street-level *éminence grise* or Celestina, the sinister, powerful go-between of the medieval Spanish masterpieces of the same name, she would hold court in her apartment and many women, never men, would come to visit her. I watched and listened with cautious fascination, although my instinct told me to be wary of her. She always had a deck of cards in her hands and also told fortune.

There was one incident in which she was involved and which I very much regret, as it proved to me it was time to return home to an actively useful life. I had become acquainted with a very attractive Czech woman at the club. She stood out among the other guests there, and I was rather surprised, with all the competition, that she decided to spend time with me. Again, it probably was because I could communicate with her reasonably well as she spoke German (although with an accent and not perfectly). I did not see her often, maybe on two or three occasions, but the second time she surprised me by telling me she would like a child from me! I totally ignored her remark, assuming I had misunderstood her imperfect German. After that she told me she was a single mother and had to visit her child near Stuttgart. She had transportation to the place. Could I give her a ride back? I promised her I would be able to manage it.

On the day I picked her up, I foolishly decided to show off and treat her to dinner at a Stuttgart club, which was strictly reserved for officers and civilians working for the military government. It was risky, but I was certain I would get away with it. After all it was full of Germans. Who knew whom they were working for? The club manager came to our table and asked me who my companion was. I brazenly told him she worked for us in Schwäbisch-Gmünd and he, to my intense relief but with doubt written all over his face, accepted my explanation. We made an arrangement to meet again later that night, but she never showed up.

Unfortunately, being a straightforward logical thinker, I liked life's patterns clearly delineated and thought I could control them. Why would she stand me up now, when I had rendered her a small service? It seemed only sensible to me that she should behave fairly, with civility. I waited and looked around the club. She was nowhere to be found. Since she was a friend of the "Celestina," I asked her whether she knew the whereabouts of my friend. She did. My Czech lady was with a certain warrant officer in his apartment! I must have been out of my mind, affected by the bad company I was keeping and the undisciplined manner in which I was spending my free time. I was senselessly angry.

Quite late at night, insisting on Celestina's cooperation and guided by her, I found the warrant officer's apartment and rang the bell. No answer. My temper rising, I rang again and started banging on the door. Finally, quite out of control, comforting myself in my actions with the thought that the warrant officer would be unable to complain without putting himself into an extremely embarrassing position, with Celestina watching in stunned silence, I broke down the door. A half-asleep warrant officer appeared in his pajamas. I asked for the Czech girl by name. I ordered her to get dressed and come with me. Somehow I must have been very convincing, and the smashed door added realism to the performance. The warrant officer, possibly suffering from a hangover, never said a word. The girl quietly obeyed.

Now that I had gone this far, I had to know why she had broken our date to go back to, evidently, her former boyfriend. Her reply was incredible: after I had ignored her request to have my child, she decided I did not want her. I began to realize that these relationships were far beyond my skill to handle them. This one could lead to a highly regrettable scandal. To avoid any repercussions from the incident — which I hoped the warrant officer wanted to cover up as much as I did — and in order to temporarily conceal my whereabouts, I moved with her for the weekend to a friend's lodgings across the river. After the weekend, she disappeared, and there were no further consequences to an affair of which I was not particularly proud.

From then on, I tried hard to stay out of trouble. However, it was like joining gangs: once in, it is hard to quit. One evening, the club officer asked me to act as an interpreter on a double date. The evening ended with another one-night stand. On another occasion, I had an unnerving sexual experience with Celestina, whom I had suspected of being a lesbian.

The end of the war with Japan fortunately came sooner than expected. XXI Corps celebrated the end of hostilities with a big bash to honor the grand occasion. There was a cocktail party, at which the guests were treated to a generous spread of *hors d'oeuvres* with plentiful drinks to wash it all down. I have often wondered why, since time immemorial and as recorded in many of the great heroic epics of early literature, mankind has measured manly valor and prowess by the amount of liquor a warrior can consume, preferably at one draft. On the other hand, why do some of us contrarians measure man's insanity by the same standards? Many years ago, an uncle of mine told me he would reward me with a gift of money should I abstain from smoking and drinking until I was 21. I kept my part of the bargain, never lighting up or imbibing. He forgot about his promise and never paid me a dime. By that time, I had lost all desire to indulge in either and never did. Did my uncle welsh on his promise or was he a Solomon-like sage who foresaw my recouping the forfeited gift a hundredfold by continued abstinence from these unwholesome habits?

We had among our guests at the XXI Corps party, a group of chemical warfare Colonels who had just returned from the Pacific and came on a special mission to Germany to probe the country's nuclear capabilities. One of them engaged me in a very significant conversation, which I often recalled in later years. The Colonel had indulged in a fair number of cocktails, but was quite lucid in his thoughts and speech. He was merely one of those inclined, when tipsy, to let it all hang out. He brought up the subject of the atomic bomb and did all the talking. He categorically condemned President Truman's decision to drop the two bombs as a major error. Why destroy all this humanity, first in Hiroshima, then in Nagasaki? With firm conviction, he referred to the action as highly unnecessary. The war was won, the Japanese were ready to surrender, and the bombs could have been dropped, if at all, on vacant real estate.

Years later, I read about a lack of communication that may have contributed to this atomic disaster. Before dropping the bomb, the United States warned the Japanese of a new weapon and gave the Japanese government a chance to surrender. Japan announced internationally that, pending cabinet discussions, it was following a policy of *mokusatsu*. The word can mean either "ignore," "withhold comment," or "have no comment." The verb was translated as "ignore" and the bomb dropped. I personally have always regretted America's being the first and only nation to take this first irretrievable step.

XXI Corps was to be deactivated in October 1945. Some time before that, Colonel Wilson asked me if I would care to guide a small group of the top brass, the same few Colonels to whom I had given German lessons, on a tour through Switzerland. Incidentally, the Colonels, being red-blooded Americans with all the characteristics of the race including an inborn lack of interest in learning foreign languages, had long before discreetly withdrawn from our lessons, claiming other pressing duties (perhaps afternoon naps) but assuring me that my teaching talents and knowledge played no part in their decision. The Red Cross or some other organization had made it possible for military personnel to take short, inexpensive tours to Switzerland, and I would prove useful as their personal interpreter and guide.

We entered Switzerland through Basel, where I had visited the zoo when I was five or six years old. From there we proceeded to Lucerne. I showed them the famous statue of the lion and the Panorama, a circular depiction of a historical scene occupying an entire building and viewed by visitors from the center. My uncle Charlie had been an importer of Swiss watches all of his life, and I thought I might, availing myself of his contacts, enable my friends to see at an appropriate jewelry store items not generally shown to every client walking in from the street. When we arrived in Geneva, my mother's birthplace, I contacted Gubelins, one of the best jewelry stores, introduced myself as Charlie Frisch's nephew, and asked whether our group could have a special show of valuable watches and clocks. The store immediately knew my uncle's name and was glad to oblige. We were treated to a dazzling display of timepieces with enlightening commentary.

In Geneva, I showed my friends the famous monument of the Reformers and, in the evening, made arrangements to take them all to a fondue. The traditional Swiss fondue is prepared by melting strips of Swiss cheese in a large tureen, adding white wine and *kirsch* or *kirschwasser*, a brandy made from distilled black cherry juice and the ground pits. The guests sit around the table, with the communal tureen in the center, and dip pieces of bread crust at the end of their forks into the same boiling hot, cholesterol-rich mixture. I am not crazy about the dish, but my companions just loved it, drinking additional cognac on the side. The evening was a great success. I took far more pleasure in watching their enjoyment than in the meal itself.

The last town on the trip was Lausanne, 50 minutes from Geneva by electric train. Lausanne is quite different from Geneva, the people, more fun-loving — more like the French. In the evening I took the group to a bar where they spent their time drinking. There was music and some single young women without partners were also present. Again, not interested in drinking, I danced with some of the girls. They were friendly and interested in meeting an American who could communicate with them. I ended up dancing frequently with the same rather shy, quiet girl. Yet she turned out not to be so shy after all, and we spent the night together not being seen, heard, or suspected by some unidentified lady with whom she boarded.

Shortly after our return to Schwäbisch-Gmünd, XXI Corps was deactivated. My team was assigned to VI Corps in Stuttgart. Colonel Wilson tried to persuade me to stay on active duty and join him on the Potsdam Mission, which he was going to command. I told him I could no longer postpone my return home. I have often wondered what my life would have been like had I followed him and stayed in the Service. Wilson rose to many key positions, including Chief of Staff of the 82nd Airborne at Fort Bragg and Chief of Infantry Career Management at the Pentagon.

But before leaving for Stuttgart with my team, I wanted to say good-bye to a friend. On his and my last night before our departure, his for home, mine for VI Corps, I drove to a nearby town where he was now temporarily housed. On the way out of town, I carelessly drove about 30 miles an hour in a 25-mile zone and was picked up by two cruising MPs.

There was a general crackdown by the Army on officers driving and especially on those exceeding the speed limit. I had permission to drive, since our team had two jeeps. I could hardly have been considered speeding at 30 miles per hour. The MPs thought differently. I could not talk them out of giving me a ticket. Unfortunately, this ticket followed me through channels to VI Corps. At the wrong time the Army can be downright efficient. After I arrived at VI Corps, I attended the weekly Monday meeting of all officers. The Chief of Staff, a gruff Colonel, brought up the subject of officers driving too much and too fast, promising to make a lasting example of the next one caught and crucify him. I knew who it was going to be, and it was.

The ticket came, and I stood at attention in front of the Chief of Staff, not expecting mercy. He was not interested in circumstances or details. He looked at me fiercely, screamed at me, and in colorful metaphorical language, acquired during many years of assiduous practice in the military, told me he was "going to fine the piss out of me." This translated, after the storm abated, into $100, a tidy sum in the 1940s, and became part of my permanent record. I was livid, but there was nothing I could say, since he abruptly dismissed me.

I was so angry I immediately raised the money by selling cartons of cigarettes, an easy thing to do at that time. Then I stormed into the AG's office and asked them how dare they violate regulations and keep me in Germany, considering my number of points. They promised to take immediate steps to send me home. Finally I told them I had been awarded the Bronze Star for my Intelligence work during the Ardennes and would like to receive it at the next ceremony held for that purpose. Such ceremonies were held periodically, and I had never received my medal.

The VI Anzio Beachhead Corps, as its personnel referred to it, would not let you forget its glorious history. Everyone in the Corps was fiercely proud of their stand on the famous beach and expected everyone else to be constantly awed by the role they had played there. In fact, the VI Corps had never fully recovered from its participation in that action, never let anyone forget it, and continued to deem itself privileged because of it. This high opinion of itself and the benefits it expected as a continuing reward for its heroism translated into some very tangible goodies for any personnel joining the Corps later, whether they spent time on the beach or not.

VI Corps had the best officer's mess I had ever experienced anywhere in the Army, seriously competing with Air Force and Navy messes. The German cooks wrought miracles with Army rations and whatever other items they scrounged up to supplement them, recalling to memory the exploits of Escoffier, the greatest chef of them all. He was the one who, during the regattas at Kiel, before World War I, told Kaiser Wilhelm II, in reply to the monarch's question as to what the chef would demand to work for him, coolly answered, "Alsace and Lorraine!" The meals prepared by the Germans at VI Corps were miraculous compared to what our GI culinary warriors produced with the same ingredients. The Officers Club was also outstanding. I almost regretted my decision to leave for home.

On the day of the presentation of medals I stood in line, waiting for the general to pin on my Bronze Star. He looked me over, noticed my overseas Service stripes, guessed that I undoubtedly had earned enough points to go home before now, and very benevolently asked me if I planned to stay in the Service. The Army was encouraging officers to stay in and even offering us permanent Master Sergeant ratings in case of a future RIF (Reduction in Force). Still angry at the fine, I rather ungraciously replied I had no intention of remaining in the Army and was awaiting my orders for shipment back to the USA. The General took it like the soldier he was.

The VI Corps G-2 section gave me one delicate job while I was with them. There had been rumors of abusive treatment of German PWs in a large PW camp near Bruchsal, north of Stuttgart. I was sent there to investigate. When I arrived, the officers attempted to distract me from my job by insisting I have lunch first. Eventually, after continued delaying actions on their part, I told them I had to inspect the camp and write a report on conditions there. The camp certainly was not as yet down to Nordhausen standards, but the emaciated German PWs were well on their way toward emulating labor camp conditions with the help of their captors. I very much doubted their rigorous diet was self-imposed. It proved to me once again that, given the opportunity, humans everywhere act pretty much the same way. My German friends still remember how some of our GIs took the wristwatch off their father's wrist before their very eyes! Conditions in the camp were not good, but I promised to write as mild a report as I could under the circumstances. I have no idea what actions were ultimately taken as a result.

I had been given quarters in a very nice private home, requisitioned from the Germans in a beautiful residential suburb of Stuttgart, Esslingen, across the river to the south. This section had been spared from Allied bombardments. I shared the home with two other officers and we all had enough space so that it might have been months before we ran into each other. I went to the club on some evenings and met a few people, but being a short-timer, refrained from any involvement. I did become acquainted with the German girl serving as bartender mainly because we could communicate.

From then on things went pretty fast. I was responsible for every piece of equipment belonging to my IPW team, from the jeeps down to weapons and wristwatches. I told my enlisted men to assemble everything, as I did not wish to pay for missing items. How they managed, I shall never know, but they outdid themselves. They had acquired a great deal of useful experience in their time. Even the wristwatches surfaced — almost a miracle. I had lost mine long ago. My men should have been in the Quartermaster Corps. They had a positive talent for literally materializing equipment, like those religious and spiritual leaders who tell their flock that wealth comes to those who really expect it — it just appears magically. I obtained a receipt for all the equipment we turned in, except the second jeep. I was going to use it to reach MIS at Bad Schwalbach, from where I would be returned to the U.S.

My orders came, I said good-bye to a few friends and the German barmaid, and drove to Bad Schwalbach near Frankfurt. My orders enabled me to obtain gas at any Army refueling station. With the caution born from experience and a fondness for gathering Intelligence, I did not immediately report to headquarters on arrival at the post. I parked my jeep in a transient parking lot and asked a few questions from officers, also awaiting shipment home. They informed me that processing was running way behind. All transportation was at a premium. Christmas was approaching and the Army was attempting to ship out as many of us as possible prior to the holidays. I could expect to be there for quite a few days.

I needed time to reflect before I got on the conveyer belt. On the spur of the moment, wishing to leave this place before someone intercepted me, especially since I had not signed in, I drove out of the camp. It was a gorgeous day. The drive back through Bruchsal to Stuttgart is very scenic, and I had a car and free gas. I drove back to VI Corps and the Officers Club, reaching it in the evening. No one noticed me much, except for one friend and the barmaid, who knew I was supposed to have left and were curious about what had happened.

I had to return to Bad Schwalbach; I knew I had to face up to it. I was afraid to return home, but the war and the postwar break were over. I had been diverted from what I considered my true purpose in life for over three years. Much of the time had been well spent, but now I was overdue to go back. I did not even have the luxury of wondering whether I wanted to or not. My whole upbringing had taught me only one way: attain the goal originally set for yourself, in this case the Ph.D. It might have been worthwhile at this point to ponder whether it was still a valid goal. But I only knew persistence, not flexibility.

From then on everything went with incredible speed and frustrating slowness. I turned in the rest of my equipment with the jeep and received a perfect clearance. The supply officer was amazed. No one in memory had turned in everything down to wristwatches and other minor items. I accepted the compliment. I did not explain to him what miracles a benevolent *laissez-faire* policy can produce with the right enlisted team. After a week or so, we traveled on the slowest train ever known to man or beast and third class, what in Russian is accurately referred to as " hard car." It was so slow, we would, to divert ourselves, jump off it, run along the tracks, then jump back on again. After almost two days, we arrived in Brussels. We could have walked the distance faster. From there, we traveled to Camp Top Hat, not far from Antwerp. We were housed in well-heated tents and waited, with thousands of others, for a ship. I felt like those emigrants of yore awaiting passage to the New World.

As an officer, I had no details. Many of the men played interminable poker games with pots as high as $1,000, which fortunately appeared to change hands, back and forth, without ever ending in one pocket. Others shot craps. Gambling was strictly prohibited, but at this point, the Army — like Justice — was blind. Once in a while we could commute in an open truck to Antwerp itself, look at store windows, and eat in cafés if we cared to spend the money. Every day we waited to be called for embarkation on an available Liberty ship. The wait seemed to last forever. It may have been ten days or more — I forget — before we were called.

We left Antwerp on November 22, 1945. I had earned my fourth overseas gold stripe, each one signifying six months outside the continental United States. The ship was no luxury liner and the trip back a very rough one. At that time of year the Atlantic is no "Pacific" in the literal meaning of the word. The vessel rolled, tossed, and pitched. I don't get seasick; besides, as an officer, I had adequate quarters. I felt sorry for the enlisted men, having been one long enough. In one of the ship's holds, 800 men were being tossed around below sea level in stifling quarters. Large GI cans were generously provided to receive the results of, if not unavoidable, quite widespread oceanic malaise, more commonly known as *mal de mer*.

The Army Major, because of rank and seniority in charge of military personnel, was a lunatic suffering from battle fatigue. He was obsessed with the fear that some enlisted man might jump overboard. Perhaps he was the one suffering from such a suicidal urge. Furthermore, he wanted a no-gambling rule enforced. Each one of the few officers was given a specific assignment. I was placed in charge of the "slave hold" ("the one with 800 men") with orders not to allow any gambling and to have periodic roll calls, thus insuring no one was AWOL and taking a forbidden dip in the ocean with no lifeguard present. It was an insane, impractical, and unenforceable order. I approached it with my usual nonmilitary logic.

First, I assembled all the First Sergeants in the hold, told them about the orders, and how I stood *vis-à-vis* their implementation. Then I proposed an alternate plan of action. Whenever I came to inspect the hold, I wanted all gambling to cease forthwith. I always took great pride in highly articulate phrasing of instructions. I had to be able to unequivocally state to the Major that I had not observed any games of chance. Second, I wanted the First Sergeants to report to me twice a day that roll calls had been carried out and that everyone was present and accounted for. The Major had requested the unfeasible. Some men in the hold had to be absent in various shifts around the clock for various details, such as KP, cleaning, and such. Besides, some were too weak to stand roll call, moaning listlessly in their bunks. I doubt they had the strength to climb up on deck to carry out any suicidal impulse. In any case, they could not all be present for roll call at any one time. Despite everything, we arrived at our destination safe and fairly sound and, to my knowledge, all accounted for on Saturday, December 1, 1945.

We were taken to Camp Shanks quite late at night and immediately informed that absolutely no passes would be granted. The Army wanted to get us all home as quickly as possible. I remember being the only one in my group to take an ice cold shower at 1 a.m. (Camp Shanks, I guess, did not wish to encourage long layovers). My entire body was beginning to show ominous signs of scabies, and I was itching all over. The next morning, a Sunday, I asked for permission to call my parents and, if possible, to see them for a few hours. My father was 75 years old, and I might never see him again. About three of us were granted exceptional three-hour passes.

We met at one of my Dad's favorite eating places, Jansen's Hofbrauhaus, on Lexington and 43rd Street, near Grand Central Station. It was indeed the last time I saw my dad alive. He died suddenly from a stroke on August 24, 1946. The day after our brief passes, those of us headed for California were taken to Camp Kilmer, New Jersey, and caught a DC-3 with bucket seats.

During the flight I looked out the window in back of me and noticed the left engine on fire. I rushed forward to the lone Army pilot and wordlessly pointed to the engine. He just laughed. We were near Boulder City, Nevada, and could glide into the airport if necessary. He switched off both engines and turned the right one on again just before landing. We waited all day in Boulder City for a plane from Fort MacArthur. Under other circumstances, this would have been an enjoyable excursion. Night came. At that time, Boulder City had no night landing facilities. We were all bussed to Las Vegas. At last, the replacement plane arrived. As it landed, the spare engine shifted in the hold, resulting in much time being spent trying to ease it out of the compartment.

We finally arrived early in the morning at Fort MacArthur. Before being processed for discharge, I talked with some officers who had just gone through the pipeline. One of them warned me, should I need any medical or dental attention, to refuse an immediate discharge and ask for proper care while still on active duty. The processing personnel tried to talk me out of it, warning me I could be forced to serve while undergoing the dental care I very much needed. I refused the immediate release and thus I remained on paid active duty, accumulated more leave time, but never had to do anything but report to a medical facility once a week until the work was completed. I had made the right choice, earning more pay and accumulating more terminal leave, while attending to my own private business.

The evening after our arrival at Fort MacArthur, I took a bus to Union Station in downtown Los Angeles. I called my wife in Montebello. She had no notion as to when I might arrive. We had been apart for well over two years, and I was hoping I could start exactly where we had left off. I would have welcomed a long drink from Hades' River Lethe, whose waters would ensure a forgetfulness and a clear conscience.

Yet, I was very grateful. I had gained a commission and come through the entire war without a scratch. The bullet hole in my shirt was made while I was not wearing it. I never had to fire at anyone, which was just as well, though I would have had no problem doing so if necessary. The only time I had fired my .45 Colt between D-Day and V-J Day was when Helmut and I were riding in a jeep from Leipzig to the PW camp. We shot at some trees while in motion and missed. As a living and emotional experience, I would not have liked to miss the war for the world. Intellectually speaking, it seemed like such a complete, and in the final analysis, unnecessary waste, at least when viewed with limited human logic, unable to grasp the larger purpose and destiny of the universe. There must be better ways!

— All things change and we change with them.
Latin Proverb

Chapter 17

Fitting Back In

CAN ONE EVER REALLY put behind one's self being in and fighting a war? Upon relief from active duty, was I exactly back where I left off, before it all began? Imagine a First Sergeant lining up and addressing a bunch of new recruits, fresh from civilian life and just reporting for duty in the Army. He has a formidable task ahead of him, molding those misfits and pathetic Sad Sacks into something the Army can use. Some may adapt better than others to their new lifestyle in the military, depending on their background and motivation, but it will take weeks of Basic Training and drilling to transform the lot into sharp-looking real soldiers.

Should not then the reverse be true? What does it take to transform a soldier back again into a civilian, especially a veteran who fought in a war? There may be a great deal for him to learn, or more likely to unlearn. Depending on the circumstances in each case and what the individual went through in training and combat, what stark realities he witnessed, might there not be need for some reverse basic physical and mental rehabilitation to help him bridge the transition back to civilian life?

Besides, not all wars are equal. The war in the Pacific was not to be compared to the war in Europe. I count myself very fortunate to have been stationed in Europe, for me a totally familiar territory. I felt at home all through the campaigns from England to Normandy to Leipzig. World War II seemed to most of us a right war — justifiable and necessary. In general, it was inescapable, although many facets thereof could have been avoided with proper foresight and more experience on the part of our leaders: the Battle of the Bulge comes to mind.

During my training in Intelligence, I had pondered the question as to who makes a better soldier: a Russian, a German, a Briton, or an American, considering the respective adjustment each one undergoes as he manages the change from civilian to military lifestyle. I developed a theory. Generally speaking, I thought the best soldier might well be the one who has to make the least adjustment when leaving civilian for military life. The one who had the lowest standard of living, hence had forsaken the least comfortable lifestyle, when entering the Service. *Eureka!* I had discovered the equation: a recruit makes the best soldier in inverse proportion to the loss in standard of living he incurs when enlisting. Carrying this formula to the limit, a Russian soldier might actually achieve a gain in living standard when joining the Red Army, transforming the latter into a hotbed of potential heroes.

How does wartime service affect a soldier? It depends on many factors, not least of them the intellectual and spiritual resources of the individual in question. Every case is different. I can only speak for myself. I was certainly no Sergeant York or Audie Murphy! I did not even dream of the Medal of Honor. Still I saw action and luck was on my side. So it is no surprise that upon my return to American soil, I was not the same individual who entered the Service on October 24, 1942. Not that I had suffered extreme physical discomfort. In that respect, I had been protected and spared. With isolated exceptions, I had never been subjected to any great physical strain or stress such as experienced on maneuvers or in prolonged front-line combat. However, emotionally, mentally, and intellectually, I had been, shall we say, "straightened out." I had progressively learned to swallow my pride, to relegate to the background any intellectual superiority I may have felt owing to my higher-than-average education. I became accustomed to taking orders I did not always deem justified from individuals I might previously not always have thought of as competent to give them. I had pulled enough KP, the ultimate humiliation in my naive way of thinking, to aspire to a place in the *Guinness Book of Records* on that score alone.

I had experienced my share of seemingly endless frustrations and disappointments, which when viewed with hindsight and in perspective were really quite bearable, could be explained by the circumstances and unavoidable confusion surrounding America's precipitous entry into the war, and presented a valuable opportunity to learn patience and cope with life's sobering lessons.

The war, nevertheless, wrought changes in me. It created pressures, opportunities, and conditions that caused me to disregard my deeply rooted principles and belief in moral values. My previously conservative strait-laced behavior was undermined, with an ensuing natural feeling of guilt toward my wife and marriage. For the first time in my life I had experienced and succumbed to casual relationships. I knew I was hardly alone in this, but each one of us has to struggle with his own conscience. Furthermore, my present position in the Army, the material benefits I now enjoyed as a commissioned officer in occupied Germany — until then the best job I had ever had — cast a cloud on my erstwhile crystal-clear resolve to return home as quickly as possible after the end of the war, to enjoy a married life I had never had the chance to start because of it, and to continue my graduate studies.

Then there was another very personal factor in my own situation. Because of my upbringing and previous life in Europe, I felt perfectly at home abroad, having up to that time actually spent more years there than in my own country. Under different circumstances, I would not have minded at all extending my tour of duty in occupied Germany for an indefinite period, enjoying the relatively carefree life and many benefits and privileges the Army offered. Before World War II, a military career was not sought after by most, unless an appointment to either West Point or the Naval Academy was forthcoming. However, a career in the military was a viable option after the war. Veterans, who had never thought of it before, depending on what prospects they had back home, were tempted. Colonel Wilson had offered me the opportunity of continuing in the Service, asking me to join him at the Potsdam Mission in Berlin — a choice assignment for an Intelligence officer. Had I been single, I would have seriously considered it. With the backing of someone like the Colonel, I could look forward to promotions and a bright future in the military. Besides, being the occupier in a conquered country is an enviable position, providing advantages and benefits with which I was already somewhat familiar. The Army was obviously going to be a part of American life for years to come.

In contrast, the alternative, except for going home to my wife after over three years of separation, offered few guarantees. What did I have to look forward to? Endless classes and studying? Satisfying the grueling requirements for a doctorate in foreign languages and literature while trying to survive on the meager subsidy of the GI Bill? Obtaining the degree, assuming I succeeded, would only be the beginning, triggering a possibly lengthy search for a job in a field that was not the most popular in America. On the other hand, I really had no choice, I had pretty much committed myself to going home and continuing my graduate work in the same field I had pursued before. My wife might not look kindly, should I think of changing fields, on being compelled to be a student's wife with little or no income for years to come.

And there were other hard facts I had to face. Although married over three years, I had never tasted married life. To tell the truth, I had only dated my wife a few times. How would I take to connubial bliss? We were almost like strangers.

I knew, however, that I had no business pondering these matters and procrastinating. Adhering to the code of conduct inculcated into me by my parents and embraced by the majority of my generation, I knew exactly what I had to do, and the sooner the better. I owed it to my wife, who had faithfully waited for me and worried about me throughout my long absence and the uncertainties of the war. "Buckle down, Winsocket, buckle down" — and get on with it! I remembered my first swimming lesson, years back, in Hamburg. Just jump into the water, the rest will follow. Then there was the ever available consolation, which had always served me so well: I was sure I was not alone in my quandary; I had lots of company.

What was it like, coming back home, a decorated veteran of World War II? By the time I returned to the United States, at the end of 1945, having delayed my separation from the Service by acceding to Colonel Wilson's request to stay on until the deactivation of XXI Corps, the euphoria generated by V-E and V-J Day had long dissipated. By that time, veterans were a dime a dozen, if not cheaper; there was no ticker-tape parade for the likes of us. I was still proud of my battlefield commission and, since I had never even had a chance to show off my Master Sergeant stripes, much less my silver Lieutenant's bars, I strutted around in my uniform the first few days, displaying on my blouse all that rhubarb our Armed Services so generously bestows upon us for our often modest deeds. I don't know about others in my situation, but I soon preferred anonymity to advertising my veteran status.

I really did not expect any special treatment for having fought in the war. In isolated cases, mostly among acquaintances and neighbors, being a veteran appeared to gain some slight favor here and there, specifically in my case the ability of securing a reasonable rental in an area where they were hard to find. Where I needed it most, namely in securing transportation, being a veteran was no help at all. New cars were almost impossible to come by without connections. The local automobile dealer in our small community, where many people knew each other and where my wife taught in the local high school, was entirely unmoved by my critical need for an automobile. His actions, or rather failure to act, made it very clear what influence my having served overseas had to gain me on his favorite client list for new cars. He soft-soaped me along for well over a year, squeezing money out of me for repairs on a hopeless lemon, until I finally shamed him into selling me a new car without any discount on the window sticker price.

In every other respect, my general impression was that most veterans did not make too much of the fact that we had served, since outwardly no one could have really told whether any one individual had risked life and limb for his country or held down some cushy desk job. How veterans remember their own war experiences is a very personal matter. For me, it was an integral part of my life. It was also a giant step in my final Americanization. The war helped me bridge the last gap from an American Yank at home abroad to an unmistakable American adult in speech, demeanor, and intercourse with my fellow Americans, no longer "abroad at home."

Index
by Lori L. Daniel